ATLAS OF GLOBAL DEVELOPMENT
second edition

Collins

THE WORLD BANK
Washington, D.C.

© 2009 The International Bank for
Reconstruction and Development /
The World Bank
1818 H Street NW
Washington DC 20433
Telephone: 202-473-1000
Internet: www.worldbank.org
E-mail: feedback@worldbank.org

Design © HarperCollins Publishers

Published for the World Bank by Collins Geo.
An imprint of HarperCollins Publishers
Westerhill Road
Bishopbriggs
Glasgow G64 2QT

www.collinsbartholomew.com

First Published 2007
Second edition 2009

The findings, interpretations, and conclusions expressed herein are those of the author(s)
and do not necessarily reflect the views of the Executive Directors of the International Bank
for Reconstruction and Development / The World Bank or the governments they represent.
The World Bank does not guarantee the accuracy of the data included in this work.
The boundaries, colors, denominations, and other information shown on any map in this
work do not imply any judgement on the part of The World Bank concerning the legal status
of any territory or the endorsement or acceptance of such boundaries.

ISBN-13: 978-0-8213-7603-4
E-ISBN-13: 978-0-8213-7604-1
DOI: 10.1596/978-0-8213-7603-4

CIP data
Printed and bound by Printing Express, Hong Kong

Contents

Acknowledgments

This *Atlas of Global Development* is a production of the World Bank's Development Economics Data Group in collaboration with the Office of the Publisher. The text and data were prepared by the Development Economics Data Group of the World Bank under the management of Shaida Badiee. The team consisted of Mehdi Akhlaghi, Azita Amjadi, Uranbileg Batjargal, David Cieslikowski, Richard Fix, Masako Hiraga, Kiyomi Horiuchi, Buyant Erdene Khaltarkhuu, Nino Kostava, Soong Sup Lee, Ibrahim Levent, Raymond Muhula, Kyoko Okamato, Sulekha Patel, Beatriz Prieto-Oramas, William Prince, Changqing Sun, Eric Swanson, and K. M. Vijayalakshmi. Sebastien Dessus, Neil Fantom, Kirk Hamilton, Santiago Herrera, Jeff Lecksell, Nadia Fernanda Piffaretti, and Giovanni Ruta made valuable contributions. Stephen McGroarty, Santiago Pombo, and Valentina Kalk Alacevich from the World Bank's Office of the Publisher managed the publication and dissemination of the book.

The Publishing, Design, Editorial, Creative Services, and Database teams at Collins Geo, HarperCollins Publishers, provided overall design direction, editorial control, mapping, and typesetting.

Picture credits

Curt Carnemark/World Bank 10, 14, 20, 22, 28, 70, 76, 86, 117, 118; **Douglas Engle/Corbis** 111 (top); **Julio Etchart/World Bank** 13; **J. Emilio Flores/Corbis** 84; **Greg Girard/IFC** 78; **Masuru Goto/World Bank** 54; **Louise Gubb/Corbis** 100; **Yosef Hadar/World Bank** 18; **Collart Herve/Corbis Sygma** 95; **Tran Thi Hoa/World Bank** 36, 50, 102; **Ed Kashi/Corbis** 62; **Kazuyoshi/Corbis** 112; **Bob Krist/Corbis** 24; **Frans Lanting/Corbis** 114; **Bill Lyons/World Bank** 40, 106; **Simone D. McCourtie/World Bank** 66; **Gideon Mendel/Corbis** 57 (bottom); **Eric Miller/World Bank** 42, 65, 72; **Viviane Moos/Corbis** 91 (bottom), 96; **Stephen Morrison/epa/Corbis** 60; **Shehzad Noorani/World Bank** 52; **Charles O'Rear/Corbis** 61; **Anatoliy Rakhimbayev/World Bank** 99, 105; **Trevor Samson/World Bank** 32; **Dominic Sansoni/World Bank** 75; **Alfredo Srur/World Bank** 46; **Shannon Stapleton/Reuters/Corbis** 82; **Eberhard Streichan/Zefa/Corbis** 120; **Wendy Stone/Corbis** 26; **William Taufic/Corbis** 57 (top); **UNCHR/T. Irwin** 88; **UNEP** 111 (bottom); **Ami Vitale/World Bank** 31; **Scott Wallace/World Bank** 58; **Ray Witlin/World Bank** 45, 49, 108; **Adam Woolfitt/Corbis** 92.

Foreword

Human and economic development cannot be separated from geography. Throughout the centuries, climate, natural resources, landscapes, and natural routes have shaped the development of political and economic institutions, nation-states, and markets. People, in return, are constantly reshaping the economic and social geography, through communication and transport infrastructure, trade and migration, and conflicts and co-operation. And their activities increasingly influence the climate, through water use, deforestation, urbanization, and the release of carbon dioxide and other greenhouse gases.

Today, location is an important predictor of a person's welfare, with one's prospects in life being decided in good measure by one's place of birth. But the diversity of outcomes across countries is great and cannot be explained by one or even a few factors. Landlocked states, for example, have a harder time participating in global markets and their development is often retarded, but Botswana has consistently grown faster than the rest of Sub-Saharan Africa. Small, island economies and those in tropical regions face other obstacles to development, but Singapore has realized the advantage of its location and prospered. Although people's welfare and prospects depend on the location and size of their countries' economies, economic success also depends on the dynamism, specialization, and openness of their political and economic institutions. It depends as well on the quality and coverage of education and health services and the degree of social and political cohesion. Countries combine these various assets and characteristics in different proportions—and these proportions are evolving rapidly.

This *Atlas* provides an overview of the world and its people as we find them in the first decade of the 21st century. Through thematic maps, it portrays in space the complexity of the development patterns. It locates development challenges and successes, and illustrates trends and comparative outcomes, relying on a large and up-to-date set of data collected by the World Bank to guide its development programs. These indicators come from many sources, but all have their origin in work carried out in individual countries, usually by statistical offices or other public agencies.

We hope that readers of this *Atlas* will find it informative and that it will provide a clearer picture of today's world. Recognizing the formidable challenges and great successes that have been achieved should strengthen our resolve to work together to create a better world for all.

Justin Lin
Senior Vice President and Chief Economist
World Bank

Classification of economies

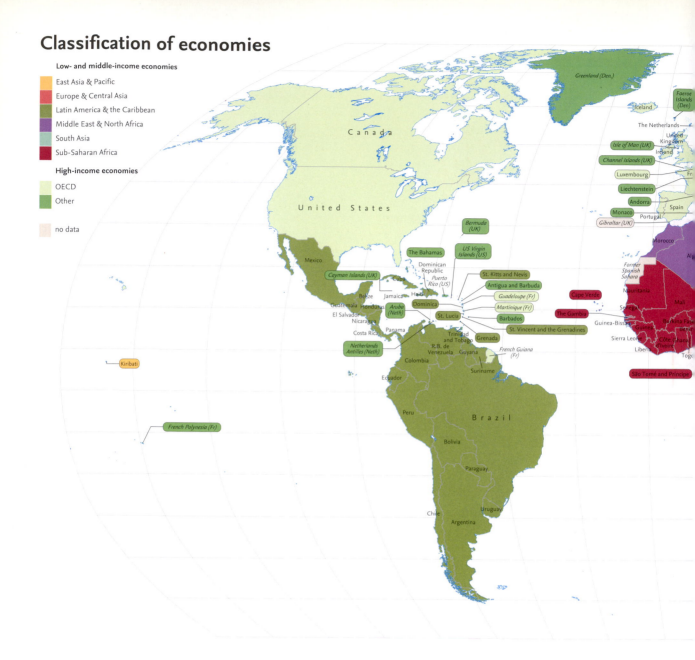

Low- and middle-income economies

- East Asia & Pacific
- Europe & Central Asia
- Latin America & the Caribbean
- Middle East & North Africa
- South Asia
- Sub-Saharan Africa

High-income economies

- OECD
- Other

- no data

The World Bank classifies economies as low-income, middle-income (subdivided into lower-middle and upper-middle), or high-income based on gross national income (GNI) per capita. Low- and middle-income economies are sometimes referred to as *developing economies*. It is not intended to imply

that all economies in the group are experiencing similar development or that other economies have reached a preferred or final stage of development.

The regions used in this atlas are based on the regions defined by the World Bank for

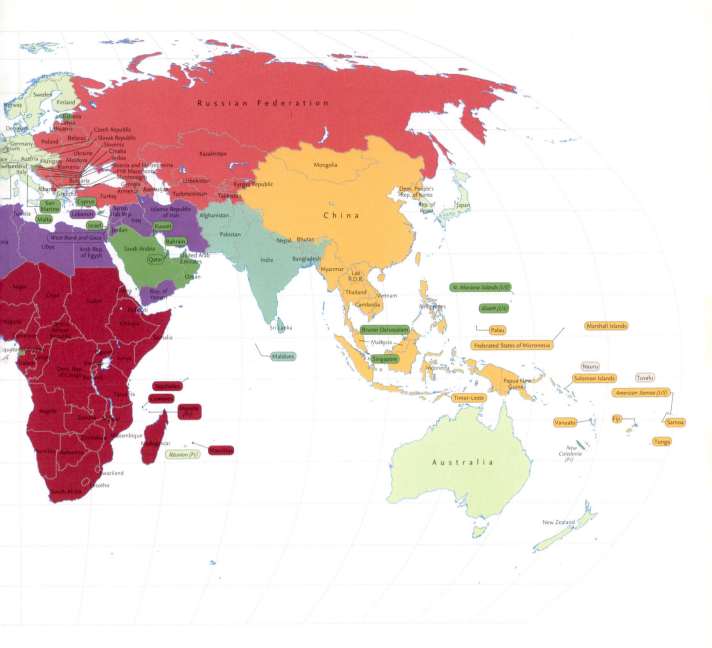

analytical and operational purposes. These regions may differ from common geographic usage or from the regions defined by other organizations. Regional groupings and the aggregate measures for regions include only low- and middle-income economies.

Data are shown for economies as they were constituted in 2007. Additional information about the data is provided in *World Development Indicators 2008* or on the World Bank web site (www.worldbank.org/data).

Standards of living vary substantially across the globe. Comparing income, consumption, or poverty levels among countries requires a common unit of measurement. Exchange rates reflect the relative value of currencies as traded in the market. Purchasing power parities (PPPs) take into account differences in price levels. Both have important roles in measuring the size of economies.

What is a developing country? Because development encompasses many factors—economic, environmental, cultural, educational, and institutional—no single measure gives a complete picture. However, the total earnings of the residents of an economy measured by its gross national income (GNI) is a good measure of its capacity to provide for the well-being of its people. The World Bank classifies countries according to their average income, or GNI per capita, converted to US dollars using three-year average market exchange rates (commonly called the *World Bank Atlas method*). Countries with average incomes of less than $11,455 in 2007 are classified as low- and middle-income (often referred to as *developing economies*). Countries with average incomes of $11,456 or more in 2007 are classified as high-income or developed economies. In 2007, the 1 billion people in high-income economies had an average income of $37,566 a person; the 4.3 billion residents in middle-income economies had average incomes of $2,872; and the 1.3 billion people in low-income economies earned only $578, with some as low as $110.

To measure differences in welfare, comparisons of income among economies should take into account differences in

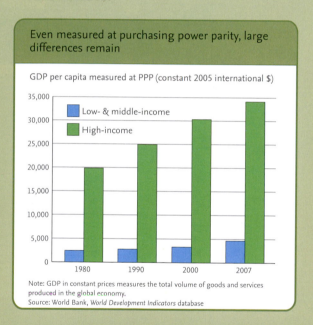

Even measured at purchasing power parity, large differences remain

GDP per capita measured at PPP (constant 2005 international $)

- Low- & middle-income
- High-income

Note: GDP in constant prices measures the total volume of goods and services produced in the global economy.
Source: World Bank, *World Development Indicators* database

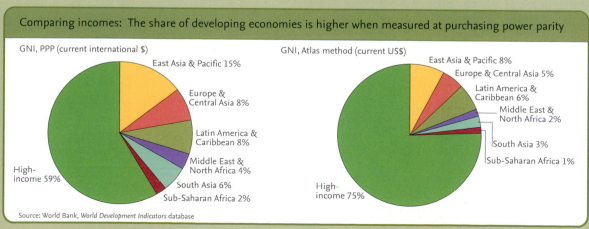

Comparing incomes: The share of developing economies is higher when measured at purchasing power parity

GNI, PPP (current international $)

- East Asia & Pacific 15%
- Europe & Central Asia 8%
- Latin America & Caribbean 8%
- Middle East & North Africa 4%
- South Asia 6%
- Sub-Saharan Africa 2%
- High-income 59%

GNI, Atlas method (current US$)

- East Asia & Pacific 8%
- Europe & Central Asia 5%
- Latin America & Caribbean 6%
- Middle East & North Africa 2%
- South Asia 3%
- Sub-Saharan Africa 1%
- High-income 75%

Source: World Bank, *World Development Indicators* database

domestic price levels. This is done using PPPs. By using PPPs instead of market exchange rates, the standard of living among countries can be compared in real terms, as if the people purchased goods and services at the same prices. Measured using PPPs, developing economies receive 42 percent of world income. But when measured using the Atlas method they receive only 25 percent (See the table on Ranking of Economies by GNI per capita on pages 128-129 for a comparison of average incomes). The difference is due to the lower cost of services and non-traded goods in developing economies, a fact that travelers frequently observe.

As the most comprehensive measure of living standards, GNI per capita is closely related to other non-monetary measures of the quality of life, such as life expectancy at birth, the mortality rate of children, and enrollment rates in school. Low incomes are both a cause and effect of low levels of health, education, and other human development outcomes. Poor people have a hard time obtaining good health care and education, while poor health and poor education leave them less able to improve their incomes.

Countries with higher GNI per capita often have higher life expectancy at birth ....

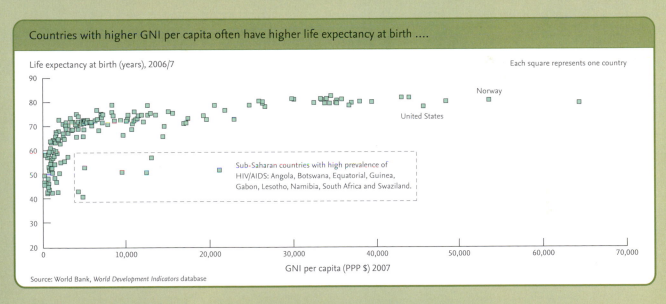

Source: World Bank, *World Development Indicators* database

.... and higher net school enrollment rates in secondary education

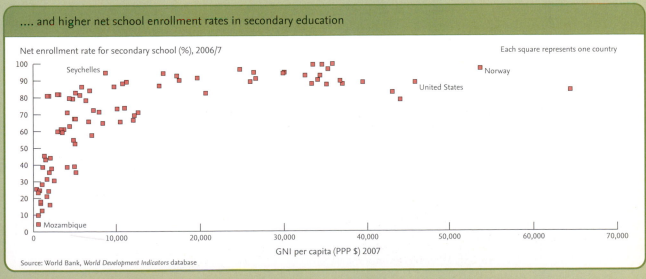

Source: World Bank, *World Development Indicators* database

Income

GNI per capita, World Bank Atlas method, 2007

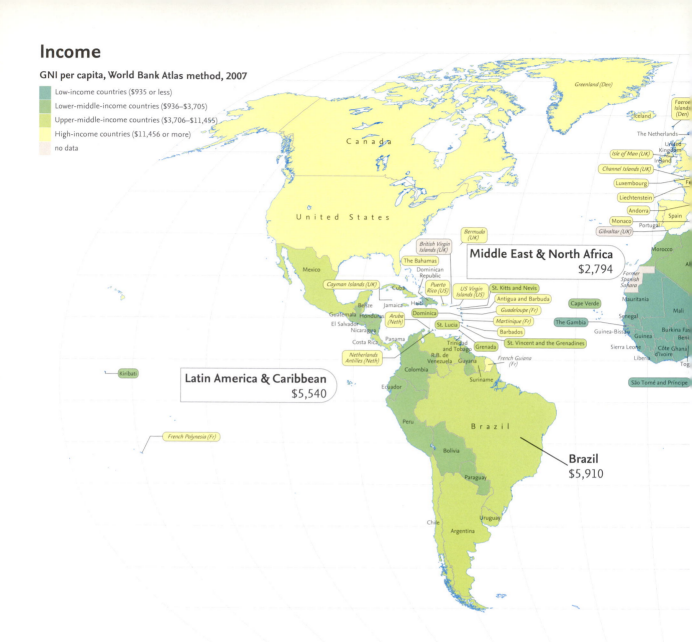

- Low-income countries ($935 or less)
- Lower-middle-income countries ($936–$3,705)
- Upper-middle-income countries ($3,706–$11,455)
- High-income countries ($11,456 or more)
- no data

Greenland (Den)

Canada

United States

Mexico

British Virgin Islands (UK)

Bermuda (UK)

The Bahamas

Dominican Republic

Cayman Islands (UK)

Cuba

Puerto Rico (US)

US Virgin Islands (US)

St. Kitts and Nevis

Antigua and Barbuda

Belize

Jamaica

Haiti

Guatemala

Honduras

El Salvador

Nicaragua

Aruba (Neth)

Dominica

Guadeloupe (Fr)

St. Lucia

Martinique (Fr)

Barbados

Costa Rica

Panama

Netherlands Antilles (Neth)

Trinidad and Tobago

R.B. de Venezuela

Grenada

St. Vincent and the Grenadines

Colombia

Guyana

Suriname

French Guiana (Fr)

Ecuador

Peru

Bolivia

Brazil
$5,910

B r a z i l

Paraguay

Chile

Argentina

Uruguay

Kiribati

Latin America & Caribbean
$5,540

French Polynesia (Fr)

Iceland

Faeroe Islands (Den)

The Netherlands

United Kingdom

Isle of Man (UK)

Ireland

Channel Islands (UK)

Fr

Luxembourg

Liechtenstein

Andorra

Spain

Monaco

Portugal

Gibraltar (UK)

Middle East & North Africa
$2,794

Morocco

Al

Former Spanish Sahara

Mauritania

Mali

Cape Verde

Senegal

Burkina Fas

Beni

The Gambia

Guinea-Bissau

Guinea

Sierra Leone

Côte d'Ivoire

Ghana

Tog

Liberia

São Tomé and Príncipe

Living conditions in Liberia, one of the world's poorest countries

Largest economies, 2007

Rank	Country	Gross national income, PPP current international $ (billions)
1	United States	13,829
2	China	7,084
3	Japan	4,421
4	India	3,079
5	Germany	2,758
6	France	2,074
7	United Kingdom	2,063
8	Russian Federation	2,039
9	Brazil	1,796
10	Italy	1,773

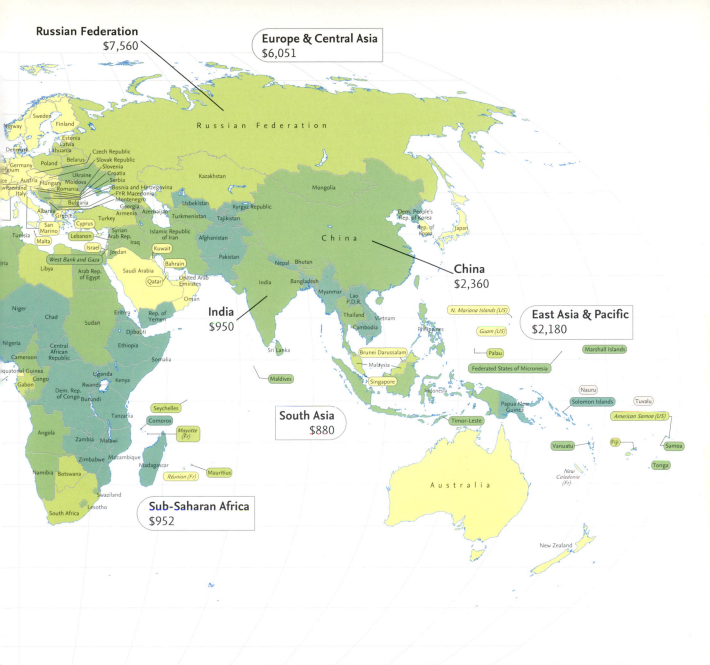

Russian Federation
$7,560

Europe & Central Asia
$6,051

China
$2,360

India
$950

East Asia & Pacific
$2,180

South Asia
$880

Sub-Saharan Africa
$952

Facts	Internet links	
▶ Of the 49 economies classified as low income in 2007, 33 are in Sub-Saharan Africa, 11 are in Asia, 3 are in Europe, 1 is in Latin America and the Caribbean, and 1 is in the Middle East.	▶ World Development Indicators	www.worldbank.org/data
▶ Most economies in Latin America and the Caribbean, the Middle East and North Africa, and Europe and Central Asia are middle-income economies.	▶ Organisation for Economic Co-operation and Development Statistics	www.oecd.org/statistics
▶ Variations within each region can also be large. For example, in 2007 Botswana's GNI per capita surpassed $5000, while GNI per capita in neighboring Mozambique was only $320.	▶ International Monetary Fund Dissemination Standards Bulletin Board	http://dsbb.imf.org/ Applications/web/dsbbhome
▶ Average GNI per capita in the low- and middle-income countries was $2,337 in 2007, while in high-income economies it was $37,566.	▶ United Nations Statistics Division	http://unstats.un.org/unsd/ snaama
▶ As of 2008, 22 economies had moved from developing to high-income status, nine of them in the last two years.	▶ International Comparison Project	www.worldbank.org/data/icp

Faster growth in developing economies is reducing poverty rates and slowly closing the income gap with high-income countries. But growth must be sustained over the long term and the gains from economic growth must be shared to make lasting improvements to the well-being of all people. To promote broad-based and sustained growth, people must be empowered and have the opportunity to make choices that improve their well-being.

Sustained growth is essential to reduce poverty. But not many developing countries—especially low-income countries—have seen strong and steady growth in the past. Only one out of five countries has increased per capita income by 3.0 percent a year or more since 1980. Moreover, only two out of five countries were able to maintain 3.0 percent or higher growth rates in five or more consecutive years. But developing countries have been growing faster. Since 2000, half of all countries achieved average growth rates of 3.0 percent a year or higher in per capita income. Many Sub-Saharan African countries experienced good economic growth despite formidable development challenges, such as conflict and epidemic disease.

Although high growth rates have helped reduce global poverty, rising income inequality has weakened the poverty reduction impact of economic growth. For a given rate of growth, the rate of poverty reduction depends on the initial level of inequality, and how the distribution of income changes with growth. Since the beginning of the 1980s, per capita incomes have risen in most countries, making most people in developing countries better

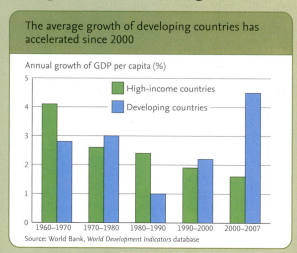

The average growth of developing countries has accelerated since 2000

Annual growth of GDP per capita (%)

Source: World Bank, *World Development Indicators* database

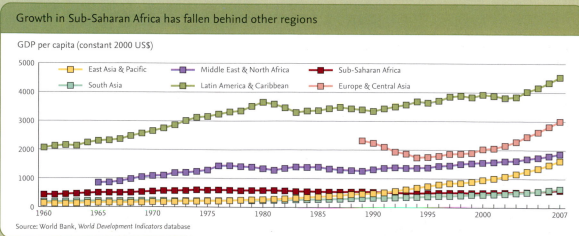

Growth in Sub-Saharan Africa has fallen behind other regions

GDP per capita (constant 2000 US$)

Source: World Bank, *World Development Indicators* database

Taroudant Province, Morocco.
New primary school funded by the World Bank

In many developing countries, children of poor families have fewer opportunities to attend school

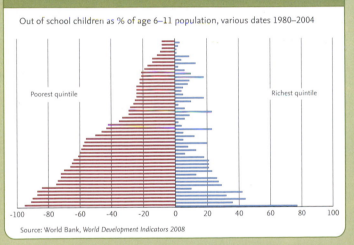

Out of school children as % of age 6–11 population, various dates 1980–2004

Poorest quintile

Richest quintile

Source: World Bank, *World Development Indicators 2008*

Inequality has increased in some countries, decreased in others

Annual change in Gini coefficient in 83 developing countries, 1995–2005
Percentage point

Less equal

More equal

Source: World Bank, *World Development Indicators database*

off. However, income inequality, as measured by the Gini coefficient, also increased in many countries. Therefore, even in fast-growing economies, poor people may not share fully in the benefits of growth. If inequality increases, poverty reduction will be slower. To achieve broad-based economic growth, all people must have equal opportunity to participate.

Equality of opportunities does not mean equal outcomes. However, if all members of society have similar chances to become socially active, politically influential, and economically productive, then sustainable long-run development is more likely because the allocation of resources is more efficient. When economic and social institutions systematically favor the interests of those with higher status and greater resources, the economy is likely to be less efficient, missing out on opportunities for innovation and investment.

There are many ways to increase the opportunities for poor people. First, access to education and health services increases productivity. Water and sanitation systems help reduce the incidence of disease. Improvements to transportation and communication systems, particularly in rural areas, improve access to markets. Secure tenure to property increases incentives for new investment by rural and urban dwellers. Protection through the rule of law reduces risks and uncertainties that undermine growth.

Economic growth

average annual growth of GDP per capita, 2000–2007

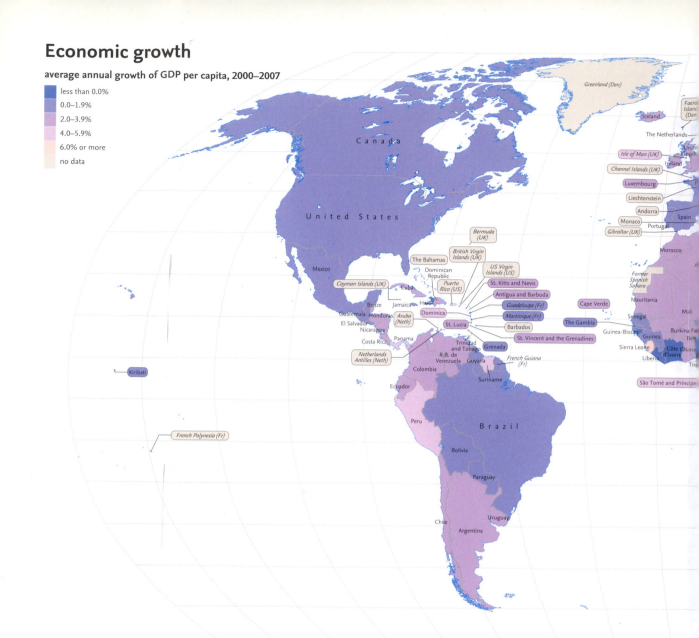

- less than 0.0%
- 0.0–1.9%
- 2.0–3.9%
- 4.0–5.9%
- 6.0% or more
- no data

China has one of the fastest GDP growth rates of the developing countries

Recent growth of GDP per capita

Rank	Country	Average annual growth rate (%), 2000–2007
1	Azerbaijan	16.1
2	Equatorial Guinea	14.1
3	Armenia	13.1
4	Angola	9.9
5	Latvia	9.7
6	China	9.5
7	Georgia	9.4
8	Kazakhstan	9.3
9	Estonia	9.0
10	Trinidad and Tobago	8.9

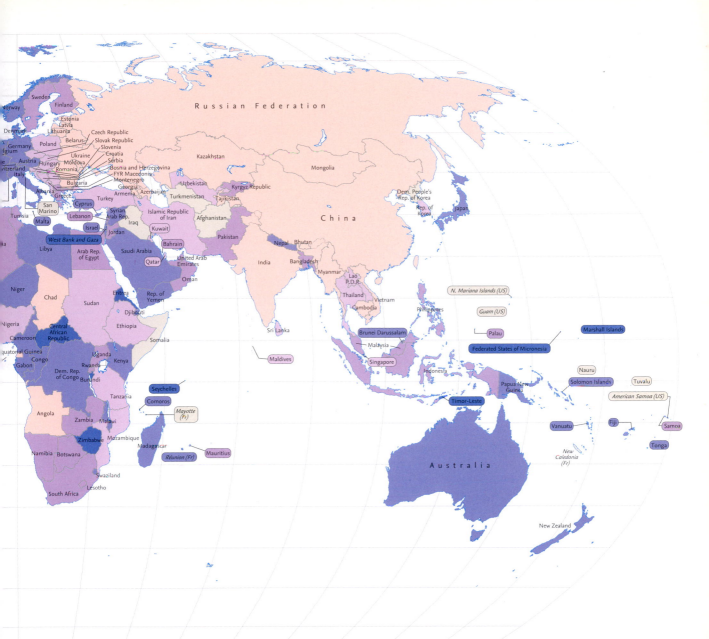

Facts

► Developing economies continued to grow faster than high-income economies. From 2000 to 2007, the annual growth of GDP per capita in developing countries averaged 4.8 percent, compared to 1.7 percent for high-income economies.

► About 80 percent of all developing economies grew faster in 2007 than their average growth rate between 1990 and 2006.

► Since 1950, only 13 economies have grown at an average rate of 7 percent a year or more for 25 years or longer.

► The last 15 years saw a surge of growth, especially among countries that opened their economies to trade and investment, maintained sound monetary and fiscal policies, and strengthened the rule of law.

Internet links	
► World Bank *Global Economic Prospects*	**www.worldbank.org/prospects**
► International Monetary Fund *World Economic Outlook*	**www.imf.org/weo**
► Organisation for Economic Co-operation and Development statistics	**www.oecd.org/statistics**
► The Commission on Growth and Development	**www.growthcommission.org**

Inequality

share of income going to the poorest quintile
1992–2005, most recent year available

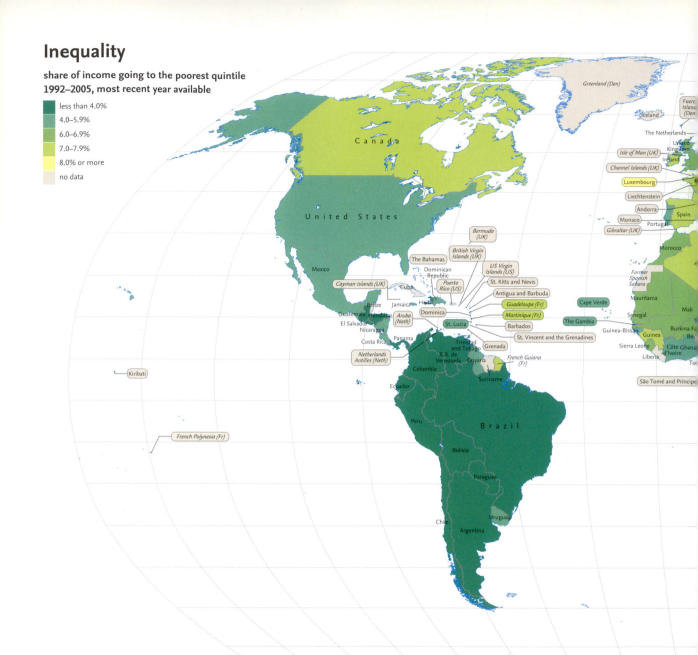

- less than 4.0%
- 4.0–5.9%
- 6.0–6.9%
- 7.0–7.9%
- 8.0% or more
- no data

Ten countries with high inequality ratios

One commonly used measure of income inequality is the inequality ratio, calculated as the ratio of income or consumption shares of the richest 20 percent to the poorest 20 percent of the population.

A ratio of 10 means that the top 20 percent of the population earns (or spends) 10 times as much as the bottom 20 percent of the population. Generally, the higher this ratio, the more unequal the income distribution. Countries with high inequality ratios are primarily in Latin America and Sub-Saharan Africa. The highest inequality ratio among Asian countries is 12.

Country	Year	Income or consumption shares	Inequality ratio
Namibia	1993	income	56
Lesotho	1995	consumption	44
Bolivia	2002	income	42
Central African Republic	1993	consumption	33
Haiti	2001	income	27
Paraguay	2003	income	26
Panama	2003	income	24
Brazil	2005	income	21
Colombia	2004	income	21
El Salvador	2002	income	21

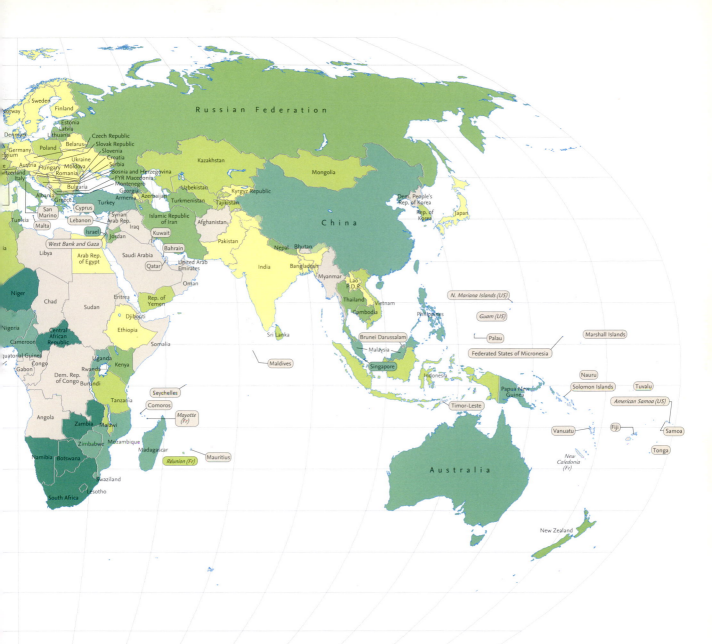

Facts	Internet links	
► Income inequalities between countries increased until the onset of rapid economic growth in China and India in the past two decades.	► World Bank *World Development Report 2006*	www.worldbank.org/wdr
► Inequality within countries has increased in many parts of the world, including Bangladesh, China, Russia, the United Kingdom, and the United States.	► United Nations *Human Development Report 2007–08*	http://hdr.undp.org
► Inequality in access to schooling has fallen as school participation rates have risen in most countries.		
► Different groups of citizens within an economy, defined by such characteristics as race or gender, often face quite different opportunities for economic and social mobility.	► World Development Indicators	www.worldbank.org/data

Poverty—the lack of income and essential goods and services—exists everywhere, but there has been progress. The proportion of people in developing countries living in extreme poverty has fallen from about 42 percent in 1990 to slightly more than 25 percent in 2005. Still, about 1.4 billion people live on less than $1.25 a day, a number that is unacceptably high. The recent increase in food and fuel prices is likely to increase the number of poor people.

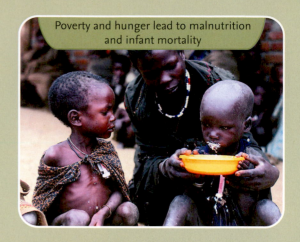

Poverty and hunger lead to malnutrition and infant mortality

Global poverty has been falling since the 1980s, perhaps for the first time in human history. A poverty line set at $1.25 a day in 2005 purchasing power (revised from the previous $1.08 a day in 1993 prices) is used as the working definition of extreme poverty. Based on this, the number of people living in extreme poverty fell from 1.9 billion in 1981 to 1.8 billion in 1990 and to about 1.4 billion in 2005. This is an important success, but greater effort will be required to further reduce poverty. Many obstacles threaten to trap hundreds of millions of people in poverty, especially in South Asia and Sub-Saharan Africa. Poor health and lack of education deprive people of productive employment; environmental resources have been depleted or spoiled; and corruption, conflict, and misgovernance waste public resources and private investment.

The significant reduction in extreme poverty over the past quarter century disguises large regional differences. The greatest decline occurred in East Asia and Pacific, led by China, where the poverty rate fell from 78 percent in 1981 to 17 percent in

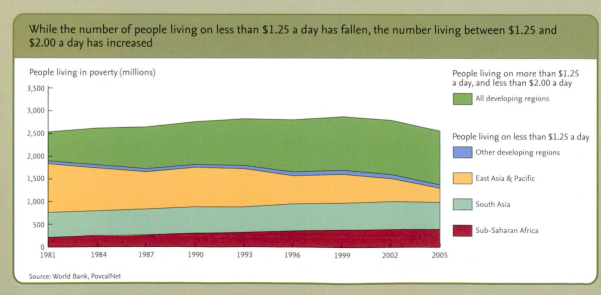

While the number of people living on less than $1.25 a day has fallen, the number living between $1.25 and $2.00 a day has increased

People living in poverty (millions)

People living on more than $1.25 a day, and less than $2.00 a day
- All developing regions

People living on less than $1.25 a day
- Other developing regions
- East Asia & Pacific
- South Asia
- Sub-Saharan Africa

Source: World Bank, PovcalNet

To measure poverty in the world as a whole, a common standard is required. Because market exchange rates tend to understate the real incomes of developing countries and overstate the extent of poverty, PPPs are used to compare income and consumption levels between countries. A PPP is the conversion rate for a given currency into a reference currency (invariably the US dollar). PPPs are calculated with the aim of assuring parity in terms of purchasing power over goods and services, both internationally traded and non-traded. In 2008, new PPP estimates for 2005 became available from the International Comparison Program.

The World Bank's "$1 a day," international poverty line was based on what "poverty" means in the world's poorest countries. By focusing on the standards of the poorest countries, the $1 a day line gives the global poverty measure a salience in focusing on the world's poorest. Using the new 2005 PPP rates, the international poverty line was revised to $1.25 a day, which is the average poverty line of 15 poorest countries in the world.

2005. Over the same period, the poverty rate in South Asia fell from 59 percent to 40 percent. In contrast, the poverty rate has fallen only slightly in Sub-Saharan Africa from 54 percent in 1981 to 51 percent in 2005, and the number of people living in poverty nearly doubled. The Millennium Development Goals (MDGs) call for 1990 poverty rates to be cut in half by 2015. At present many countries are falling short of that goal.

The average daily income of those living on less than $1.25 a day increased slightly in most regions during the 1990s. However, a marked exception is Sub-Saharan Africa where average incomes of the poor did not increase—remaining at a meager $0.73 a day—pointing to the severity and depth of poverty in this region.

Undernourishment and extreme poverty often go hand in hand. Hunger and malnutrition cause tremendous human suffering, killing millions of children every year, and costing developing countries billions of dollars through lost productivity. It is estimated that 864 million people worldwide were undernourished in 2002–2004, and 96 percent of undernourished people lived in developing countries.

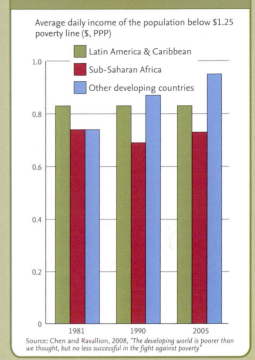

Average daily incomes of the extremely poor have stagnated in Sub-Saharan Africa and Latin America and the Caribbean

Average daily income of the population below $1.25 poverty line ($, PPP)

Source: Chen and Ravallion, 2008, "The developing world is poorer than we thought, but no less successful in the fight against poverty"

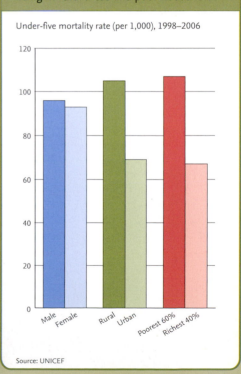

Child mortality is higher among children living in rural areas and poor households

Under-five mortality rate (per 1,000), 1998–2006

Source: UNICEF

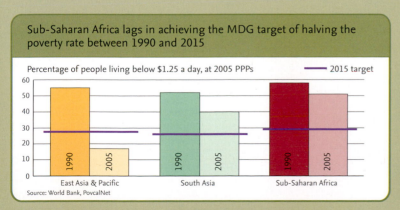

Sub-Saharan Africa lags in achieving the MDG target of halving the poverty rate between 1990 and 2015

Percentage of people living below $1.25 a day, at 2005 PPPs — 2015 target

Source: World Bank, PovcalNet

Poverty

share of population living on less than $1.25 a day, 2005

- 50.0% or more
- 25.0–49.9%
- 10.0–24.9%
- 2.0–9.9%
- less than 2.0%
- no data

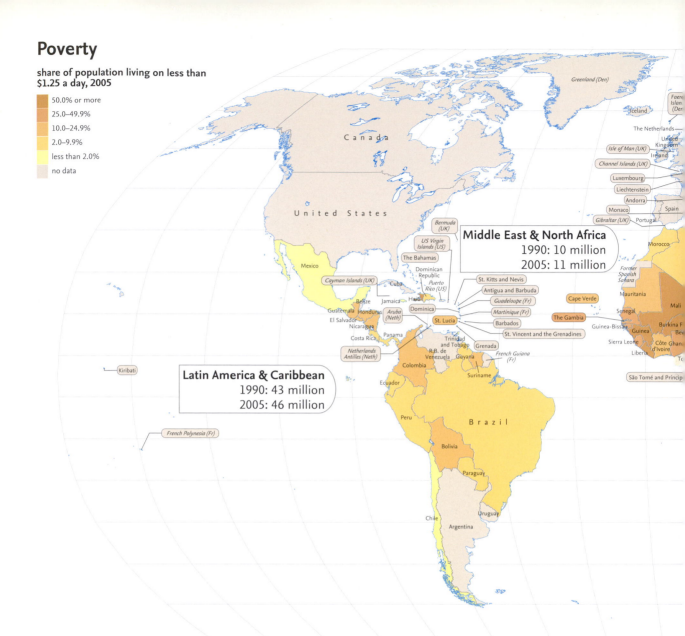

Greenland (Den)

Canada

United States

Middle East & North Africa
1990: 10 million
2005: 11 million

Latin America & Caribbean
1990: 43 million
2005: 46 million

Mexico

Cayman Islands (UK)

The Bahamas

Cuba

Dominican Republic

Puerto Rico (US)

Belize

Jamaica

Haiti

Honduras

Guatemala

Aruba (Neth)

Dominica

El Salvador

Nicaragua

Costa Rica

Panama

Netherlands Antilles (Neth)

Bermuda (UK)

US Virgin Islands (US)

St. Kitts and Nevis

Antigua and Barbuda

Guadeloupe (Fr)

Martinique (Fr)

St. Lucia

Barbados

St. Vincent and the Grenadines

Grenada

Trinidad and Tobago

R.B. de Venezuela

Guyana

Suriname

French Guiana (Fr)

Colombia

Ecuador

Peru

Brazil

Bolivia

Paraguay

Chile

Uruguay

Argentina

Kiribati

French Polynesia (Fr)

Iceland

Faeroe Islan (Den)

The Netherlands

United Kingdom

Isle of Man (UK)

Ireland

Channel Islands (UK)

Luxembourg

Liechtenstein

Andorra

Monaco

Spain

Gibraltar (UK)

Portugal

Morocco

Former Spanish Sahara

Mauritania

Mali

Cape Verde

The Gambia

Senegal

Guinea-Bissau

Guinea

Sierra Leone

Liberia

Côte d'Ivoire

Burkina F

Be

Ghana

São Tomé and Príncip

Garbage surrounds run-down buildings in rural Indonesia

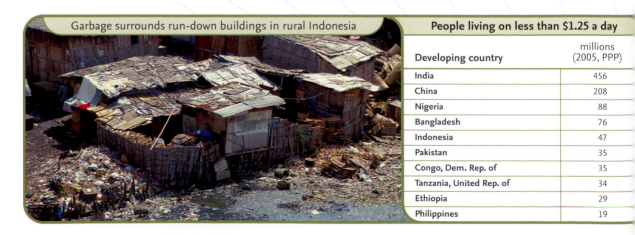

People living on less than $1.25 a day	
Developing country	**millions (2005, PPP)**
India	456
China	208
Nigeria	88
Bangladesh	76
Indonesia	47
Pakistan	35
Congo, Dem. Rep. of	35
Tanzania, United Rep. of	34
Ethiopia	29
Philippines	19

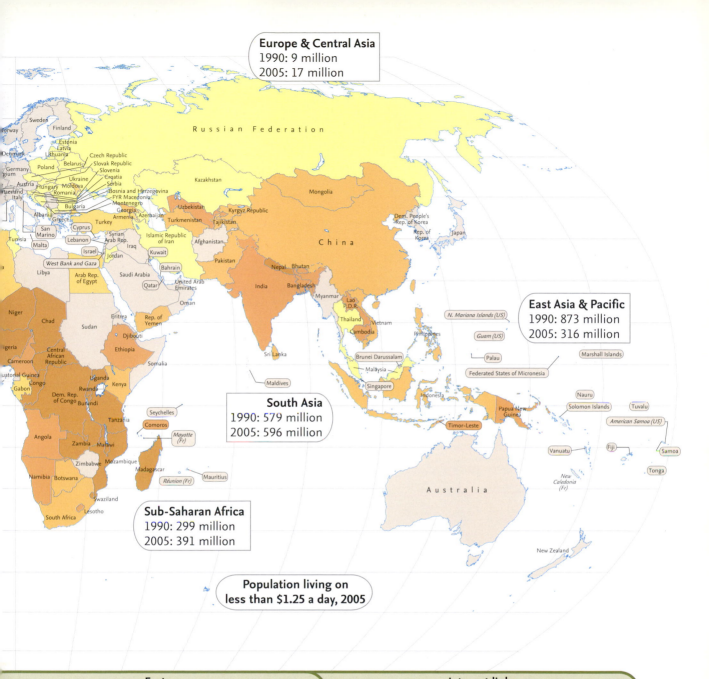

Europe & Central Asia
1990: 9 million
2005: 17 million

Russian Federation

East Asia & Pacific
1990: 873 million
2005: 316 million

South Asia
1990: 579 million
2005: 596 million

Sub-Saharan Africa
1990: 299 million
2005: 391 million

Population living on less than $1.25 a day, 2005

Facts	Internet links	
▶ Africa has more countries with high poverty rates than any other developing region, but Asia has the most people living in extreme poverty.	▶ World Bank: PovcalNet	**iresearch.worldbank.org/ PovcalNet**
▶ Although extreme poverty occurs mostly in rural areas, urban slum populations can also have a high poverty ratio.	▶ World Bank: Country poverty assessments	**www-wds.worldbank.org** (go to "By doc type" in left hand bar and select "Poverty assessment" from "Economic & Sector Work")
▶ If economic growth rates in developing countries are sustained, the poverty target of the Millennium Development Goal of halving poverty by 2015 is likely to be achieved at the global level.	▶ United Nations Millennium Project	**www.unmillenniumproject.org**
▶ But, many developing countries are not on track to achieve the poverty reduction target.	▶ World Development Report	**econ.worldbank.org/wdr**

Malnourished children

proportion of children under five who are underweight, 2000–2006, most recent year available

- 30% or more
- 20–29%
- 10–19%
- 5–9%
- less than 5%
- no data

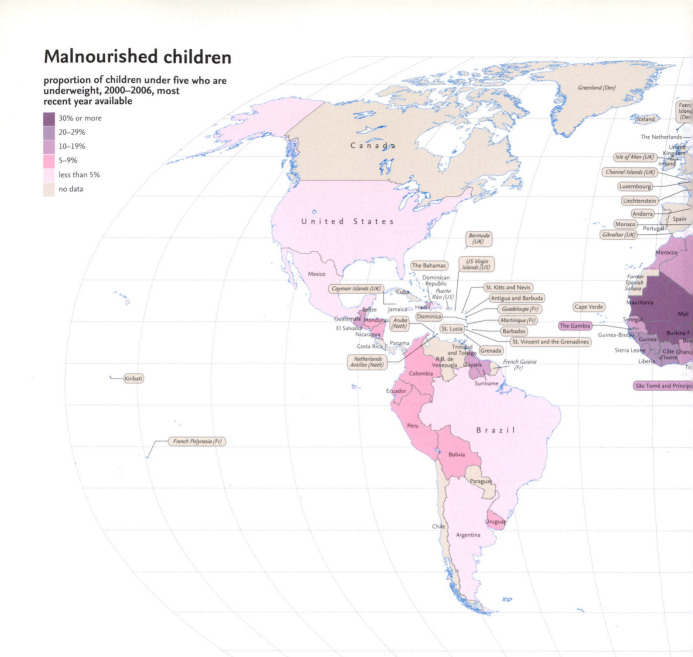

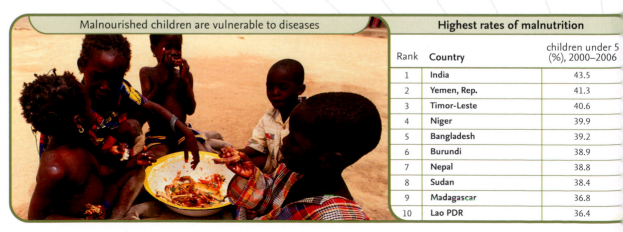

Malnourished children are vulnerable to diseases

Highest rates of malnutrition

Rank	Country	children under 5 (%), 2000–2006
1	India	43.5
2	Yemen, Rep.	41.3
3	Timor-Leste	40.6
4	Niger	39.9
5	Bangladesh	39.2
6	Burundi	38.9
7	Nepal	38.8
8	Sudan	38.4
9	Madagascar	36.8
10	Lao PDR	36.4

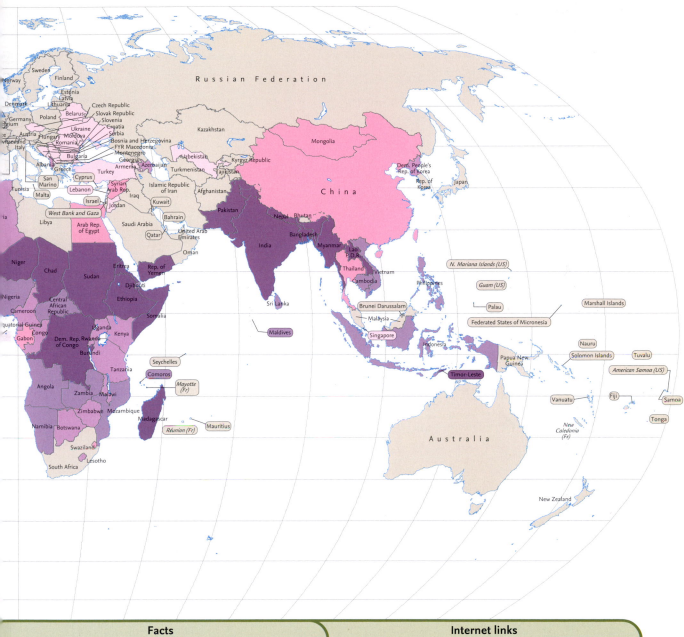

Facts	Internet links	
► Malnutrition is an underlying cause for around half of all child deaths worldwide. 75 percent of the children who die from causes related to malnutrition were only mildly or moderately undernourished, showing the vulnerability of these children.	► World Health Organization	**www.who.int/nutgrowthdb/en/**
► More than one-quarter of children ages under 5 (about 140 million) in developing countries are underweight. Of these children, nearly three-quarters live in only 10 countries.	► UNICEF Childinfo	**www.childinfo.org/ undernutrition.html**
► South Asia has the highest prevalence of underweight children, where more than 40 percent of children under five are underweight.	► UNICEF	**www.unicef.org/health/ index_statistics.html**
► On average, children in rural areas are twice as likely to be underweight as children in urban areas, and poor children are more than twice as likely to be underweight as rich children.	► Food and Agriculture Organization	**www.fao.org/faostat/ foodsecurity/**

Global trends in population

Demography will shape the world of our children and grandchildren. Failure to slow population growth in the poorest countries is likely to mean a lower quality of life for millions of people. The key determinants of population size and structure are fertility, mortality, and migration.

Crowded street, Shanghai, China

The twentieth century witnessed extraordinary growth of world population—from 1.6 billion in 1900 to 6.1 billion in 2000. Most of this growth—80 percent since 1950—was in developing countries. The uneven regional growth reduced the developed countries' share of world population from one-third to one-fifth over the century. Europe's relative share of world population fell most—from one-quarter in 1900 to merely one-eighth in 2000.

In contrast, Asia, with over half the world's population in 1950, added over two billion people to its population over the next 40 years.

But Sub-Saharan Africa, whose population nearly tripled in the same time period, had the highest growth rate.

The fertility and mortality trends that shaped the current population profiles of countries will influence their demographic futures. In the industrial world, increasing life expectancy has coincided with income growth and healthier lifestyles. But with a fertility rate of 1.7 births per woman—well below replacement level—the average age of the population will rise, and population size may fall in the absence of immigration. In

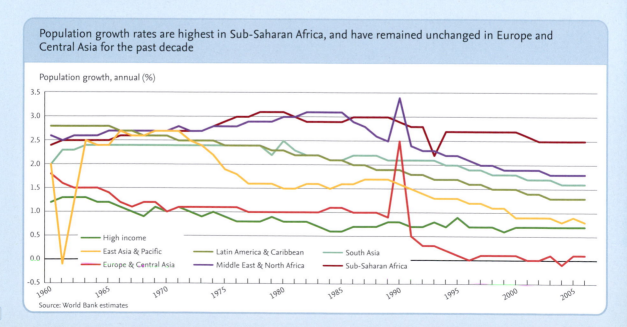

Population growth rates are highest in Sub-Saharan Africa, and have remained unchanged in Europe and Central Asia for the past decade

Population growth, annual (%)

Legend:
- High income
- East Asia & Pacific
- Europe & Central Asia
- Latin America & Caribbean
- Middle East & North Africa
- South Asia
- Sub-Saharan Africa

Source: World Bank estimates

	Population (millions)			Growth rate (%)	
	1965	1980	2006	1965–1980	1980–2006
East Asia & Pacific	980.6	1,359.1	1,898.8	2.18	1.34
Europe & Central Asia	331.1	389.0	445.0	1.07	0.54
Latin America & Caribbean	246.6	356.6	556.1	2.46	1.78
Middle East & North Africa	110.7	167.2	308.1	2.75	2.45
South Asia	634.7	903.3	1,499.4	2.35	2.03
Sub-Saharan Africa	254.8	386.0	781.3	2.77	2.82
High income	755.4	869.8	1,049.5	0.94	0.75
World	3,313.9	4,431.0	6,538.2	1.94	1.56

Source: World Bank estimates

fact, large increases in migration will be needed to stabilize the labor force and maintain current levels of welfare. In developing countries, life expectancy at birth increased steadily for the developing region as a whole, from 41 years in 1950 to 66 years in 2006. Fertility rates have declined, but at 2.7 births per woman, they remain well above those in high-income countries, fueling population growth as births exceed deaths.

With about 30 percent of the population in developing countries below age 15, the working-age population will bear the burden of dependent children for some time to come. In high-income countries with declining birth rates and 14 percent of the population over the age of 65, the dependency burden is increasingly that of the elderly population.

Although fertility and mortality are the largest factors affecting demographic change, migration can be important. A majority of international migrants are from developing countries. These migrants make up a significant part of population growth in industrial countries where fertility is so low that annual deaths exceed annual births. However, the total number of migrants is too small to have much impact on population growth in most developing countries.

Most people in developing countries are living longer

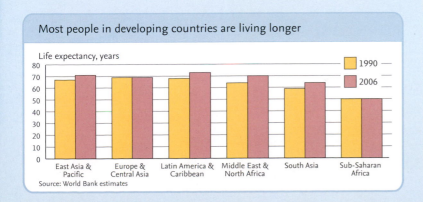

Life expectancy, years

Source: World Bank estimates

In high-income countries, the dependency burden is increasingly that of the elderly population, as birth rates decline

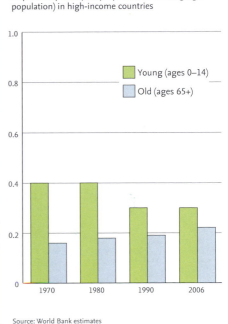

Dependency ratio (as a proportion of working-age population) in high-income countries

- Young (ages 0–14)
- Old (ages 65+)

Source: World Bank estimates

In contrast, the working-age population in developing countries will continue to support young children for some time to come

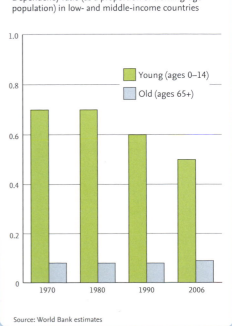

Dependency ratio (as a proportion of working-age population) in low- and middle-income countries

- Young (ages 0–14)
- Old (ages 65+)

Source: World Bank estimates

Population growth

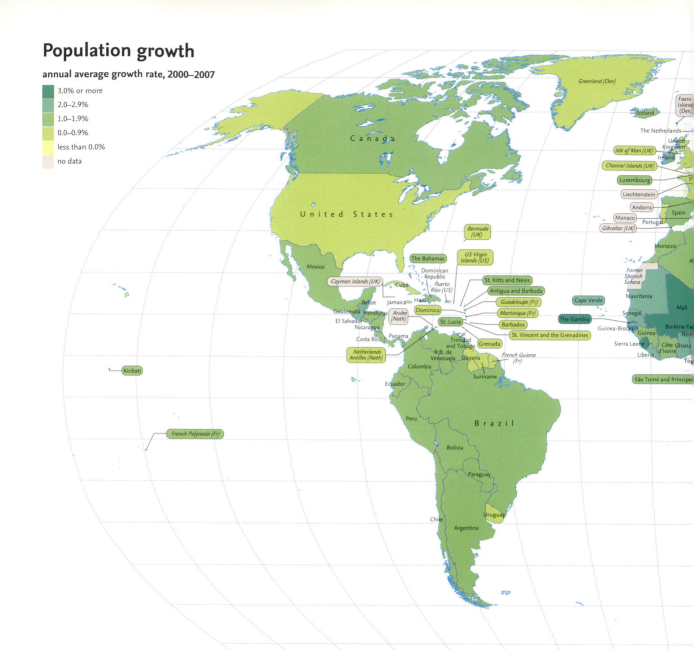

annual average growth rate, 2000–2007

- ■ 3.0% or more
- ■ 2.0–2.9%
- ■ 1.0–1.9%
- ■ 0.0–0.9%
- ■ less than 0.0%
- ■ no data

Greenland (Den)

Faeroe Islands (Den)

Iceland

The Netherlands

United Kingdom

Ireland

Isle of Man (UK)

Channel Islands (UK)

Luxembourg

Liechtenstein

Andorra

Monaco   Portugal   Spain

Gibraltar (UK)

Canada

United States

Mexico

Bermuda (UK)

The Bahamas

US Virgin Islands (US)

Cayman Islands (UK)   Cuba

Dominican Republic

Puerto Rico (US)

St. Kitts and Nevis

Antigua and Barbuda

Guadeloupe (Fr)

Martinique (Fr)

Dominica

St. Lucia

Barbados

St. Vincent and the Grenadines

Grenada

Belize   Jamaica   Haiti

Guatemala   Honduras   Aruba (Neth)

El Salvador   Nicaragua

Costa Rica   Panama

Netherlands Antilles (Neth)

Trinidad and Tobago

R.B. de Venezuela   Guyana

Colombia

Ecuador

Suriname

French Guiana (Fr)

Peru

Bolivia

Brazil

Paraguay

Chile   Argentina   Uruguay

Kiribati

French Polynesia (Fr)

Morocco

Former Spanish Sahara

Mauritania   Mali

Cape Verde

Senegal   Burkina Faso

The Gambia

Guinea-Bissau   Guinea   Côte   Ghana

Sierra Leone   d'Ivoire

Liberia

São Tomé and Príncipe

Countries with the highest population in 2015

Rank	Country	Projected population (millions)
1	China	1,383
2	India	1,233
3	United States	324
4	Indonesia	245
5	Brazil	209
6	Pakistan	192
7	Bangladesh	180
8	Nigeria	176
9	Russian Federation	135
10	Japan	125

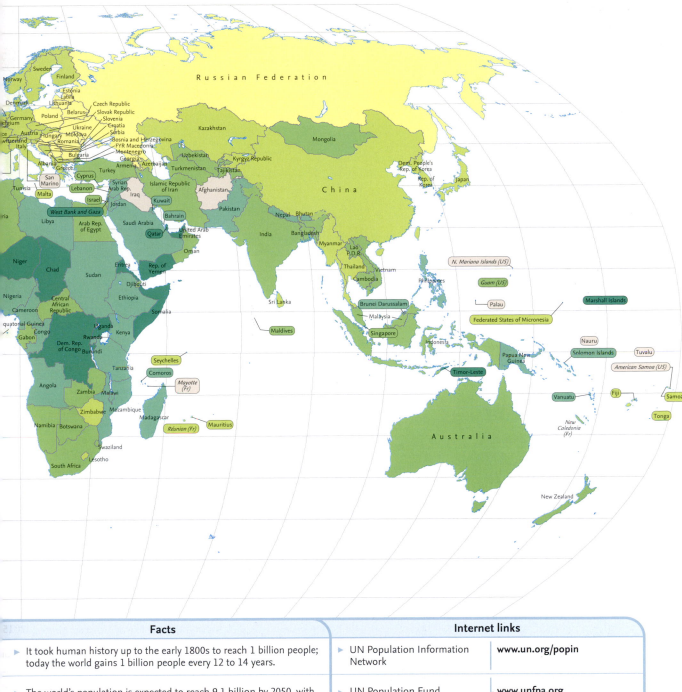

Facts
▶ It took human history up to the early 1800s to reach 1 billion people; today the world gains 1 billion people every 12 to 14 years.
▶ The world's population is expected to reach 9.1 billion by 2050, with virtually all population growth occurring in developing countries.
▶ Sub-Saharan Africa will experience the largest proportional increase, from 13 percent of the world's population today to 19 percent by 2050.
▶ Population growth over the next few decades will be determined by two factors which are difficult to predict: the pace of fertility decline in some developing countries and the course of the HIV/AIDS epidemic.

Internet links	
▶ UN Population Information Network	**www.un.org/popin**
▶ UN Population Fund	**www.unfpa.org**
▶ Demographic and Health Surveys	**www.measuredhs.com**
▶ World Bank HNPstats	**www.worldbank.org/hnpstats**
▶ Population Reference Bureau	**www.prb.org**

Life expectancy

life expectancy at birth, 2006

- less than 50 years
- 50–59 years
- 60–69 years
- 70–74 years
- 75 years or more
- no data

Canada

United States

Greenland (Den)

Iceland

The Netherlands

United Kingdom

Ireland

Isle of Man (UK)

Channel Islands (UK)

Luxembourg

Liechtenstein

Andorra

Monaco

Gibraltar (UK)

Spain

Portugal

Morocco

Bermuda (UK)

Mexico

The Bahamas

US Virgin Islands (US)

Cayman Islands (UK)

Cuba

Dominican Republic

Puerto Rico (US)

Haiti

Jamaica

Belize

Guatemala

Honduras

El Salvador

Nicaragua

Costa Rica

Panama

Aruba (Neth)

Dominica

St. Kitts and Nevis

Antigua and Barbuda

Guadeloupe (Fr)

Martinique (Fr)

St. Lucia

Barbados

St. Vincent and the Grenadines

Grenada

Cape Verde

The Gambia

Former Spanish Sahara

Mauritania

Mali

Senegal

Guinea-Bissau

Guinea

Burkina Faso

Benin

Sierra Leone

Côte d'Ivoire

Liberia

Togo

São Tomé and Príncipe

Netherlands Antilles (Neth)

Trinidad and Tobago

R.B. de Venezuela

Colombia

Guyana

French Guiana (Fr)

Suriname

Kiribati

Ecuador

Peru

Brazil

Bolivia

French Polynesia (Fr)

Paraguay

Chile

Argentina

Uruguay

A child in Botswana can only expect to reach, on average, the age of 50

Countries with the highest and lowest life expectancies, 2006

Highest countries	years
Japan	82
Hong Kong, China	82
Switzerland	82
Italy	81
Australia	81
Lowest countries	
Mozambique	42
Angola	42
Sierra Leone	42
Zambia	42
Swaziland	41

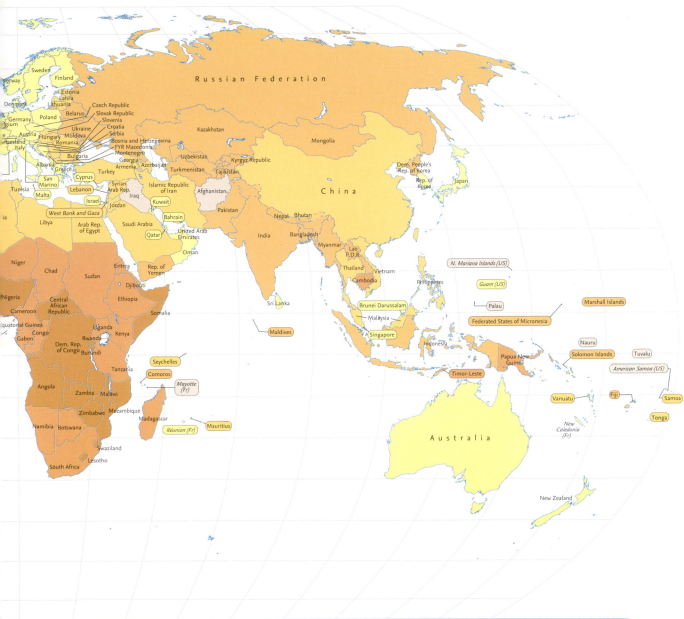

Facts

► Life expectancies for Lesotho, Swaziland, and Zimbabwe declined by over 15 years between 1990 and 2006, the result of the HIV/AIDS epidemic.

► In Japan, Italy, and Germany, over 20 percent of the population are 65 years and older; combined with total fertility rates of only 1.3 births per women, this potentially promotes labor shortages in the absence of in-migration.

► Today, only 11 countries have a median age above 40 years. By 2050, it is projected that there will be 89 countries in that group, 45 in the developing world.

► In most countries fertility rates, rather than mortality rates, will determine future population size.

Internet links

► UN Population Information Network	www.un.org/popin
► UN Population Fund	www.unfpa.org
► Demographic and Health Surveys	www.measuredhs.com
► World Bank HNPstats	www.worldbank.org/hnpstats
► Population Reference Bureau	www.prb.org

Education opens doors

Education prepares children to participate in their society and in the global economy. School enrollment rates are rising, but many children still do not enroll or complete primary schooling. Ensuring that all children receive a good quality education is the foundation of sustainable development and poverty alleviation.

Since 1990, the world has promised that by 2015 all children would be able to complete a full course of primary education. Primary completion rates—the proportion of children completing the last year of primary school—directly measure progress towards this goal. Two regions, Latin America and the Caribbean, and East Asia and Pacific, have already reached this goal, and Europe and Central Asia are on track. But Sub-Saharan Africa and South Asia, with primary completion rates of just 60 and 80 percent respectively, are in danger of falling short.

Worldwide, an estimated 75 million primary school-age children remained out of school in 2005. About 75 percent of these are in Sub-Saharan Africa and South Asia.

Primary completion rates have improved, but regional differences remain

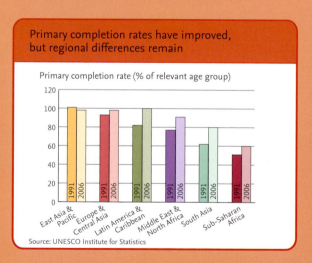

Primary completion rate (% of relevant age group)

Source: UNESCO Institute for Statistics

And many children continue to be outside the school system

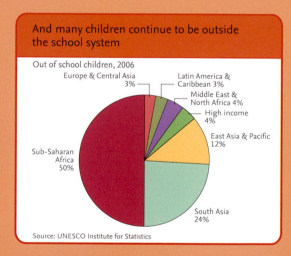

Out of school children, 2006

Source: UNESCO Institute for Statistics

Girls, children from poor families, and those living in rural areas, are less likely to complete schooling

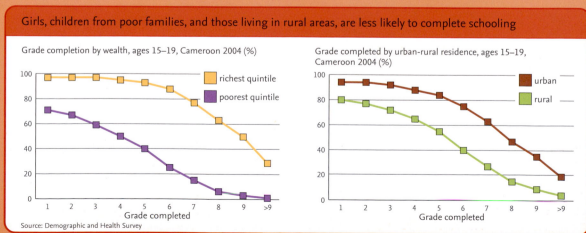

Grade completion by wealth, ages 15–19, Cameroon 2004 (%)

Source: Demographic and Health Survey

Grade completed by urban-rural residence, ages 15–19, Cameroon 2004 (%)

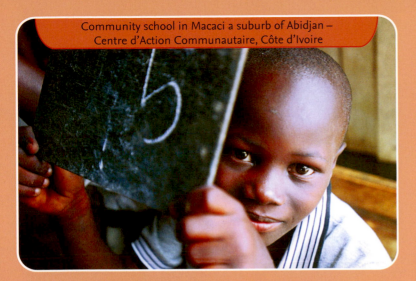

More boys than girls are enrolled in and complete primary school. Children in poor families and those living in rural areas are less likely to enroll in school and more likely to drop out earlier. There are many reasons why children drop out and stay out of school or never enroll in school. Schools may be inaccessible or of poor quality, especially in rural areas; parents may keep children at home because of high school costs; or there may be demands for children's labor and their income. In Burkina Faso, 50 percent of children ages 7 to 14 worked in 2004. Almost all of these worked full time, with only two percent combining work with school. In contrast, while over 50 percent of children in Cambodia are economically active, nearly 85 percent manage to combine work with schooling.

Beyond primary schooling

To compete in today's knowledge-driven economy and shifting global markets, countries need a flexible, skilled work force, able to create and apply knowledge. This is usually achieved through strong secondary and tertiary education systems. While all regions have made progress in expanding secondary and tertiary enrollments between 1991 and 2005, only two regions—Europe and Central Asia, and Latin America and the Caribbean—have an enrollment rate of over 80 percent in secondary education. In East Asia and Pacific, which has achieved universal primary education, about 70 percent of children are enrolled in secondary schools. In Sub-Saharan Africa, where primary enrollment is lower than all other regions, secondary enrollment ratio is even lower, about 30 percent. Only Europe and Central Asia has tertiary enrollment reaching 50 percent.

Children in many countries work, making the goal of universal primary education elusive

	Year	Economically active children % of children ages 7–14	Work only % of children ages 7–14	Study and work % of total working children
Burkina Faso	2004	50	98	2
Cambodia	2001	52	16	84
Chile	2003	4	3	97
India	2000	5	90	10

Source: Understanding Children's Work (UCW)

Secondary and tertiary enrollment in all regions lag behind those of developed countries

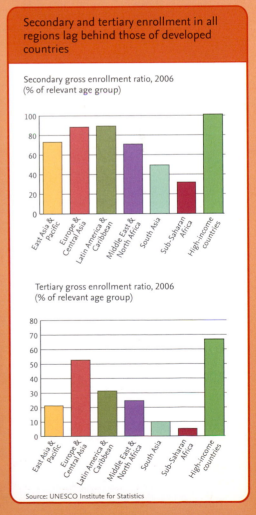

Secondary gross enrollment ratio, 2006 (% of relevant age group)

Tertiary gross enrollment ratio, 2006 (% of relevant age group)

Source: UNESCO Institute for Statistics

Education for all

primary completion rate, 2003–2006,
most recent year available

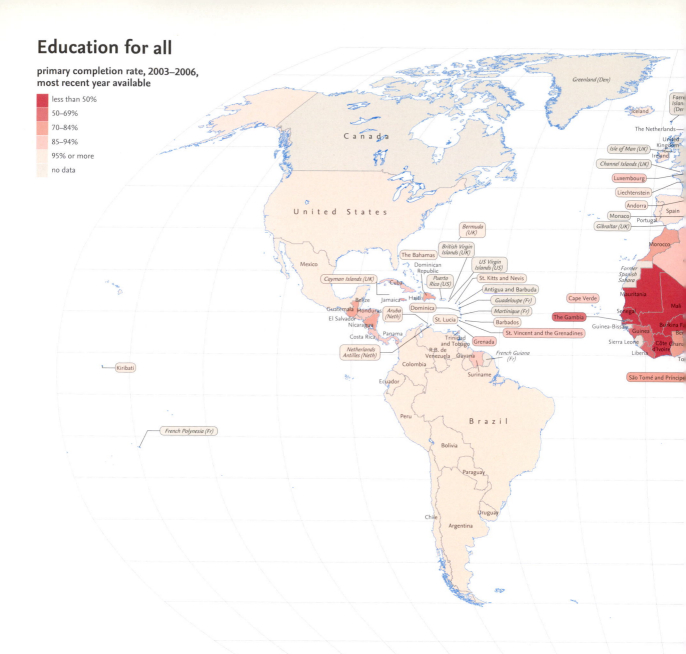

	less than 50%
	50–69%
	70–84%
	85–94%
	95% or more
	no data

In rural areas children often face a long walk to school

Lowest primary completion rates, 2003–2006

Rank	Country	%
1	Central African Republic	24
2	Chad	31
3	Burkina Faso	31
4	Niger	33
5	Rwanda	35
6	Burundi	36
7	Congo, Dem. Rep.	38
8	Mozambique	42
9	Côte d'Ivoire	43
10	Ethiopia	43

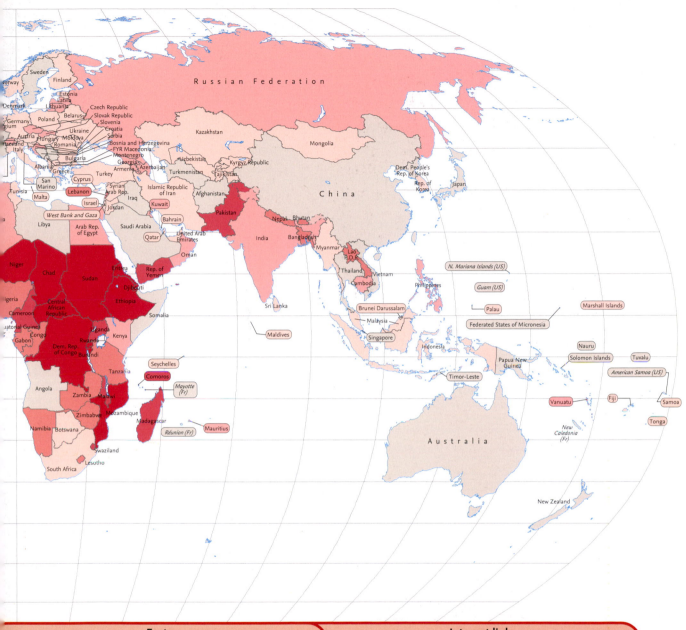

Facts	Internet links	
▶ Approximately 63 percent of the countries in the world have achieved gender parity at the primary level, compared with 37 percent at secondary and less than 3 percent at the tertiary level.	▶ UNESCO	**www.unesco.org**
▶ Globally, about 130 million students were enrolled in tertiary education in 2004, up from 68 million in 1991. Over half of the world's tertiary students live in East Asia and the Pacific, North America, and Western Europe.	▶ UNESCO Institute for Statistics	**www.uis.unesco.org**
	▶ World Bank Edstats	**www.edstats.worldbank.org**
▶ On average, the literacy gaps between adult men and women are largest in South Asia (70 percent vs. 46 percent), followed by Middle East and North Africa (83 percent vs. 63 percent), and Sub-Saharan Africa (69 percent vs. 50 percent).	▶ Demographic and Health Survey	**www.measuredhs.com**

Children at work

About 200 million children ages 5 to 14 work. The type of children's work ranges widely—from simple tasks within the family, to long hours of harmful and damaging work. Children's work often interferes with education, and could damage normal physical and mental development, reducing their future opportunities to join the productive workforce and get out of poverty.

Children living in the poorest households and in rural areas are most likely to be involved in child labor. Those burdened with household chores are overwhelmingly girls. The majority of working children, around 70 percent, is in the agricultural sector. Many work for long hours on farms and plantations owned by their families, often without pay. They plant and harvest crops using sharp tools designed for adults, spray toxic pesticides, and tend livestock. Agriculture is one of the three most hazardous sectors—along with mining and construction—in terms of fatalities, accidents, and ill health.

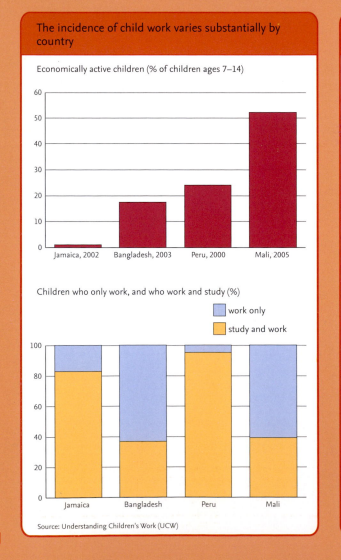

The incidence of child work varies substantially by country

Economically active children (% of children ages 7–14)

Children who only work, and who work and study (%)

- work only
- study and work

Source: Understanding Children's Work (UCW)

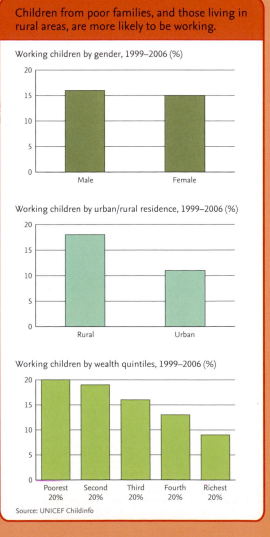

Children from poor families, and those living in rural areas, are more likely to be working.

Working children by gender, 1999–2006 (%)

Working children by urban/rural residence, 1999–2006 (%)

Working children by wealth quintiles, 1999–2006 (%)

Source: UNICEF Childinfo

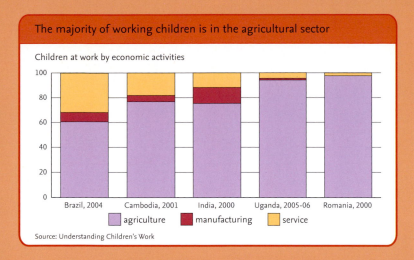

The majority of working children is in the agricultural sector

Children at work by economic activities

agriculture manufacturing service

Source: Understanding Children's Work

Labor interferes with children's education

Many poor families are unable to afford school fees or other school costs. The family may depend on the income that a working child brings to the household and may place more importance on children's work than on education. If children work long hours, they cannot find sufficient time to go to school, even though many of them try to juggle work and education. Girls are particularly disadvantaged, as they often undertake household chores after work. In many countries, the schools in poor areas are under-resourced and of low quality, with poor facilities, oversized classes, and inadequately trained teachers. Families will often keep children at home rather than send them to schools in poor conditions. The Millennium Development Goal of providing universal primary education to all children by 2015 cannot be attained unless the factors that push children to work and prevent poor families from sending children to school are addressed.

Working children are less likely to be enrolled in schools and more likely to repeat grades

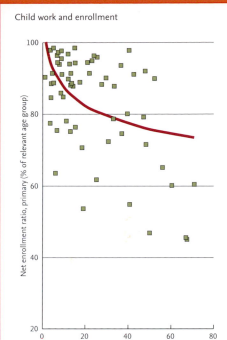

Child work and enrollment

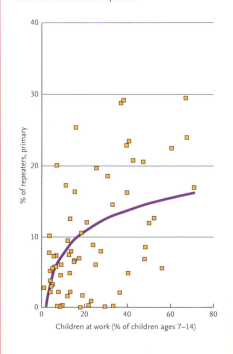

Child work and school repeaters

Source: Understanding Children's Work (UCW) and UNESCO Institute for Statistics

In developing countries, the majority of child workers is involved in unpaid family work

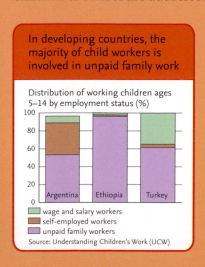

Distribution of working children ages 5–14 by employment status (%)

wage and salary workers
self-employed workers
unpaid family workers

Source: Understanding Children's Work (UCW)

Most children work long hours

Average weekly working hours, children ages 7–14 (children who work only)	
Dominican Republic, 2002[a]	53.3
Guatemala, 2003	43.8
Zimbabwe, 1999	43.3
Mali, 2005	41.5
Turkey, 1999	41.3
Mexico, 2004[b]	40.9

a Data are for children ages 10–14
b Data are for children ages 12–14

Source: Understanding Children's Work (UCW)

Children at work

economically active children as a percentage of children
ages 7–14, 1994–2006, most recent year available

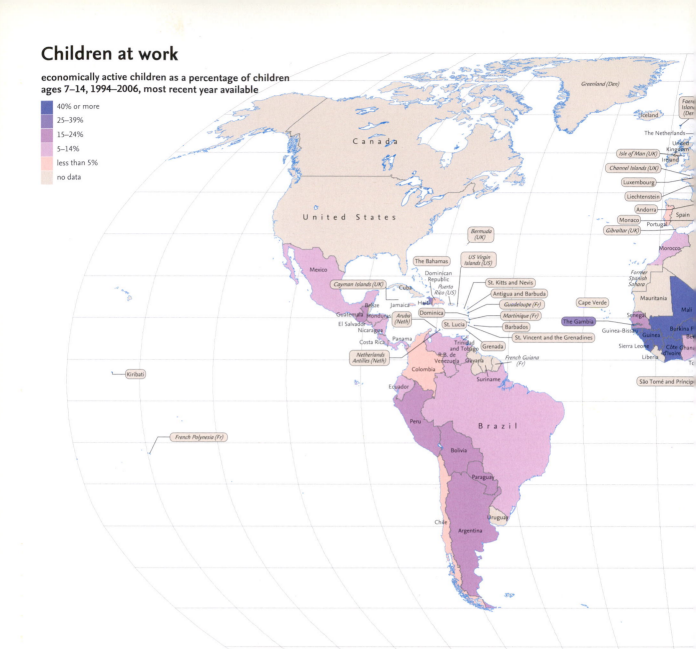

- **40% or more**
- **25–39%**
- **15–24%**
- **5–14%**
- **less than 5%**
- **no data**

Children on their way home from farm-work,
Son La province, northern Vietnam.

Highest proportion of working children

Rank	Country	Children at work (% of children ages 7–1
1	Guinea-Bissau	67.5
2	Central African Rep.	67.0
3	Sierra Leone	65.0
4	Chad	60.4
5	Ethiopia	56.0
6	Cambodia	52.3
7	Mali	52.3
8	Burkina Faso	50.0
9	Guinea	48.3
10	Zambia	47.9

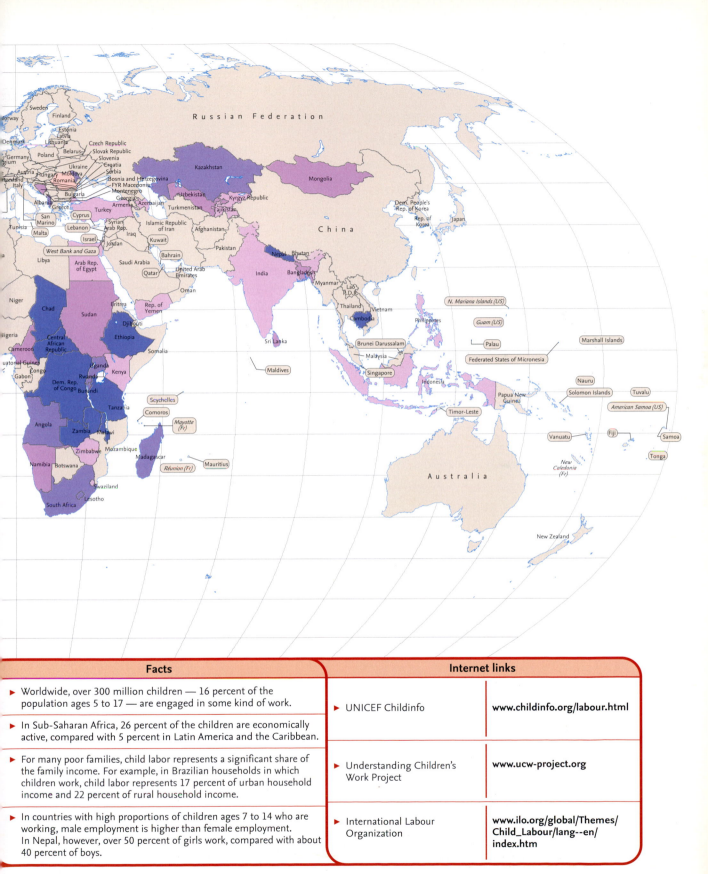

Facts	Internet links	
▶ Worldwide, over 300 million children — 16 percent of the population ages 5 to 17 — are engaged in some kind of work.	▶ UNICEF Childinfo	**www.childinfo.org/labour.html**
▶ In Sub-Saharan Africa, 26 percent of the children are economically active, compared with 5 percent in Latin America and the Caribbean.		
▶ For many poor families, child labor represents a significant share of the family income. For example, in Brazilian households in which children work, child labor represents 17 percent of urban household income and 22 percent of rural household income.	▶ Understanding Children's Work Project	**www.ucw-project.org**
▶ In countries with high proportions of children ages 7 to 14 who are working, male employment is higher than female employment. In Nepal, however, over 50 percent of girls work, compared with about 40 percent of boys.	▶ International Labour Organization	**www.ilo.org/global/Themes/ Child_Labour/lang--en/ index.htm**

The economic and social status of women has improved. More girls than ever before are completing primary school, women's labor force participation is increasing, and fertility rates are declining. But persistent inequalities also keep women at a disadvantage and limit the ability of societies to grow, reduce poverty, and govern effectively.

Despite great improvement in girls' enrollment rates, in 2005 over 40 million girls—55 percent of all children out of school—did not attend primary school. About two-thirds of all illiterate adults—almost 500 million—were women. In some countries, girls are less likely to receive medical treatment than boys because of parental discrimination and neglect. Mothers' illiteracy and lack of schooling disadvantage their young children. For example, in Nepal, children of mothers with no education are three times more likely to die before their fifth birthday, compared with the children of mothers with secondary or higher education.

Does better access to education mean more opportunities and better pay for women?

For women to realize the full benefits of improved educational opportunities, more attention must be paid to ensuring equality of economic opportunities, especially

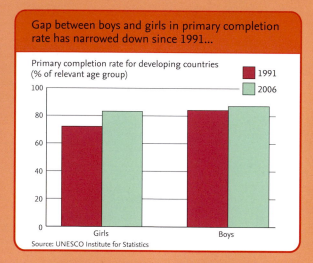

Gap between boys and girls in primary completion rate has narrowed down since 1991...

Primary completion rate for developing countries (% of relevant age group)

Source: UNESCO Institute for Statistics

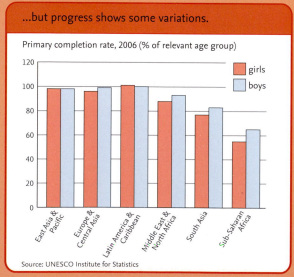

...but progress shows some variations.

Primary completion rate, 2006 (% of relevant age group)

Source: UNESCO Institute for Statistics

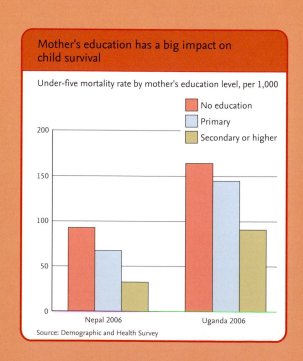

Mother's education has a big impact on child survival

Under-five mortality rate by mother's education level, per 1,000

Source: Demographic and Health Survey

The education gap has narrowed...

Gap between male and female gross primary enrollment ratios (percentage point)

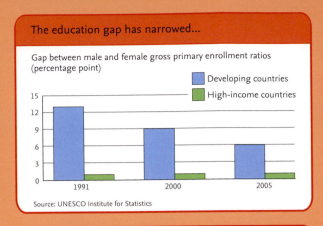

Source: UNESCO Institute for Statistics

... but women's labor force participation remains far below that of men

Gap between male and female labor force participation rate (percentage point)

Source: ILO KILM 5th edition

during the transition from school to work. Improvements in labor force participation have lagged behind enrollment ratios. Too often women work as unpaid family workers or occupy low-paid, low-status jobs. Women's earnings tend to be lower than men's, especially in manufacturing. In East Asia and Pacific, women's hourly earnings in manufacturing are only 39 percent of those of men's.

Less rewarding employment opportunities and lower wages mean that women face a high risk of poverty. In no region of the developing world do women have equal access to social services and productive resources, and women's participation in politics and government also remains limited, making it difficult for them to influence policy. In the Middle East and North Africa region, women occupy less than 10 percent of parliamentary seats.

This is because more women than men work in family enterprises with no pay

Unpaid family workers, 2005 (% of employment)

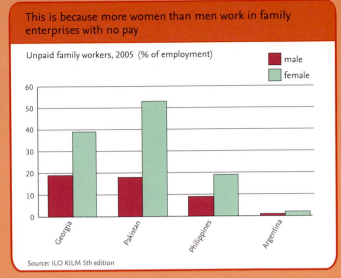

Source: ILO KILM 5th edition

And when women work, they earn less than men

Ratio of female to male hourly earnings by region, 1992–2006

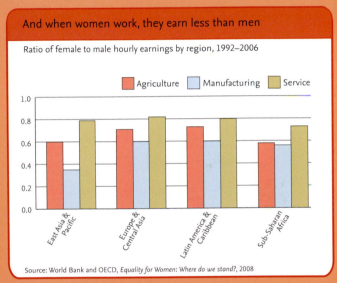

Source: World Bank and OECD, *Equality for Women: Where do we stand?*, 2008

Women's political participation has increased, but is still low everywhere

Women in parliaments (% of total seats)

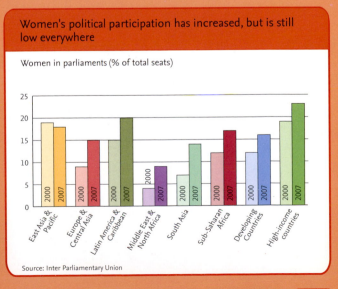

Source: Inter Parliamentary Union

Gender equity

ratio of girls to boys in primary and secondary
education, 2003–2006, most recent year available

- less than 80%
- 80–89%
- 90–97%
- 98–100%
- 101% or more
- no data

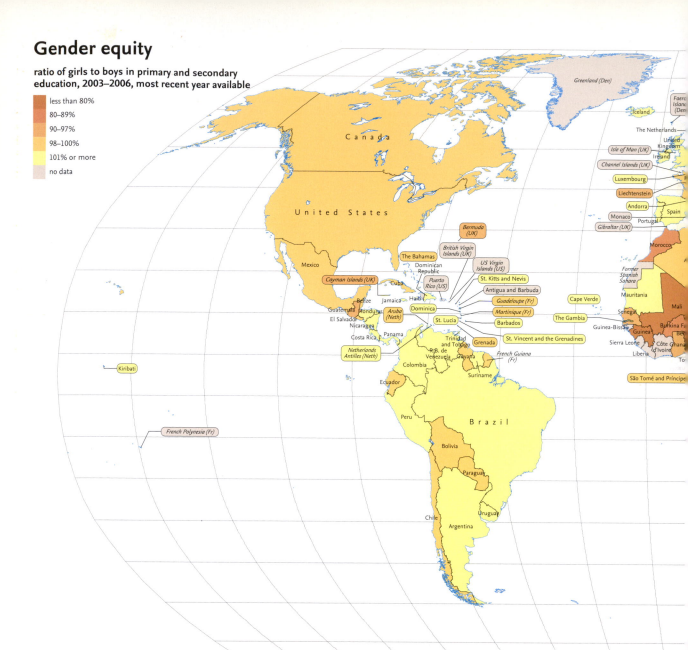

Countries and territories labeled on map include: Greenland (Den), Iceland, Faeroe Islands (Den), The Netherlands, United Kingdom, Isle of Man (UK), Ireland, Channel Islands (UK), Luxembourg, Liechtenstein, Andorra, Monaco, Spain, Portugal, Gibraltar (UK), Morocco, Former Spanish Sahara, Mauritania, Mali, Canada, United States, Mexico, Bermuda (UK), The Bahamas, Dominican Republic, British Virgin Islands (UK), US Virgin Islands (US), Cayman Islands (UK), Cuba, Puerto Rico (US), St. Kitts and Nevis, Antigua and Barbuda, Cape Verde, Belize, Jamaica, Haiti, Guadeloupe (Fr), Martinique (Fr), The Gambia, Senegal, Guatemala, Honduras, Aruba (Neth), Dominica, St. Lucia, Barbados, Guinea-Bissau, Guinea, Burkina Faso, El Salvador, Nicaragua, Costa Rica, Panama, Grenada, St. Vincent and the Grenadines, Sierra Leone, Côte d'Ivoire, Ghana, Liberia, Netherlands Antilles (Neth), Trinidad and Tobago, R.B. de Venezuela, Guyana, French Guiana (Fr), Colombia, Suriname, São Tomé and Príncipe, Kiribati, Ecuador, Peru, Brazil, French Polynesia (Fr), Bolivia, Paraguay, Chile, Uruguay, Argentina

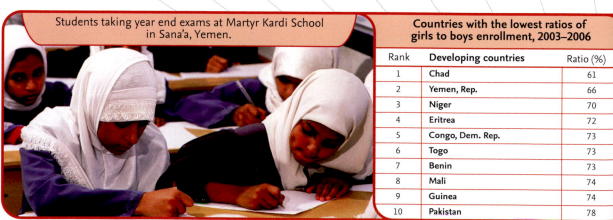

Students taking year end exams at Martyr Kardi School in Sana'a, Yemen.

Countries with the lowest ratios of girls to boys enrollment, 2003–2006

Rank	Developing countries	Ratio (%)
1	Chad	61
2	Yemen, Rep.	66
3	Niger	70
4	Eritrea	72
5	Congo, Dem. Rep.	73
6	Togo	73
7	Benin	73
8	Mali	74
9	Guinea	74
10	Pakistan	78

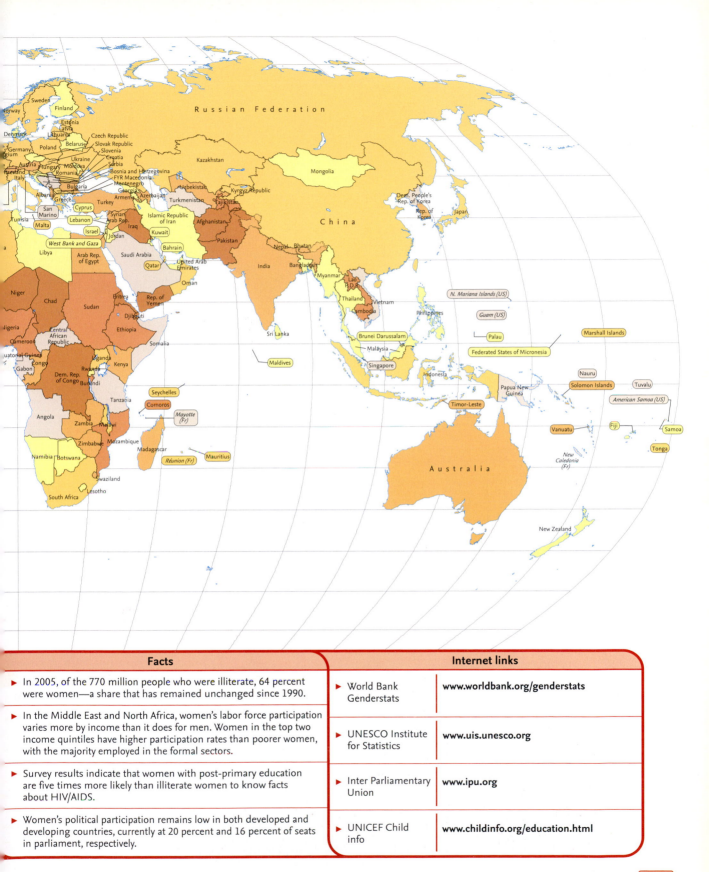

Facts		Internet links	
▶ In 2005, of the 770 million people who were illiterate, 64 percent were women—a share that has remained unchanged since 1990.		▶ World Bank Genderstats	**www.worldbank.org/genderstats**
▶ In the Middle East and North Africa, women's labor force participation varies more by income than it does for men. Women in the top two income quintiles have higher participation rates than poorer women, with the majority employed in the formal sectors.		▶ UNESCO Institute for Statistics	**www.uis.unesco.org**
▶ Survey results indicate that women with post-primary education are five times more likely than illiterate women to know facts about HIV/AIDS.		▶ Inter Parliamentary Union	**www.ipu.org**
▶ Women's political participation remains low in both developed and developing countries, currently at 20 percent and 16 percent of seats in parliament, respectively.		▶ UNICEF Child info	**www.childinfo.org/education.html**

Women in employment

share of women in total employment, 2006

- less than 25%
- 25–34%
- 35–39%
- 40–44%
- 45% or more
- no data

Maputo-Fapel, paper mill and paper recycling factory; women working in the recycling section

Countries with the lowest share of women in total employment, 2006

Rank	Country	Share of women (%
1	Saudi Arabia	14
2	West Bank and Gaza	14
3	United Arab Emirates	14
4	Oman	17
5	Egypt, Arab Rep.	18
6	Sudan	24
7	Jordan	25
8	Kuwait	26
9	Morocco	26
10	Pakistan	26

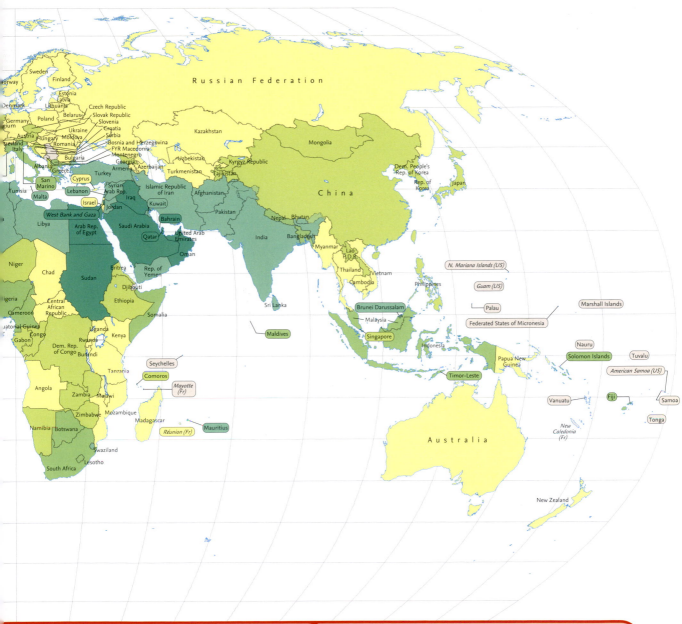

Facts	Internet links	
▶ In six countries, almost all of them in Middle East and North Africa, less than 25 percent of women ages 15 and over were in the labor force.	▶ World Bank Genderstats	www.worldbank.org/genderstats
▶ In South Asia and Sub-Saharan Africa, about two-thirds of women work in the agricultural sector, while usually more women work in service sectors in other regions.	▶ Inter Parliamentary Union	www.ipu.org
▶ Women often work as unpaid family workers. In Ethiopia, almost 70 percent of women are unpaid family workers.	▶ International Labour Organization	http://laborsta.ilo.org/ www.ilo.org/public/english/employment/ strat/kilm
▶ In many countries women's access to paid employment is limited. In Pakistan, only 10 percent of women are in paid employment in industry and service sectors.	▶ Demographic and Health Surveys	www.measuredhs.com

Each year, almost 10 million children die before their fifth birthday. Of these, the vast majority dies from causes that are preventable through a combination of good care, nutrition, and simple medical treatment. Child mortality is thus closely linked to poverty, with child malnutrition implicated in more than half of the deaths worldwide.

Child mortality has declined in every region since 1960, when 1 in 5 children died before the age of 5. By 1990, this rate had fallen to 1 in 10 children. Since then, progress has slowed, and a few countries in Sub-Saharan Africa actually experienced increases in child mortality. In 2006, 41 countries had under-5 mortality rates greater than 100 per 1,000. Ten countries—all of them in Sub-Saharan Africa—had under-5 mortality rates greater than 200. In developing countries today, 1 in 13 children dies before their fifth birthday, compared with 1 in 143 in high-income countries.

In developing countries, many children still die before their fifth birthday

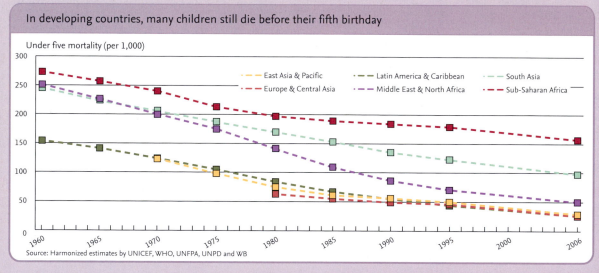

Under five mortality (per 1,000)

East Asia & Pacific · Latin America & Caribbean · South Asia · Europe & Central Asia · Middle East & North Africa · Sub-Saharan Africa

Source: Harmonized estimates by UNICEF, WHO, UNFPA, UNPD and WB

Immunizations are a cheap and effective way to reduce childhood deaths, yet many children in developing countries are not vaccinated

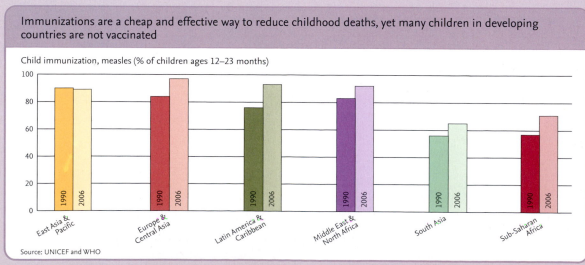

Child immunization, measles (% of children ages 12–23 months)

Source: UNICEF and WHO

Children of a slum-dwelling family have a high risk of dying before the age of five

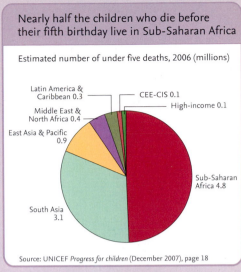

Nearly half the children who die before their fifth birthday live in Sub-Saharan Africa

Estimated number of under five deaths, 2006 (millions)

Latin America & Caribbean 0.3
Middle East & North Africa 0.4
East Asia & Pacific 0.9
CEE-CIS 0.1
High-income 0.1
Sub-Saharan Africa 4.8
South Asia 3.1

Source: UNICEF *Progress for children* (December 2007), page 18

Under-5 mortality is significantly lower among children living in urban areas and in richer households. These children are more likely to have access to better health care and to avail themselves of these services.

Just five diseases—pneumonia, diarrhea, malaria, measles, and AIDS—account for half of all deaths in children under age 5. Malnutrition is implicated in more than half of all child deaths worldwide. It weakens children's immune systems and reduces resistance to disease. The process often begins at birth, when poorly nourished mothers give birth to underweight babies. Improper feeding and child care practices contribute to worsen malnutrition.

Low-cost treatments and interventions such as early and exclusive breast feeding, antibiotics for respiratory infections, oral rehydration for diarrhea, immunization, and the use of treated bed nets and appropriate drugs in malarial regions could prevent many unnecessary deaths. In 2006, almost 80 percent of children in developing countries were immunized against measles, but regional differences remain. Improved public services, such as safe water and sanitation and education, especially for girls and mothers, can help save children's lives. Greater effort is needed to make sure the services reach people in rural areas and in poor families, because these people suffer the most but are the hardest to reach.

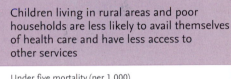

Children living in rural areas and poor households are less likely to avail themselves of health care and have less access to other services

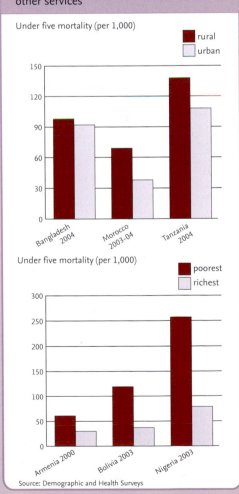

Under five mortality (per 1,000)

rural
urban

Under five mortality (per 1,000)

poorest
richest

Source: Demographic and Health Surveys

Child mortality

under five mortality rate per 1,000, 2006

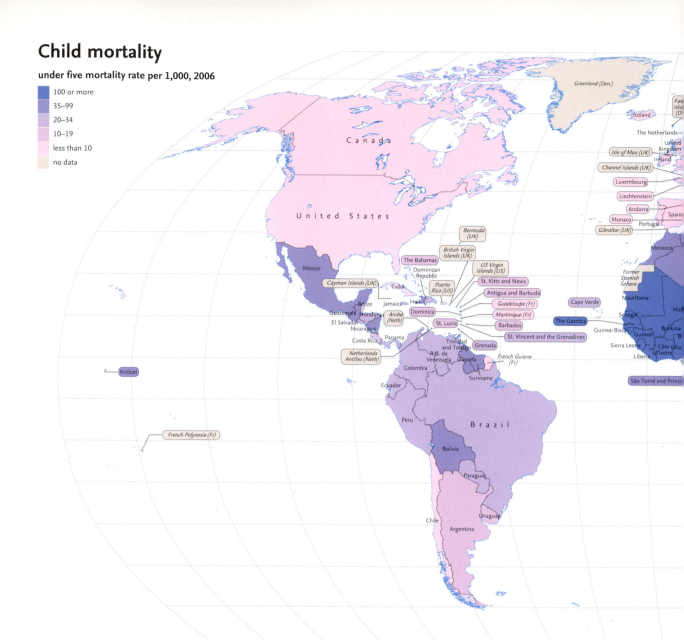

Legend:
- 100 or more
- 35–99
- 20–34
- 10–19
- less than 10
- no data

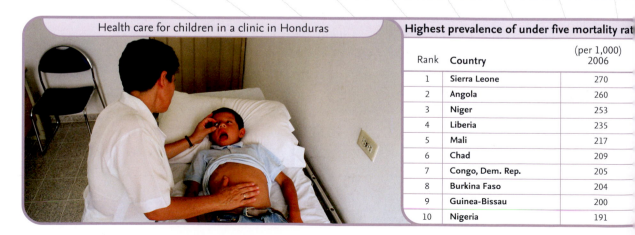

Health care for children in a clinic in Honduras

Rank	Country	(per 1,000) 2006
1	Sierra Leone	270
2	Angola	260
3	Niger	253
4	Liberia	235
5	Mali	217
6	Chad	209
7	Congo, Dem. Rep.	205
8	Burkina Faso	204
9	Guinea-Bissau	200
10	Nigeria	191

Highest prevalence of under five mortality rat

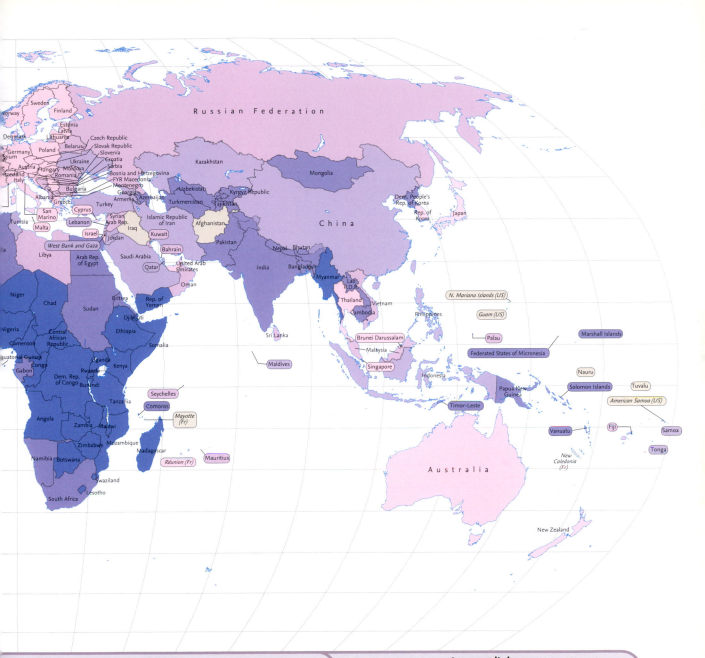

Facts	Internet links	
▶ Every hour, more than 1,000 children die before their fifth birthday.	▶ UNICEF Childinfo	**www.childinfo.org/ mortality.html**
▶ Of the approximately 10 million deaths annually to children under age 5, half occur in Sub-Saharan Africa.	▶ World Health Organization	**www.who.int/child_adolescent_ health/data/child/en**
▶ In South Asia, almost half the children are underweight. Its long term consequences are diminished productive capacity in adulthood.	▶ World Bank, HNPstats	**www.worldbank.org/hnpstats**
▶ Almost 70 percent of children under the age of 5 die in the first 12 months.	▶ Demographic and Health Surveys	**www.measuredhs.com**

Complications from pregnancy and childbirth are a leading cause of death and disability among women of reproductive age in developing countries. In 2005, more than half a million women died from pregnancy-related causes, and about 200 million women suffered life-threatening complications and disabilities. Over 99 percent of all maternal deaths occur in developing counties, the majority in Sub-Saharan Africa and South Asia.

Because of high maternal mortality and fertility rates, women in Africa face a 1 in 22 risk of a pregnancy-related death, and risks to women from the poorest families are even greater. In contrast, the lifetime risk to women in high-income countries is only 1 in 6,700.

High maternal mortality rates in many countries are the result of inadequate health care before, during, and after pregnancy. The situation is improving, but only 70 percent of pregnant women in South Asia had at least one prenatal care visit during pregnancy. Access to skilled care during childbirth is lower still. Only about 45 percent of births in South Asia and Sub-Saharan Africa are attended by skilled health staff, compared with 99 percent in high-income countries. In any country, poor women are much less likely to receive skilled care during childbirth.

Compounding the risks of poor reproductive health care are poorly timed and inadequately spaced births, which expose women to frequent pregnancies in short intervals. Although cheap and easy methods of preventing unwanted pregnancies are available, every year 120 million couples hoping to avoid pregnancy do not use contraception. As a result, 80 million women

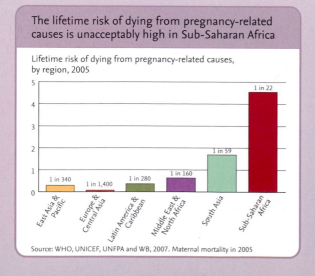

Women are at much higher risk of dying in childbirth in South Asia and Sub-Saharan Africa

Maternal mortality ratio (per 100,000 live births)

Source: WHO, UNICEF, UNFPA and WB, 2007. Maternal mortality in 2005

The lifetime risk of dying from pregnancy-related causes is unacceptably high in Sub-Saharan Africa

Lifetime risk of dying from pregnancy-related causes, by region, 2005

Source: WHO, UNICEF, UNFPA and WB, 2007. Maternal mortality in 2005

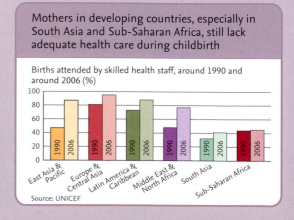

Mothers in developing countries, especially in South Asia and Sub-Saharan Africa, still lack adequate health care during childbirth

Births attended by skilled health staff, around 1990 and around 2006 (%)

Source: UNICEF

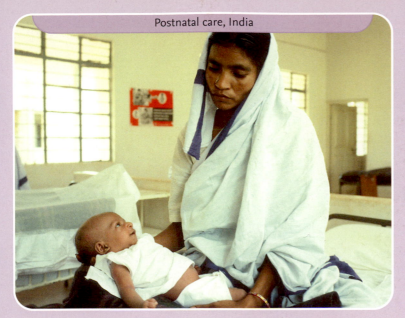
Postnatal care, India

30 percent are mothers or are pregnant. Many adolescent pregnancies are unintended, but young girls may continue their pregnancies, giving up opportunities for education and employment, or seek unsafe abortions. Forty percent of all abortions are performed on women under age 25.

become pregnant against their will, and 45 million seek abortions; about 20 million of these abortions are performed by untrained providers. Contraceptive use among women in developing countries has risen, from 14 percent of married women ages 15 to 49 in 1965 to 60 percent in 2006. But there is much variation. In Sub-Saharan Africa, only about 20 percent of women plan their pregnancies.

Teenage mothers

Teenage pregnancies are high risk for both mother and child. They are more likely to result in premature delivery, low birth weight, delivery complications, and death. In Sub-Saharan Africa, South Asia, and Latin America and the Caribbean, more than 10 percent of girls ages 15 to 19 are mothers. In Bangladesh and Mozambique, more than

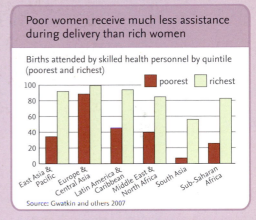
Poor women receive much less assistance during delivery than rich women

Births attended by skilled health personnel by quintile (poorest and richest)

■ poorest　■ richest

Source: Gwatkin and others 2007

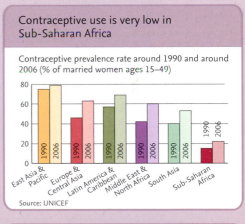
Contraceptive use is very low in Sub-Saharan Africa

Contraceptive prevalence rate around 1990 and around 2006 (% of married women ages 15–49)

Source: UNICEF

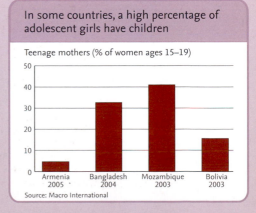
In some countries, a high percentage of adolescent girls have children

Teenage mothers (% of women ages 15–19)

Source: Macro International

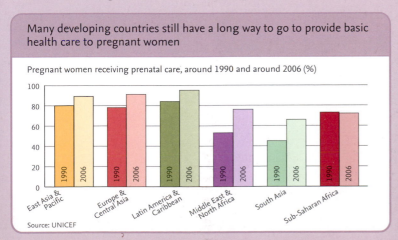
Many developing countries still have a long way to go to provide basic health care to pregnant women

Pregnant women receiving prenatal care, around 1990 and around 2006 (%)

Source: UNICEF

Total fertility rate

births per woman, 2006

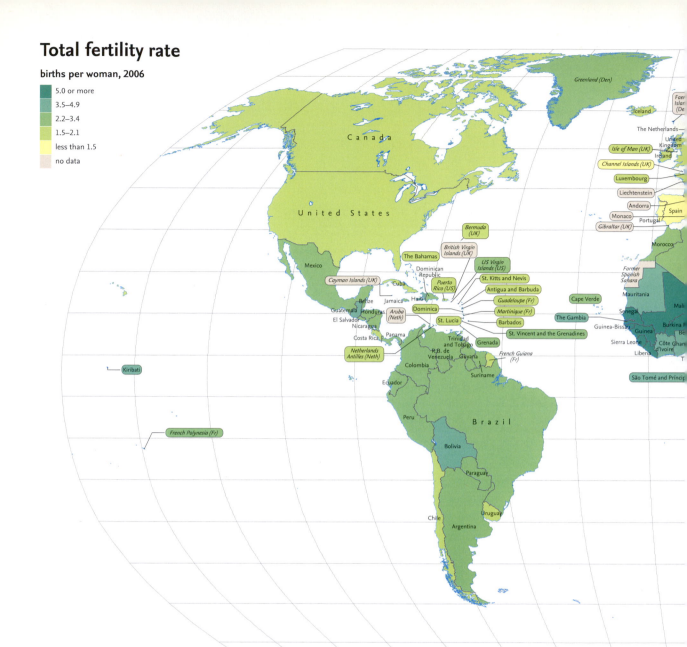

■	5.0 or more
■	3.5–4.9
■	2.2–3.4
■	1.5–2.1
■	less than 1.5
■	no data

A mother and child receive free vitamin A at a government health clinic, Hanoi

Countries with low level of contraceptive use, 2000–2007, most recent year available

Country	(% of women, ages 15–49)
Chad	3
Sierra Leone	5
Angola	6
Sudan	8
Eritrea	8
Mauritania	8
Mali	8
Burundi	9
Guinea	9
Liberia	10

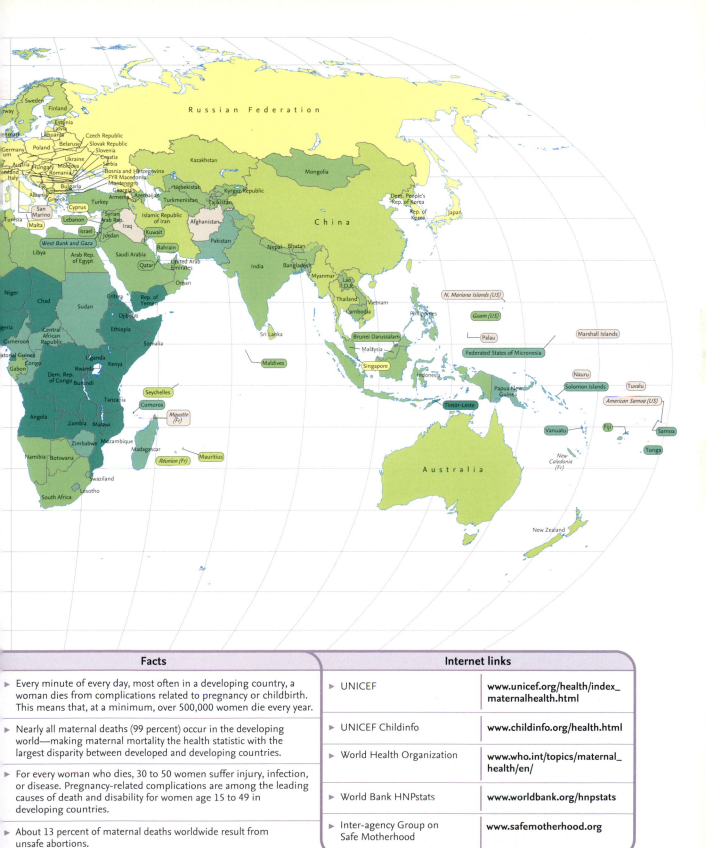

Facts

▶ Every minute of every day, most often in a developing country, a woman dies from complications related to pregnancy or childbirth. This means that, at a minimum, over 500,000 women die every year.

▶ Nearly all maternal deaths (99 percent) occur in the developing world—making maternal mortality the health statistic with the largest disparity between developed and developing countries.

▶ For every woman who dies, 30 to 50 women suffer injury, infection, or disease. Pregnancy-related complications are among the leading causes of death and disability for women age 15 to 49 in developing countries.

▶ About 13 percent of maternal deaths worldwide result from unsafe abortions.

Internet links

▶ UNICEF	**www.unicef.org/health/index_ maternalhealth.html**
▶ UNICEF Childinfo	**www.childinfo.org/health.html**
▶ World Health Organization	**www.who.int/topics/maternal_ health/en/**
▶ World Bank HNPstats	**www.worldbank.org/hnpstats**
▶ Inter-agency Group on Safe Motherhood	**www.safemotherhood.org**

Communicable diseases such as HIV/AIDS, tuberculosis, and malaria kill millions of people each year. They exact a terrible toll on society and the economy of developing countries. Although international awareness and funding to fight epidemic diseases have increased, much remains to be done.

A Bangladeshi health worker giving antibiotic tablets to a tuberculosis patient

Every day, over 6,800 people are infected with HIV, and more than 5,700 die from AIDS. The number of people living with HIV reached 33.2 million in 2007, even though the global HIV prevalence rate has leveled off in recent years. Over 60 percent of people living with HIV/AIDS are in Sub-Saharan Africa, where women and children are especially vulnerable to the disease. Women constitute almost 61 percent of adults ages 15 to 49 living with HIV, and about 90 percent of all HIV-positive children ages 0 to 14 live in the region. Orphans and vulnerable children face grave risks to their health and well-being. Many cannot attend school, and assistance for them is minimal. While treatment to those living with HIV and AIDS has increased, only 28 percent of people in developing regions who needed antiretroviral therapy received treatment in 2006.

Tuberculosis, still a major cause of illness and death worldwide, is becoming more dangerous with the spread of drug-resistant strains. Twenty-two countries, which are seriously affected by tuberculosis and are

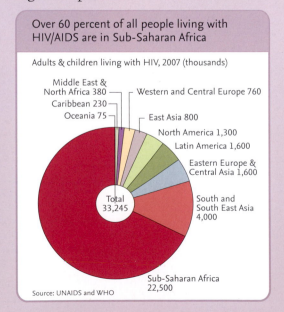

Over 60 percent of all people living with HIV/AIDS are in Sub-Saharan Africa

Adults & children living with HIV, 2007 (thousands)

Middle East & North Africa 380
Caribbean 230
Oceania 75
Western and Central Europe 760
East Asia 800
North America 1,300
Latin America 1,600
Eastern Europe & Central Asia 1,600
South and South East Asia 4,000
Total 33,245
Sub-Saharan Africa 22,500

Source: UNAIDS and WHO

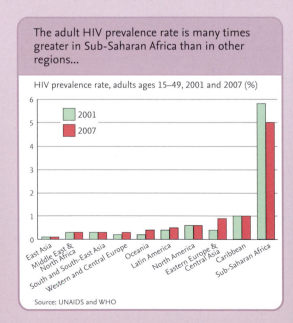

The adult HIV prevalence rate is many times greater in Sub-Saharan Africa than in other regions...

HIV prevalence rate, adults ages 15–49, 2001 and 2007 (%)

2001
2007

East Asia
Middle East & North Africa
South and South-East Asia
Western and Central Europe
Oceania
Latin America
North America
Eastern Europe & Central Asia
Caribbean
Sub-Saharan Africa

Source: UNAIDS and WHO

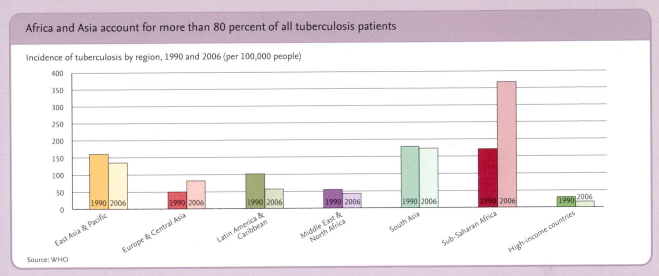

Incidence of tuberculosis by region, 1990 and 2006 (per 100,000 people)

Source: WHO

mostly in Asia and Africa, collectively account for 80 percent of all tuberculosis cases. Poor people are especially vulnerable to the disease due to underlying health problems and limited access to treatment. Tuberculosis is the leading cause of death among people who are HIV-positive, accounting for about 15 percent of AIDS deaths worldwide. Drug resistant tuberculosis strains are caused by inconsistent or partial treatment, wrong treatment regimens, or unavailability of drugs.

Malaria causes more than 1 million deaths each year, primarily among children below age 5 and pregnant women, mainly in Africa. The emergence of drug-resistant parasites and insecticide-resistant mosquitoes is exacerbating the impact of malaria. About 40 percent of the world's population is at risk from malaria—the largest share is composed of those living in the poorest countries. Insecticide-treated mosquito nets can

Treated bed nets combat malaria but are still not widely used

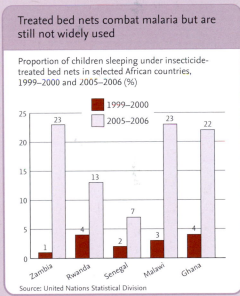

Proportion of children sleeping under insecticide-treated bed nets in selected African countries, 1999–2000 and 2005–2006 (%)

Source: United Nations Statistical Division

reduce malaria transmission by up to 90 percent. The availability of treated bed nets has increased recently, but the use of treated bed nets among children under age 5 is still very low—only 5 percent in Sub-Saharan Africa.

In addition to the use of treated bed nets, malaria control depends on surveillance, efficient public health measures, education, and access to medications.

... but only 25 percent of those infected receive treatment

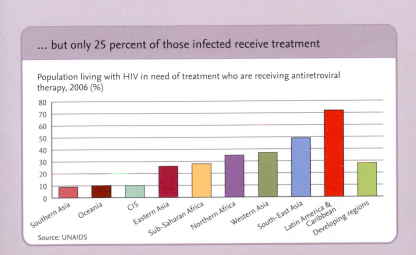

Population living with HIV in need of treatment who are receiving antiretroviral therapy, 2006 (%)

Source: UNAIDS

HIV/AIDS

adult HIV prevalence, 2005

- 15.0% or more
- 5.0–14.9%
- 1.0–4.9%
- 0.5–0.9%
- less than 0.5%
- no data

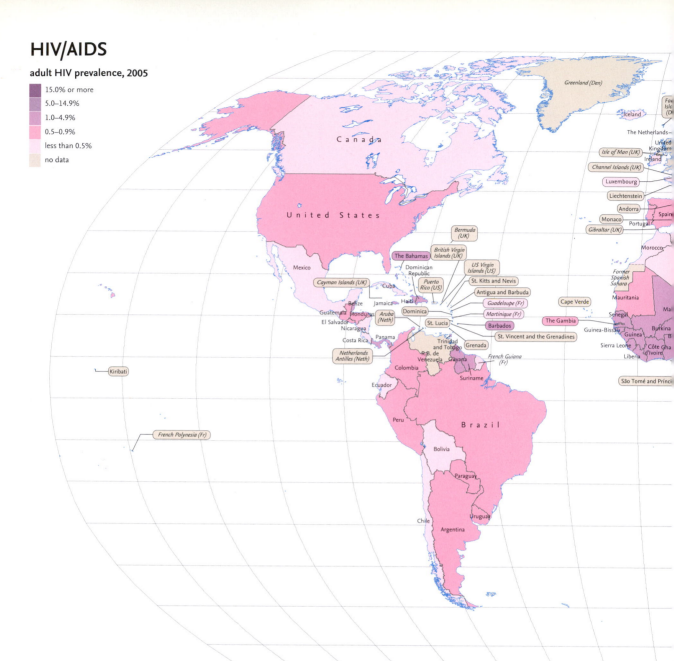

Greenland (Den)

Canada

Iceland

The Netherlands

United Kingdom

Isle of Man (UK)
Ireland

Channel Islands (UK)

Luxembourg

Liechtenstein

Andorra

Monaco

Spain

Gibraltar (UK)
Portugal

United States

Morocco

Mexico

Bermuda (UK)

Dominican Republic

British Virgin Islands (UK)

The Bahamas

US Virgin Islands (US)

Cayman Islands (UK)

Cuba

Puerto Rico (US)

St. Kitts and Nevis

Antigua and Barbuda

Former Spanish Sahara

Mauritania

Cape Verde

Belize

Jamaica

Haiti

Guadeloupe (Fr)

Senegal

Mali

Guatemala

Honduras

Aruba (Neth)

Dominica

Martinique (Fr)

The Gambia

Guinea-Bissau

Burkina

El Salvador

Nicaragua

St. Lucia

Barbados

Guinea

Costa Rica

Panama

Trinidad and Tobago

St. Vincent and the Grenadines

Sierra Leone

Côte d'Ivoire

Netherlands Antilles (Neth)

R.B. de Venezuela

Grenada

Guyana

Liberia

Kiribati

Colombia

Suriname

French Guiana (Fr)

São Tomé and Príncipe

Ecuador

Peru

Brazil

French Polynesia (Fr)

Bolivia

Paraguay

Chile

Uruguay

Argentina

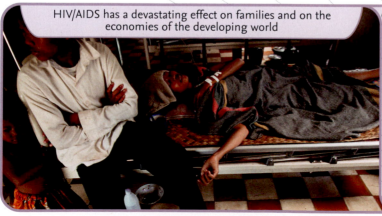

Countries with the highest prevalence rates, 200

Rank	Country	Prevalence of HIV (% of population ages 15–49)
1	Swaziland	26.1
2	Botswana	23.9
3	Lesotho	23.2
4	South Africa	18.1
5	Zimbabwe	15.3
6	Namibia	15.3
7	Zambia	15.2
8	Mozambique	12.5
9	Malawi	11.9
10	Kenya	7.8

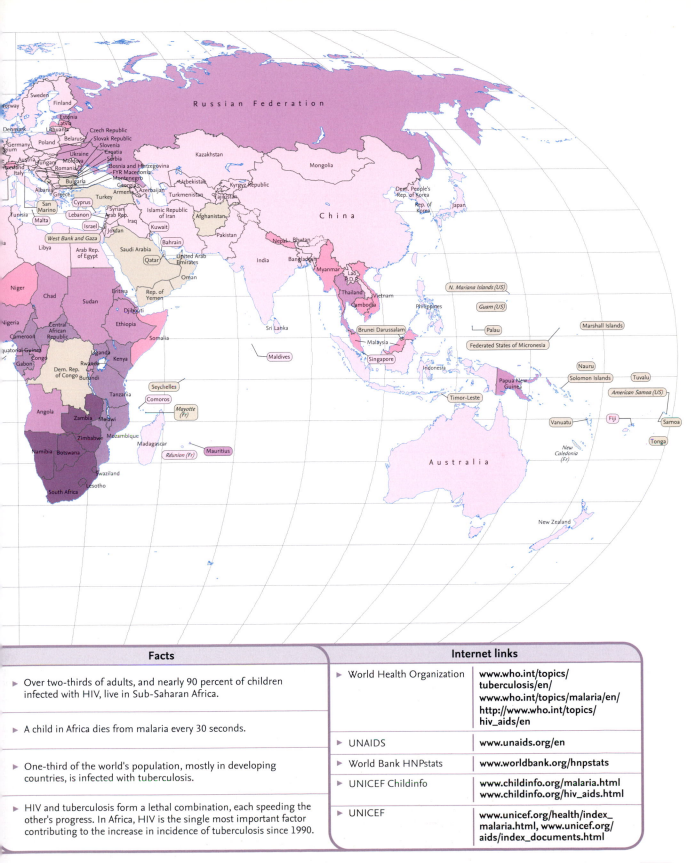

Facts

▶ Over two-thirds of adults, and nearly 90 percent of children infected with HIV, live in Sub-Saharan Africa.

▶ A child in Africa dies from malaria every 30 seconds.

▶ One-third of the world's population, mostly in developing countries, is infected with tuberculosis.

▶ HIV and tuberculosis form a lethal combination, each speeding the other's progress. In Africa, HIV is the single most important factor contributing to the increase in incidence of tuberculosis since 1990.

Internet links

▶ World Health Organization	www.who.int/topics/ tuberculosis/en/ www.who.int/topics/malaria/en/ http://www.who.int/topics/ hiv_aids/en
▶ UNAIDS	www.unaids.org/en
▶ World Bank HNPstats	www.worldbank.org/hnpstats
▶ UNICEF Childinfo	www.childinfo.org/malaria.html www.childinfo.org/hiv_aids.html
▶ UNICEF	www.unicef.org/health/index_ malaria.html, www.unicef.org/ aids/index_documents.html

Services, the most rapidly growing sector of the global economy, now accounts for almost 70 percent of world output. Developing economies are also becoming important producers of manufactured goods. However, the natural resource sectors, especially agriculture and mining, continue to be the main sources of income for many developing economies.

Gross domestic product (GDP) measures the output of an economy. It is the sum of value added in agriculture (including forestry and fisheries), industry (including mining and manufacturing), and services (including government and private services). As economies develop, they typically shift from the production and export of agricultural and mining commodities to manufactured goods, and later to services. In many high-income economies more than 70 percent of GDP is produced in the service sector. The income elasticity of demand for services is generally greater than that of agricultural products.

Services now account for 54 percent of the output of middle-income economies, although some, such as Jordan and Panama,

Services now account for two-thirds of global output

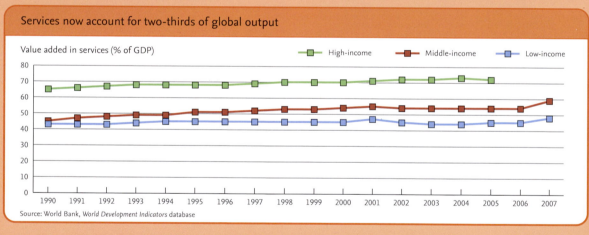

Source: World Bank, *World Development Indicators* database

Service sectors are growing rapidly in both East Asia and Pacific, and South Asia

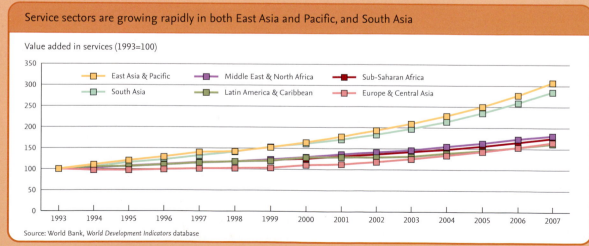

Source: World Bank, *World Development Indicators* database

Agricultural employment as a share to total employment, 2003–2005 (%)

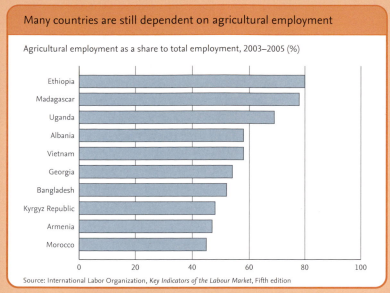

Ethiopia	80
Madagascar	78
Uganda	68
Albania	58
Vietnam	58
Georgia	54
Bangladesh	52
Kyrgyz Republic	48
Armenia	47
Morocco	45

Source: International Labor Organization, *Key Indicators of the Labour Market*, Fifth edition

Although the service sector can contribute more than 70 percent of GDP in high-income economies...

have maintained large service sectors for some time. In low-income economies, the service sectors are growing and now produce slightly less than 50 percent of the output. The East Asia and Pacific region, led by China, and the South Asia region, led by India, have increased their service output in real terms more than three-fold since 1990.

Although the service sector is growing everywhere, agriculture remains of great importance to developing economies. Agriculture not only feeds a growing population, it produces raw materials for industries, such as rubber and timber. Increases in oil prices have resulted in additional demand for food crops, such as corn and sugar cane, used to produce biofuels. Higher prices for agricultural products will raise the incomes of producers, but higher food prices also reduce the welfare of consumers.

In 2007, value added in agriculture as a share of GDP was over 40 percent in 10 low-income economies, nine of them in Africa. Agriculture is also an important source of employment. It employs over 40 percent of the labor force in 16 countries, over 50 percent in seven countries, and as much as 80 percent in Ethiopia. Not only low-income economies, but also some middle-income economies remain dependent on agriculture. In Albania, agriculture accounts for 58 percent of the total employment. In comparison, agricultural employment made up 4 percent of total employment in Japan, 2 percent in the United States and Germany, and only 1 percent in the United Kingdom.

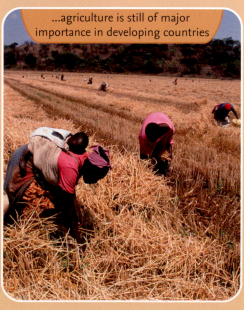

...agriculture is still of major importance in developing countries

Agricultural output

share of value added in agriculture in GDP,
2002–2007, most recent year available

- 25% or more
- 15–24%
- 10–14%
- 3–9%
- less than 3%
- no data

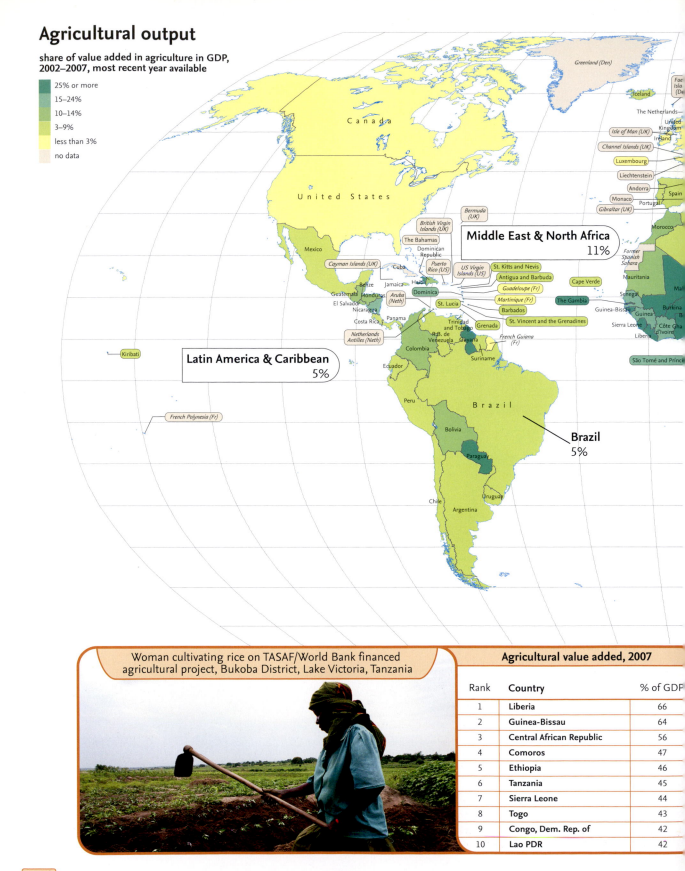

Greenland (Den)

Iceland

Faeroe Islands (Den)

The Netherlands

United Kingdom

Ireland

Isle of Man (UK)

Channel Islands (UK)

Luxembourg

Liechtenstein

Andorra

Monaco

Gibraltar (UK)

Portugal

Spain

C a n a d a

U n i t e d   S t a t e s

Bermuda (UK)

Middle East & North Africa
11%

Morocco

Former Spanish Sahara

Mexico

British Virgin Islands (UK)

The Bahamas

Dominican Republic

Cayman Islands (UK)

Cuba

Puerto Rico (US)

US Virgin Islands (US)

St. Kitts and Nevis

Antigua and Barbuda

Cape Verde

Mauritania

Jamaica

Haiti

Dominica

Guadeloupe (Fr)

Belize

Guatemala

Honduras

Aruba (Neth)

St. Lucia

Martinique (Fr)

The Gambia

Senegal

Mali

El Salvador

Nicaragua

Barbados

Guinea-Bissau

Guinea

Burkina

Costa Rica

Panama

Grenada

St. Vincent and the Grenadines

Sierra Leone

Côte d'Ivoire

Netherlands Antilles (Neth)

Trinidad and Tobago

R.B. de Venezuela

Guyana

Liberia

Kiribati

Colombia

Suriname

French Guiana (Fr)

São Tomé and Príncipe

Ecuador

Latin America & Caribbean
5%

Peru

B r a z i l

Brazil
5%

French Polynesia (Fr)

Bolivia

Paraguay

Uruguay

Chile

Argentina

Woman cultivating rice on TASAF/World Bank financed
agricultural project, Bukoba District, Lake Victoria, Tanzania

Agricultural value added, 2007		
Rank	Country	% of GDP
1	Liberia	66
2	Guinea-Bissau	64
3	Central African Republic	56
4	Comoros	47
5	Ethiopia	46
6	Tanzania	45
7	Sierra Leone	44
8	Togo	43
9	Congo, Dem. Rep. of	42
10	Lao PDR	42

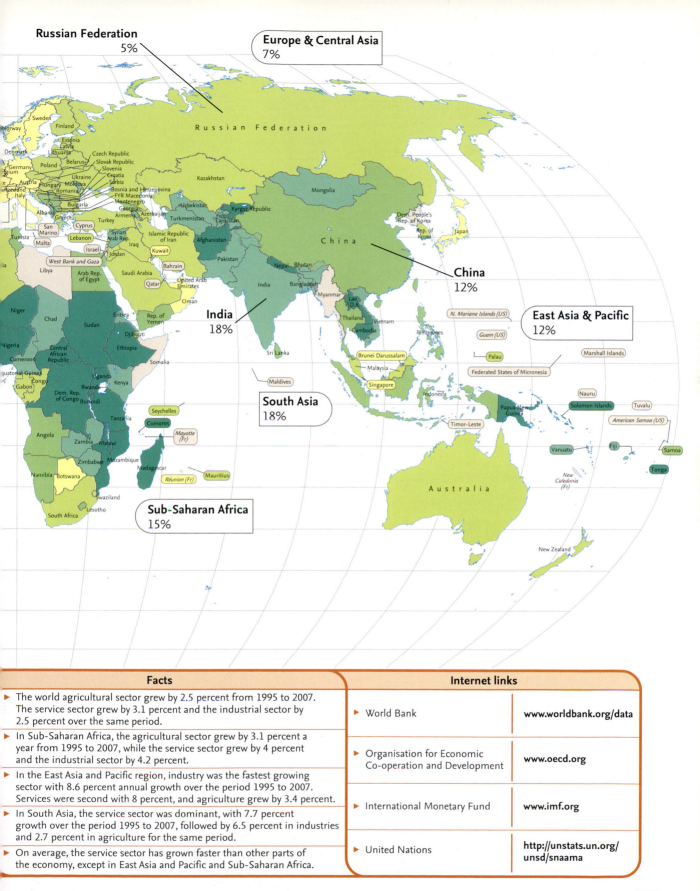

Russian Federation
5%

Europe & Central Asia
7%

China
12%

East Asia & Pacific
12%

India
18%

South Asia
18%

Sub-Saharan Africa
15%

Facts	Internet links	
▶ The world agricultural sector grew by 2.5 percent from 1995 to 2007. The service sector grew by 3.1 percent and the industrial sector by 2.5 percent over the same period.	▶ World Bank	www.worldbank.org/data
▶ In Sub-Saharan Africa, the agricultural sector grew by 3.1 percent a year from 1995 to 2007, while the service sector grew by 4 percent and the industrial sector by 4.2 percent.	▶ Organisation for Economic Co-operation and Development	www.oecd.org
▶ In the East Asia and Pacific region, industry was the fastest growing sector with 8.6 percent annual growth over the period 1995 to 2007. Services were second with 8 percent, and agriculture grew by 3.4 percent.	▶ International Monetary Fund	www.imf.org
▶ In South Asia, the service sector was dominant, with 7.7 percent growth over the period 1995 to 2007, followed by 6.5 percent in industries and 2.7 percent in agriculture for the same period.	▶ United Nations	http://unstats.un.org/ unsd/snaama
▶ On average, the service sector has grown faster than other parts of the economy, except in East Asia and Pacific and Sub-Saharan Africa.		

Governance describes the way public officials and institutions acquire and exercise authority to provide public goods and services, including education, health care, infrastructure, and a sound investment climate. Good governance is associated with increased citizen participation and improved accountability of public officials. It is fundamental to development and economic growth.

Governance has several dimensions:

- the process by which governments are selected, monitored, and replaced;
- the capacity of government to effectively formulate and implement sound policies;
- the respect of citizens and the state for the institutions that govern interactions between them.

Features of good governance—such as free and fair elections, respect for individual liberties and property rights, a free and vibrant press, open and impartial judiciary, and well-informed and effective legislative structures—all contribute to strong and capable institutions of the state.

Although bad governance is often equated with corruption, the concepts, while related, are different. Corruption—the abuse of public office for private gain—is an outcome of poor governance, reflecting the breakdown of accountability. Corruption undermines the legitimacy of governments and may reduce the quality and availability of public services if funds are diverted to private use. Excessive "red tape" and poor bureaucratic performance can also become

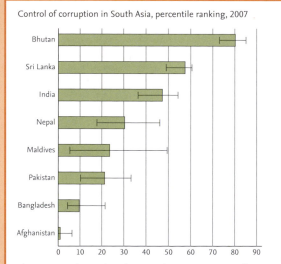

Control of corruption varies even within the same region

Control of corruption in South Asia, percentile ranking, 2007

The percentile rank indicates the percentage of countries worldwide that rate below the selected country (subject to a margin of error). Higher values indicate better governance ratings. Error bars, showing the statistically likely range of estimates, are shown as thin black lines. For instance, a bar extending to 75 percent with error bars showing a range of 60 to 85 percent means that an estimated 75 percent of countries rate worse and an estimated 25 percent rate better than that country. At the 90 percent confidence level, only 60 percent of countries rate worse, while 15 percent of countries rate better.

Source: Kaufmann, D., A. Kraay and M. Mastruzzi 2008: *Governance Matters VII: Aggregated and Individual Governance Indicators 1996-2007*

Democratic elections are one aspect of good governance

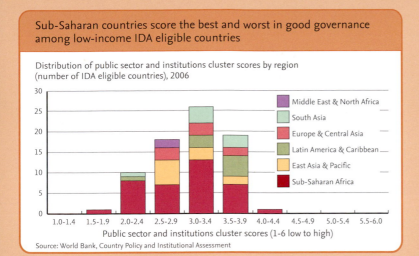

Sub-Saharan countries score the best and worst in good governance among low-income IDA eligible countries

Distribution of public sector and institutions cluster scores by region (number of IDA eligible countries), 2006

Legend:
- Middle East & North Africa
- South Asia
- Europe & Central Asia
- Latin America & Caribbean
- East Asia & Pacific
- Sub-Saharan Africa

x-axis: Public sector and institutions cluster scores (1–6 low to high)
values: 1.0-1.4, 1.5-1.9, 2.0-2.4, 2.5-2.9, 3.0-3.4, 3.5-3.9, 4.0-4.4, 4.5-4.9, 5.0-5.4, 5.5-6.0

Source: World Bank, Country Policy and Institutional Assessment

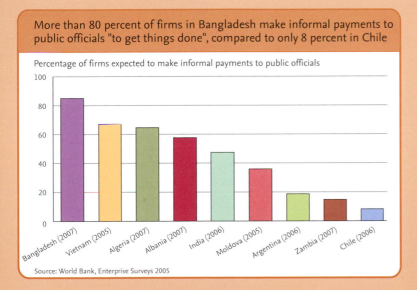

More than 80 percent of firms in Bangladesh make informal payments to public officials "to get things done", compared to only 8 percent in Chile

Percentage of firms expected to make informal payments to public officials

Countries: Bangladesh (2007), Vietnam (2005), Algeria (2007), Albania (2007), India (2006), Moldova (2005), Argentina (2006), Zambia (2007), Chile (2006)

Source: World Bank, Enterprise Surveys 2005

The World Bank's Country Policy and Institutional Assessment (CPIA) is an annual exercise by World Bank staff to measure the extent to which a country's policy and institutional framework supports sustainable growth and poverty reduction. Scores of these assessments are disclosed only for low-income countries that are eligible for lending by the World Bank's International Development Association (IDA). CPIA indicators examine policies and institutions, not development outcomes, which can depend on forces outside a country's control. There are 16 criteria grouped into four clusters; one of the clusters (shown in the top left chart) is the public sector management and institutions cluster. This cluster includes five criteria: property rights and rule-based governance; quality of budgetary and financial management; efficiency of revenue mobilization; quality of public administration; and transparency, accountability, and control of corruption in the public sector.

Parliament in session in South Africa

excuses for unofficial payments "to get things done," raising the cost of doing business. Fighting corruption requires addressing underlying failures of governance.

Measuring the quality of institutions and governance outcomes is difficult and often subject to large margins of error, (see the margins of error shown in the chart on the left). Data for one dimension of governance—control of corruption—are presented in the map. The data are an aggregate measure derived from several sources of informed views of individuals from both the private and public sectors. The map represents data on control of corruption by percentile ranges, from the best performing (90th to 100th percentile) to the poorest performing (0 to 9th percentile). Some developing countries have better scores on some governance measures than developed countries.

Controlling corruption

control of corruption from the Worldwide Governance Indicators, percentile rank, 2007

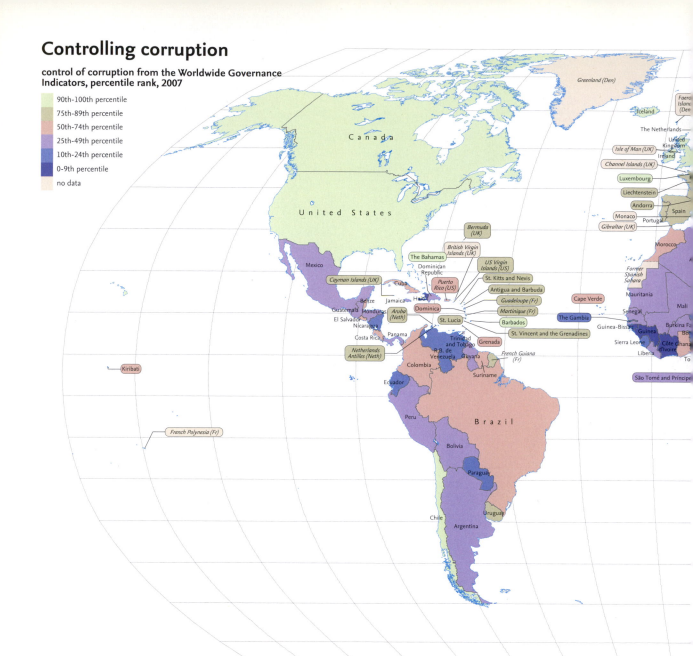

- 90th-100th percentile
- 75th-89th percentile
- 50th-74th percentile
- 25th-49th percentile
- 10th-24th percentile
- 0-9th percentile
- no data

People in many countries are fighting against corruption

Control of corruption

Approximate rank	Developing countries, population over 1 million	percentile rank, 2007	Lower percentile range
1	Chile	90	84
2	Uruguay	81	74
3	Botswana	80	74
4	Hungary	71	64
5	Mauritius	70	62
6	Costa Rica	69	62
7	South Africa	67	61
8	Jordan	67	61
9	Latvia	66	61
10	Namibia	63	59

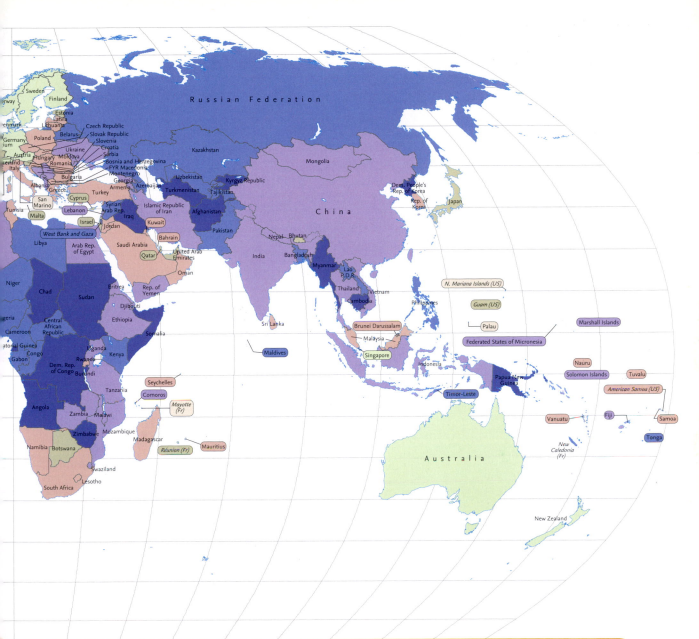

	Facts		Internet links	
Upper percentile range	▶ Nine Sub-Saharan African countries rank in the 50th percentile or higher in the Worldwide Governance Indicators measure of *control of corruption*.		▶ World Bank: Worldwide Governance Indicators	**www.govindicators.org**
92	▶ Research shows a relationship between low levels of income and higher levels of corruption. But some middle-income countries, such as Botswana, Chile, and Uruguay, perform as well as some high-income countries on measures of governance.		▶ World Bank: Enterprise Surveys	**www.enterprisesurveys.org**
84				
83			▶ World Bank: Doing Business	**www.doingbusiness.org**
74				
74				
73	▶ Good governance has been found to significantly enhance the effectiveness of development assistance.		▶ United Nations Development Programme (UNDP): Democratic Governance	**www.undp.org/governance**
73				
73	▶ When governance is improved by one standard deviation, infant mortality declines by two-thirds and incomes rise about threefold in the long run.		▶ Transparency International	**www.transparency.org**
73				
70				

Infrastructure services—transport, energy, water and sanitation, and information and communications technology—are the backbone of a functioning economy, facilitating growth and binding communities together. Some infrastructure is built and maintained by governments; some is privately owned; and some comes about through public-private partnerships.

Infrastructure services play a key role in the most important development objective—reducing poverty and bringing real improvements in the lives of billions of people in developing countries. These services affect people in many ways—what they consume and produce; how they heat and light their homes; how they travel to work, to school, or to visit family and friends, and how they communicate. Without passable roads, farmers cannot deliver their products to markets. Without reliable electricity, manufacturers cannot compete in today's markets. And information and communications are essential in an integrated world.

Physical isolation is a strong contributor to poverty. People living in remote places have less access to health and education services, employment, and markets. Problems are particularly severe in rural areas. An estimated 1 billion rural dwellers in developing countries, most of them poor, are without reliable access to affordable means of transportation.

Despite global efforts, improvements in water and sanitation infrastructure have barely kept pace with population growth and migration in the developing world, and will

---

Rural road projects in Vietnam improved people's access to all-weather roads from about 30 percent in 1993 to more than 80 percent in 2004

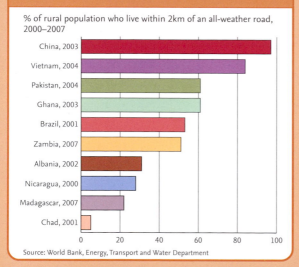

% of rural population who live within 2km of an all-weather road, 2000–2007

Source: World Bank, Energy, Transport and Water Department

Water-related deaths and diseases can be sharply reduced with improvements in drinking water, sanitation, and good hygiene

- 2.6 billion people—more than 40 percent of the world population—do not use a toilet, but instead use open or unsanitary places.
- Every year, unsafe water, coupled with a lack of basic sanitation, kills at least 1.6 million children under the age of 5 years—more than eight times the number of people who died in the Asian tsunami in 2004.
- Although 73 percent of rural dwellers have access to an improved source of drinking water, only 30 percent have access to piped water in the home.

Source: WHO/UNICEF Joint Monitoring Programme for Water Supply and Sanitation, 2006. *Meeting the MDG Drinking Water and Sanitation Target: the Urban and Rural Challenge of the Decade*

Telecommunications infrastructure projects attract high levels of private sector participation but there is much less in water and sanitation

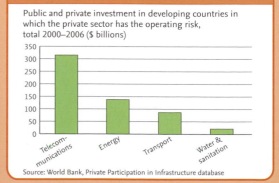

Public and private investment in developing countries in which the private sector has the operating risk, total 2000–2006 ($ billions)

Source: World Bank, Private Participation in Infrastructure database

Women collecting water from a pump in Mozambique

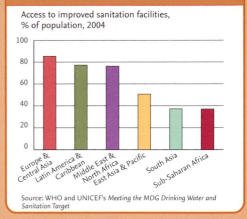

Improved sanitation facilities range from simple but protected pit latrines to flush toilets with a sewerage connection

Access to improved sanitation facilities, % of population, 2004

Source: WHO and UNICEF's *Meeting the MDG Drinking Water and Sanitation Target*

require more public and private investment. Investment commitments in water and sanitation projects with private participation from 2000–2006 were only $22 billion, compared to $315 billion in investments in telecommunications. The challenge in reducing disease transmission lies not only in providing better water and sanitation facilities, but also in promoting good hygiene practices, such as hand washing. Globally, approximately 1.1 billion people remain without access to safe water, 2.4 billion without sanitation, and 1.6 billion without electricity.

Information and communication technology has vast potential for fostering growth in developing countries by helping to increase productivity in a wide range of economic activities, from agriculture to manufacturing and services. Mobile phones keep families and communities in contact and provide market information for farmers and business people. By the end of 2007, there were over 3 billion mobile phone subscribers in the world, compared to 1.3 billion fixed telephone lines. The Internet delivers information to schools and hospitals, and computers improve public and private services and increase productivity and participation.

The global supply of infrastructure services is not able to meet the needs of today. With another 2 billion people arriving in the next 25 years, the challenges of tomorrow will be even greater. Infrastructure investment in developing countries will need to double to more than $400 billion per year. Increased investment also needs to be accompanied by improved policies and institutions to deliver quality services to citizens.

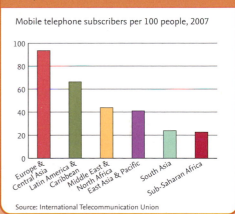

The Europe and Central Asia region leads developing countries in mobile telephone subscribers

Mobile telephone subscribers per 100 people, 2007

Source: International Telecommunication Union

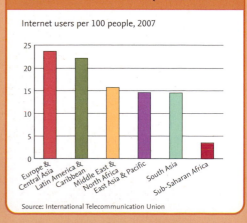

Among developing country regions, Internet use is highest in Europe & Central Asia and in Latin America & the Caribbean

Internet users per 100 people, 2007

Source: International Telecommunication Union

Internet users

Internet users per 100 people, 2007 or latest available data

■	less than 2
■	2–9
■	10–24
■	25–49
■	50 or more
■	no data

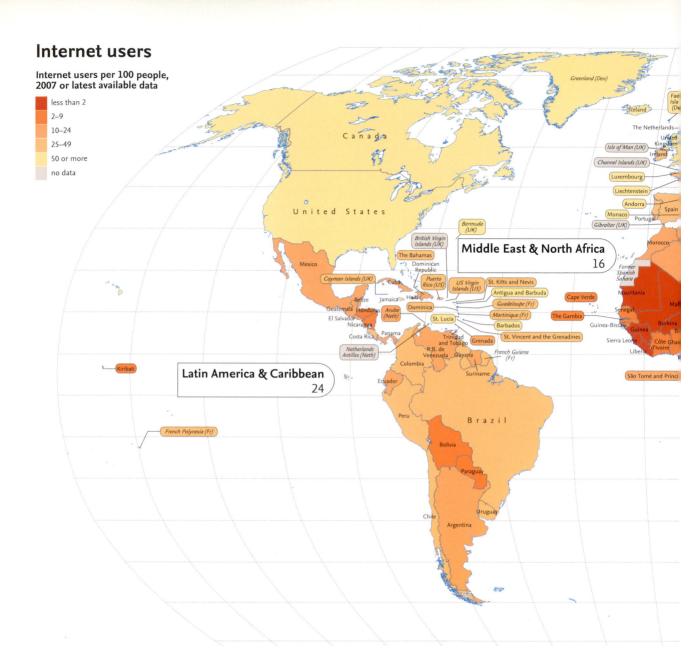

Greenland (Den)

Iceland

The Netherlands

United Kingdom

Isle of Man (UK)

Ireland

Channel Islands (UK)

Luxembourg

Liechtenstein

Andorra

Spain

Monaco

Portugal

Gibraltar (UK)

Morocco

Canada

United States

Bermuda (UK)

Middle East & North Africa
16

Former Spanish Sahara

Mauritania

Mexico

British Virgin Islands (UK)

The Bahamas

Dominican Republic

Cayman Islands (UK)

Cuba

Puerto Rico (US)

US Virgin Islands (US)

St. Kitts and Nevis

Antigua and Barbuda

Cape Verde

Belize

Jamaica

Haiti

Dominica

Guadeloupe (Fr)

The Gambia

Senegal

Mali

Guatemala

Honduras

Aruba (Neth)

St. Lucia

Martinique (Fr)

Guinea-Bissau

Guinea

Burkina

El Salvador

Nicaragua

Barbados

Sierra Leone

Côte d'Ivoire

Costa Rica

Panama

Trinidad and Tobago

Grenada

St. Vincent and the Grenadines

Liberia

Netherlands Antilles (Neth)

R.B. de Venezuela

Guyana

French Guiana (Fr)

Colombia

São Tomé and Príncipe

Kiribati

Suriname

Ecuador

Latin America & Caribbean
24

Peru

B r a z i l

French Polynesia (Fr)

Bolivia

Paraguay

Uruguay

Chile

Argentina

Students continue their language lessons in the computer laboratory at Hanoi University, Vietnam

Internet users

Rank	Countries with population of 1 million or more	(per 100 people) 2007
1	Netherlands	92
2	Canada	85
3	Norway	81
4	New Zealand	79
5	Sweden	77
6	Japan	74
7	United States	73
8	Korea, Rep.	72
9	Finland	68
10	United Kingdom	66

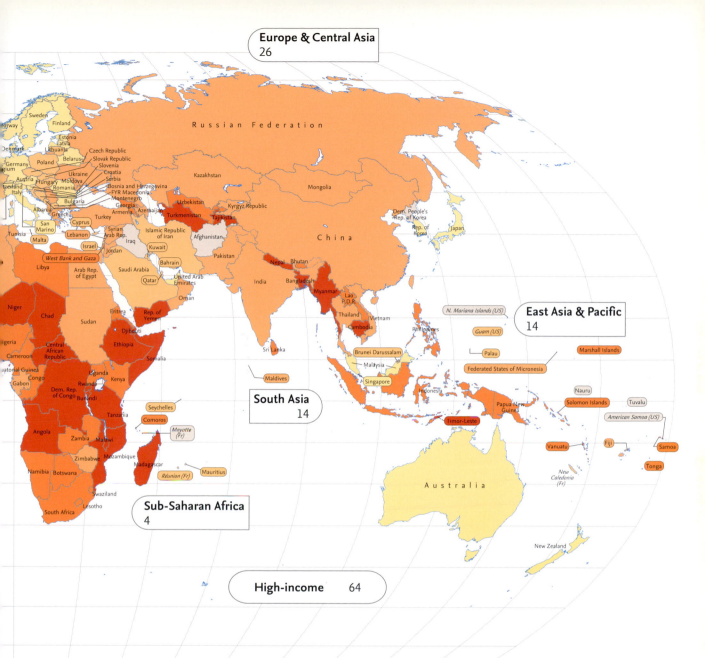

Europe & Central Asia
26

R u s s i a n   F e d e r a t i o n

Kazakhstan

Mongolia

C h i n a

East Asia & Pacific
14

South Asia
14

Sub-Saharan Africa
4

High-income   64

Australia

New Zealand

Facts

▶ Worldwide, from 2000–2007, the number of Internet users more than tripled, increasing from 390 million users in 2000 to almost 1.5 billion in 2007.

▶ There are still wide gaps in Internet users in different regions in the world: Latin America and the Caribbean has about 24 Internet users per 100 people; South Asia has about 14; and Sub-Saharan Africa has about 4 users per 100 people. The average for high-income countries is 64.

▶ Internet prices (for 20 hours of service per month) in developing countries dropped from about $31 per month to $23 per month from 2003–2006.

▶ Internet prices are more affordable in some developing country regions than others: in Europe and Central Asia, Internet service (for 20 hours of service per month) is just 2.8 percent of monthly income, but in Sub-Saharan Africa monthly Internet service is 23 percent of monthly income.

Internet links

▶ International Telecommunication Union	**www.itu.int**
▶ International Road Federation	**www.irfnet.org**
▶ World Resources Institute	**earthtrends.wri.org** (click on Energy and Resources)
▶ World Bank	**www.worldbank.org** (click on Topics, then select Sustainable Development)
▶ Organisation for Economic Co-operation and Development	**www.oecd.org** (click on By Topic, then select Information and Communications Technologies)
▶ World Health Organization	**http://www.who.int/water_sanitation_health/en**

Investment is expenditure to replenish capital stocks, both physical and human, used up in production, and to increase the total capital stock. Without investment there would be no sustainable economic growth. A good investment climate is one in which government policies encourage firms and entrepreneurs to invest their resources productively, create jobs, and contribute to growth and poverty reduction. On average, 21 percent of world output is used for investment purposes. But high rates of investment alone do not ensure rapid economic growth because the productivity of capital varies with the sector, the project, and the level of development.

Physical investment takes many forms: buildings, machinery, and equipment; improvements to property; and additions to inventories. Investment is financed out of domestic savings or external savings. However, external financing is limited and generally more volatile than domestic savings. Countries that have high savings and investment rates are likely to produce high rates of economic growth. Growth is also spurred by improved efficiency as a result of technological advances and investments in people, as well as through better education and health care. To sustain growth, government policies must create a climate that encourages productive investment.

Government policies play a key role in shaping the investment climate. They influence the security of property rights, the effectiveness of regulation, the impact of taxation, the quality and accessibility of infrastructure, and the functioning of financial and labor markets. The quality of the investment climate also contributes strongly to increased productivity and employment creation, both necessary for

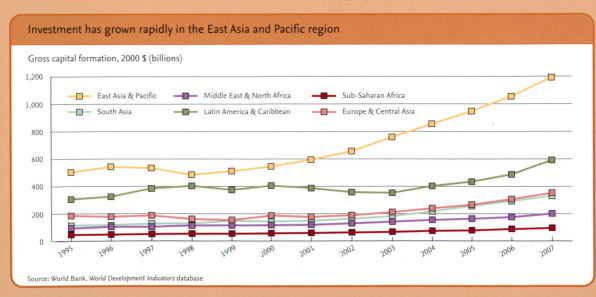

Investment has grown rapidly in the East Asia and Pacific region

Gross capital formation, 2000 $ (billions)

Source: World Bank, *World Development Indicators* database

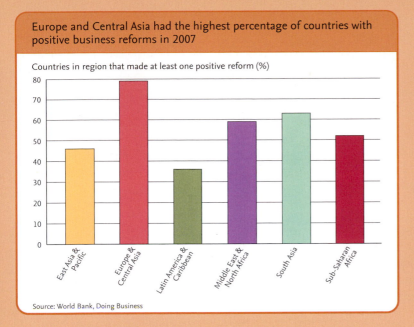

Europe and Central Asia had the highest percentage of countries with positive business reforms in 2007

Countries in region that made at least one positive reform (%)

Source: World Bank, Doing Business

poverty reduction. Poor governance increases transaction costs, encourages unproductive activities such as lobbying, and reduces transparency. Hence, it leads to misallocation of resources and discourages new investment.

Between 2006 and 2007, 79 percent of the countries in the Europe and Central Asia region implemented at least one positive reform to make doing business easier, while 63 percent of the countries in South Asia had such reforms.

In the most recent year, the East Asia and Pacific region has had the highest investment rate, averaging 38 percent of gross domestic product (GDP). South Asia invested 35 percent of its output. Sub-Saharan Africa had the lowest investment rate, at 21 percent of GDP, but this has been increasing since 2001.

The level of investment in the East Asia and Pacific region has been the highest since 1995. It now invests more than twice as much as the Latin America and the Caribbean region. Similarly, the South Asia, and Middle East and North Africa regions had about the same level of investment in 1995, but now South Asia invests 36 percent more than the Middle East and North Africa.

Although China and some of the other "tigers" in the East Asia and Pacific region have obtained spectacular growth rates, high levels of investment do not guarantee high growth rates. Investment produces growth, but investment also chases growth. More investment is likely in places where high returns are possible.

Over the period from 1995 through 2007, most developing regions invested an average of 18 to 36 percent of their GDP each year. The results obtained have varied, from Latin America and the Caribbean, where an investment ratio of 20 percent produced an average annual growth rate of only 3.5 percent, to South Asia, where an investment ratio of a little more than 26 percent resulted in annual growth of 9.2 percent. Sub-Saharan Africa is an interesting exception: a low investment ratio of 18 percent led to an annual growth rate of 6.1 percent, better than several regions with higher investment ratios.

Not everyone obtains the same result

GDP growth rate (%), annual average 1995–2007

East Asia & Pacific

South Asia

Europe & Central Asia

Middle East & North Africa

Sub-Saharan Africa

Latin America & Caribbean

High-income

Gross capital formation (% of GDP)

Source: World Bank, *World Development Indicators* database

Investment for growth

gross capital formation as a share of GDP,
2002–2007, most recent year available

- less than 15%
- 15–19%
- 20–24%
- 25–29%
- 30% or more
- no data

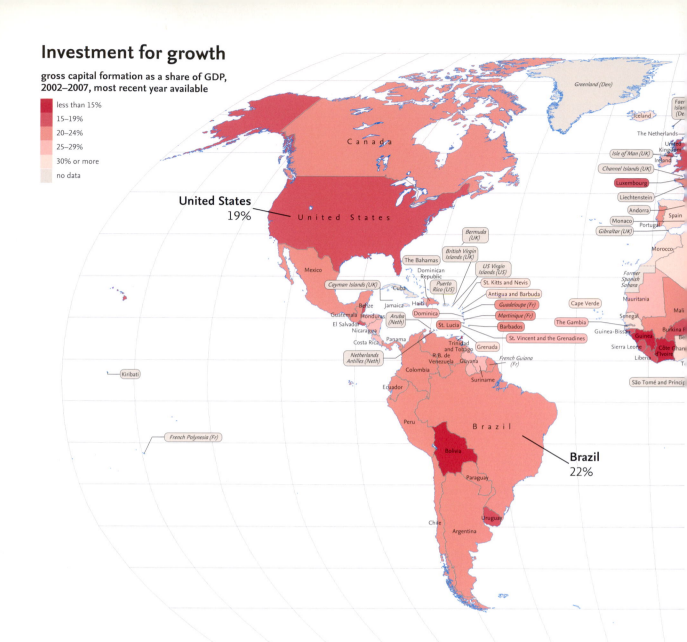

United States
19%

Brazil
22%

Greenland (Den)

Faer Islan (De

Iceland

The Netherlands

United Kingdom

Isle of Man (UK)

Ireland

Channel Islands (UK)

Luxembourg

Liechtenstein

Andorra

Spain

Monaco

Portugal

Gibraltar (UK)

Morocco

Former Spanish Sahara

Mauritania

Mali

Senegal

Burkina F

Cape Verde

The Gambia

Guinea-Bissau

Guinea

Sierra Leone

Côte d'Ivoire

Liberia

Be

Ghan

São Tomé and Princip

Canada

United States

Mexico

Bermuda (UK)

The Bahamas

Dominican Republic

Cayman Islands (UK)

Cuba

British Virgin Islands (UK)

Puerto Rico (US)

US Virgin Islands (US)

St. Kitts and Nevis

Antigua and Barbuda

Guadeloupe (Fr)

Dominica

Martinique (Fr)

St. Lucia

Barbados

St. Vincent and the Grenadines

Grenada

Belize

Jamaica

Haiti

Guatemala

Honduras

Aruba (Neth)

El Salvador

Nicaragua

Costa Rica

Panama

Netherlands Antilles (Neth)

Trinidad and Tobago

R.B. de Venezuela

Guyana

Suriname

French Guiana (Fr)

Colombia

Ecuador

Kiribati

French Polynesia (Fr)

Peru

Brazil

Bolivia

Paraguay

Uruguay

Chile

Argentina

China's rapidly growing economy has benefited from foreign investment

Highest average gross capital formation

Rank	Countries greater than 1 million in population	% of GDP 1995–2007
1	Lesotho	44
2	China	40
3	Iran, Islamic Rep. of	34
4	Turkmenistan	34
5	Azerbaijan	33
6	Botswana	33
7	Mongolia	32
8	Vietnam	32
9	Estonia	31
10	Korea, Rep. of	31

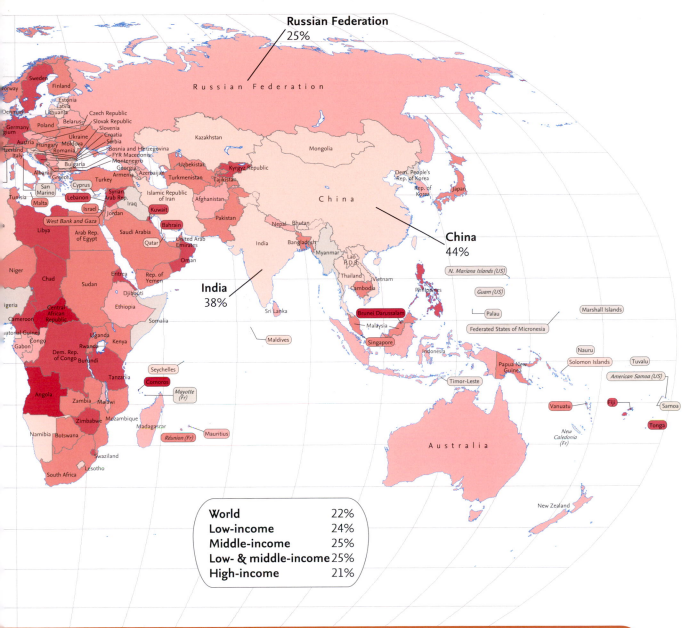

Russian Federation
25%

Russian Federation

China
44%

India
38%

World	22%
Low-income	24%
Middle-income	25%
Low- & middle-income	25%
High-income	21%

Facts	Internet links	
▶ Growth in investment has been the fastest in the South Asia region. Between 2000 and 2007, it has been increasing at an average rate of 13.8 percent per year.	▶ World Bank data and statistics	**www.worldbank.org/data**
▶ Investment has grown most slowly in the Latin America and the Caribbean region, averaging 5.5 percent a year between 2000 and 2007.	▶ Organisation for Economic Co-operation and Development	**www.oecd.org/statistics**
▶ Investment declined in 19 countries between 2000 and 2007.	▶ International Monetary Fund statistics	**www.imf.org/external/data.htm**
▶ Azerbaijan had the highest growth in investment, averaging an increase of 36 percent per year between 2000 and 2007.	▶ International Monetary Fund Dissemination Standards Bulletin Board	**http://dsbb.imf.org/ Applications/web/dsbbhome**
▶ In China, investment grew at an average of 13.5 percent a year between 2000 and 2007.	▶ United Nations Statistics Division	**http://unstats.un.org/unsd/ snaama**

Starting a business

time required to start a new business, 2007

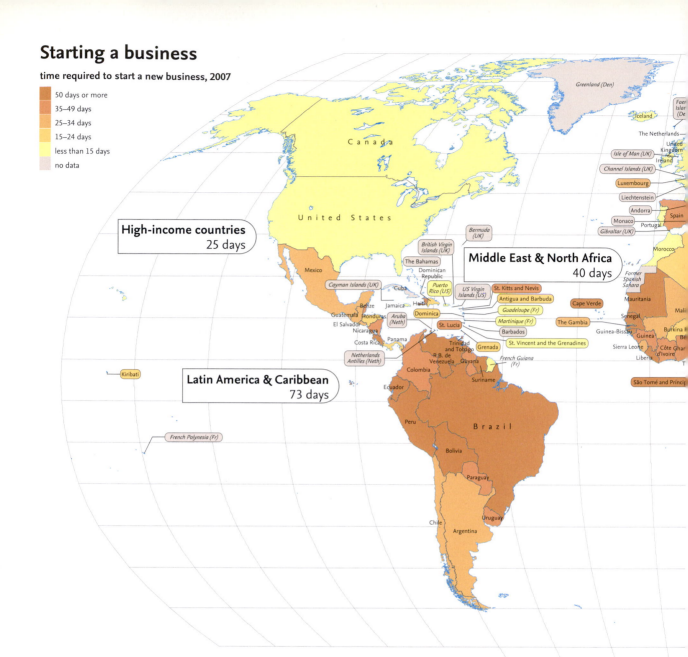

Legend:
- 50 days or more
- 35–49 days
- 25–34 days
- 15–24 days
- less than 15 days
- no data

High-income countries
25 days

Middle East & North Africa
40 days

Latin America & Caribbean
73 days

Greenland (Den)

Iceland

The Netherlands

United Kingdom

Isle of Man (UK)

Ireland

Channel Islands (UK)

Luxembourg

Liechtenstein

Andorra

Monaco   Portugal   Spain

Gibraltar (UK)   Morocco

Former Spanish Sahara

Mauritania

Canada

United States

Mexico

Cayman Islands (UK)

Bermuda (UK)

British Virgin Islands (UK)

The Bahamas

Dominican Republic

Cuba   Puerto Rico (US)

Belize   Jamaica   Haiti

Guatemala   Honduras   Aruba (Neth)

El Salvador   Nicaragua   Dominica

Costa Rica   Panama   St. Lucia

US Virgin Islands (US)

St. Kitts and Nevis

Antigua and Barbuda

Guadeloupe (Fr)

Martinique (Fr)

Barbados

St. Vincent and the Grenadines

Grenada

Netherlands Antilles (Neth)

Trinidad and Tobago

R.B. de Venezuela   Guyana

Colombia   Suriname   French Guiana (Fr)

Ecuador

Peru

B r a z i l

Bolivia

Paraguay

Chile   Uruguay

Argentina

Kiribati

French Polynesia (Fr)

Cape Verde

The Gambia

Senegal

Guinea-Bissau

Guinea   Sierra Leone

Liberia   Côte d'Ivoire

Mali   Burkina

São Tomé and Príncipe

Business meeting, Mozambique

Best performers—starting a business in developing countries

Rank	Country	(days) 2007
1	Turkey	6
2	Madagascar	7
3	Mauritius	7
4	Jamaica	8
5	Afghanistan	9
6	Egypt	9
7	Maldives	9
8	Georgia	11
9	Tunisia	11
10	Morocco	12

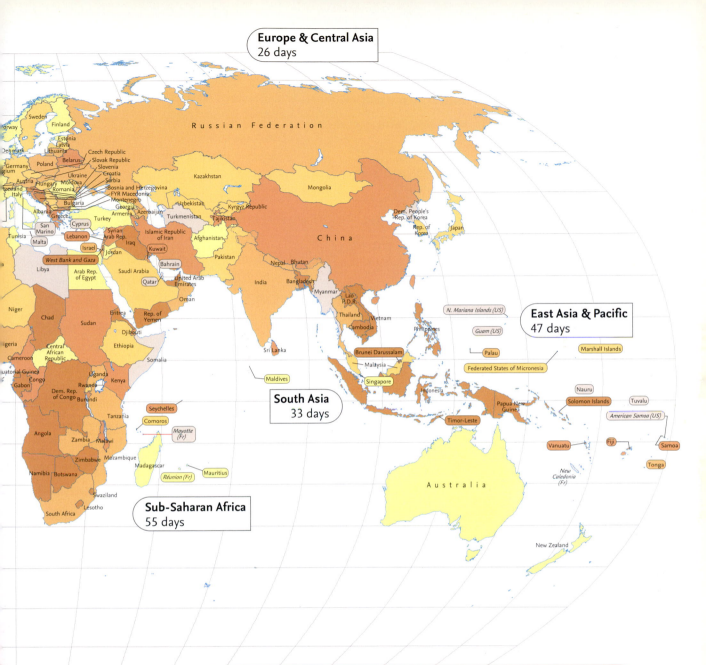

Europe & Central Asia
26 days

East Asia & Pacific
47 days

South Asia
33 days

Sub-Saharan Africa
55 days

Facts	Internet links	
► Between 2003 and 2007, Turkey cut the number of procedures to start a business from 13 to 6, and the time to complete the process from 38 days to 6 days.	► World Bank Doing Business project	**www.doingbusiness.org**
► El Salvador slashed the time required to register a business from 40 days in 2005 to 26 days in 2007.	► World Bank Enterprise Surveys	**www.enterprisesurveys.org**
► Business entry was eased in 39 countries in 2007, making starting a business simpler, faster, and cheaper.		
► In 2007, Kenya, Ghana, Mozambique, Madagascar, and Burkina Faso were the best African reformers in ease of doing business.	► Private Participation in Infrastructure database	**http://ppi.worldbank.org/**
► If it is easy to set up a business, more businesses are set up—and business investment increases and new jobs are created.		
► Countries that introduce standardized business application forms save their entrepreneurs time, and fewer applications are rejected for flawed or insufficient paperwork.	► Privatization database	**http://rru.worldbank.org/ Privatization/**

Economies have become increasingly dependent on each other for goods, services, labor, and capital. Advances in information and communications technology, expanding financial markets, and cheaper transportation systems enable easier movement of inputs and outputs among countries, accelerating global integration, but many barriers remain. The benefits from global integration need to be equitably shared both among and within economies.

Traditional patterns of production and employment have given way to new modes of production and distribution, which are often spread over multiple locations. Developing countries offering higher returns are attracting foreign investment in manufacturing. Skilled as well as unskilled labor is seeking employment in economies that offer higher wages. High-income economies are looking at the developing world to meet the increasing demand for service and technology workers.

As the global economy becomes more integrated, the importance of trade has increased. Goods equivalent to 51 percent of global gross domestic product (GDP) were traded in 2007, up from 32 percent in 1990. Over the same period, trade in services increased from 8 percent to 12 percent of global GDP.

The international service sector has grown rapidly in the new century. Between 2000 and 2006, trade in services by developing countries grew at an annual average rate of 17 percent (in nominal terms)—5 percentage points higher than that in high-income countries. South Asia led the way, growing at an average annual rate of 25 percent.

But agricultural and industrial goods still

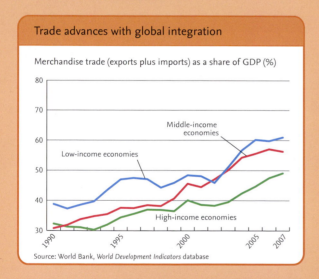

Trade advances with global integration

Merchandise trade (exports plus imports) as a share of GDP (%)

Source: World Bank, *World Development Indicators* database

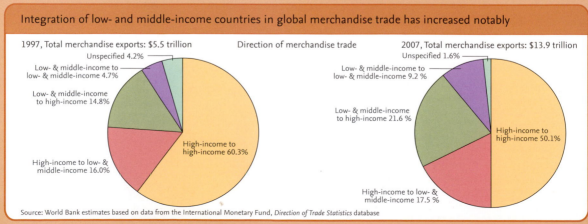

Integration of low- and middle-income countries in global merchandise trade has increased notably

Source: World Bank estimates based on data from the International Monetary Fund, *Direction of Trade Statistics* database

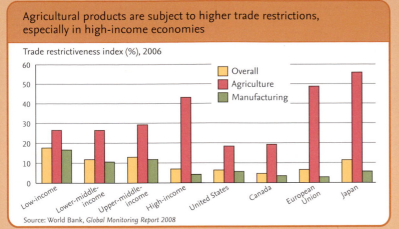

Agricultural products are subject to higher trade restrictions, especially in high-income economies

Trade restrictiveness index (%), 2006

Source: World Bank, *Global Monitoring Report 2008*

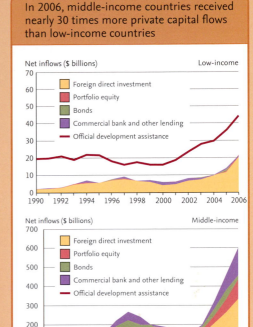

In 2006, middle-income countries received nearly 30 times more private capital flows than low-income countries

Net inflows ($ billions) — Low-income

- Foreign direct investment
- Portfolio equity
- Bonds
- Commercial bank and other lending
- Official development assistance

Net inflows ($ billions) — Middle-income

- Foreign direct investment
- Portfolio equity
- Bonds
- Commercial bank and other lending
- Official development assistance

Source: World Bank, *Global Development Finance*, and Organisation for Economic Co-operation and Development, Development Assistance Committee, *International Development Statistics*

dominate world trade, accounting for 81 percent of total trade in 2006. While some developing countries, such as China and India, are making rapid progress as exporters, the high-income economies account for 68 percent of world merchandise exports. Of these, exports to the developing countries amounted to 18 percent in 2007. Between 1997 and 2007, merchandise exports of the developing countries grew at 14.8 percent a year in nominal terms, while high-income country exports grew at 8.3 percent a year.

Reductions in tariff and nontariff barriers have helped to spur trade, but many trade barriers remain. Trade barriers are costly to both consumers in developed countries and producers in developing countries. The poorest countries impose higher barriers across a broad range of goods to protect their producers and raise revenues for their governments. But rich countries often impose their highest barriers specifically on the exports of developing countries, especially agricultural products. In addition to tariff protection, they provide subsidies and other forms of support to domestic producers. Total agricultural support in countries in the Organisation for Economic Co-operation and Development (OECD) exceeded $372 billion in 2006, encouraging greater production in OECD countries and undercutting developing country producers.

Since 1990, the number of bilateral and multilateral preferential trade agreements has increased rapidly. Such agreements, especially bilateral free trade agreements, are increasingly made among countries with different levels of development. These agreements provide developing countries with new trading opportunities and contribute toward their integration to the global economy. But these agreements also raise trade barriers to exports from non-member economies and may hinder the overall integration of world economies.

Effective global integration requires the free flow of goods, services, investment, labor, and technology, not merely the reduction of tariffs and import quotas. An open and equitable trading system enhances growth opportunities and encourages domestic and foreign investment. As countries have reduced restrictions on foreign investment, capital flows have increased. Middle-income countries with improved credit have more access to the international financial markets and can raise large amounts of capital through bond issuance and commercial borrowing. The main source of external financing for low-income countries remains official development assistance.

Merchandise trade

exports and imports as a share of GDP, 2007 or latest available data

- less than 40%
- 40–59%
- 60–74%
- 75–99%
- 100% or more
- no data

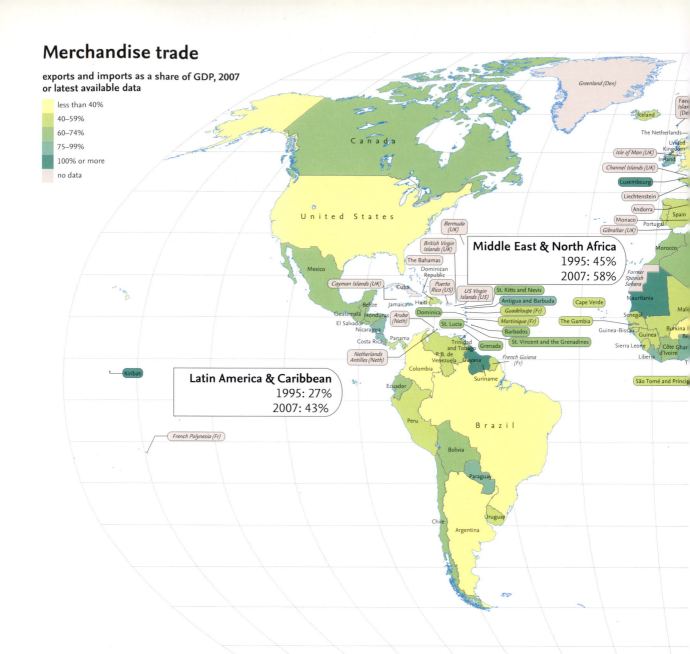

Middle East & North Africa
1995: 45%
2007: 58%

Latin America & Caribbean
1995: 27%
2007: 43%

Map labels include: Greenland (Den), Iceland, Faeroe Islands (De), The Netherlands, United Kingdom, Isle of Man (UK), Ireland, Channel Islands (UK), Luxembourg, Liechtenstein, Andorra, Monaco, Spain, Portugal, Gibraltar (UK), Morocco, Former Spanish Sahara, Mauritania, Mali, Senegal, Burkina, Cape Verde, The Gambia, Guinea-Bissau, Guinea, Sierra Leone, Liberia, Côte d'Ivoire, São Tomé and Príncipe, Canada, United States, Mexico, Bermuda (UK), British Virgin Islands (UK), The Bahamas, Dominican Republic, Cuba, Cayman Islands (UK), Puerto Rico (US), US Virgin Islands (US), St. Kitts and Nevis, Antigua and Barbuda, Guadeloupe (Fr), Belize, Jamaica, Haiti, Dominica, Guatemala, Honduras, Aruba (Neth), St. Lucia, Martinique (Fr), Barbados, El Salvador, Nicaragua, Costa Rica, Panama, Netherlands Antilles (Neth), Trinidad and Tobago, Grenada, St. Vincent and the Grenadines, R.B. de Venezuela, Guyana, Colombia, Suriname, French Guiana (Fr), Ecuador, Peru, Brazil, Bolivia, Paraguay, Chile, Argentina, Uruguay, Kiribati, French Polynesia (Fr)

Singapore relies heavily on trade with the rest of the world

Merchandise trade					
Largest merchandise exporters, 2007			**Largest merchandise importers, 2007**		
Rank	Developing countries	$ billions	Rank	Developing countries	$ billion
1	China	1,218	1	China	956
2	Russian Federation	355	2	Mexico	297
3	Mexico	272	3	Russian Federation	223
4	Malaysia	176	4	India	217
5	Brazil	161	5	Turkey	170

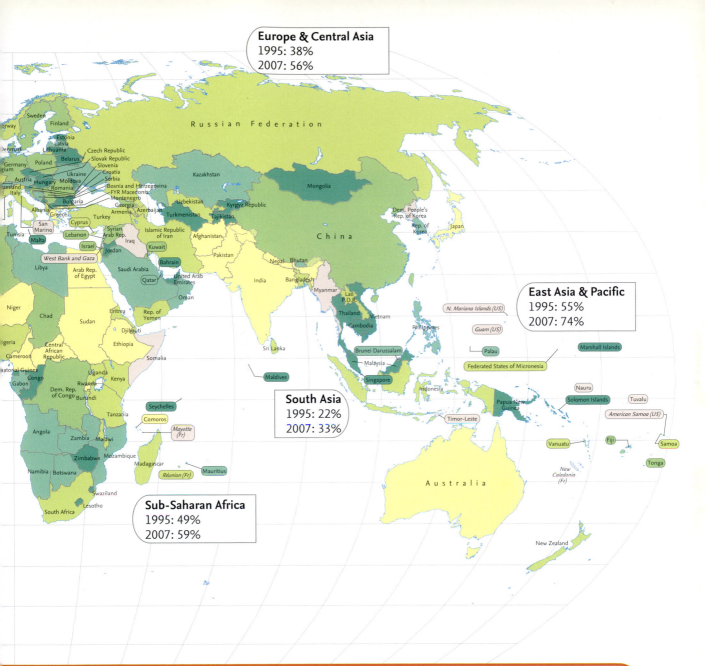

Europe & Central Asia
1995: 38%
2007: 56%

East Asia & Pacific
1995: 55%
2007: 74%

South Asia
1995: 22%
2007: 33%

Sub-Saharan Africa
1995: 49%
2007: 59%

Facts	Internet links	
▶ The 10 largest exporters in 2007 accounted for more than two-thirds of the merchandise exports from developing countries.	▶ Organisation for Economic Co-operation and Development	**www.oecd.org/trade**
▶ World exports of services grew from $863 billion in 1990, to over $3.3 trillion in 2007.	▶ International Monetary Fund	**www.imfstatistics.org/dot** **www.imfstatistics.org/bop**
▶ The total number of bilateral and multilateral trade agreements in force and notified to the World Trade Organization increased from 21 in 1990, to 193 in 2008; of these, 119 were free trade agreements.	▶ World Trade Organization	**www.wto.org** (go to Resources, select Trade Statistics)
▶ The United States imports more goods than any other country, followed by Germany and China.	▶ United Nations Conference on Trade and Development	**www.unctad.org** (go to Statistics, select Statistical databases online)
▶ Equatorial Guinea increased its merchandise exports by more than 156 times between 1990 and 2007. Cambodia's merchandise exports for the same period increased more than 51 times.	▶ United Nations Trade Statistics	**http://unstats.un.org/unsd/trade** **http://unstats.un.org/unsd/ servicetrade**

Foreign direct investment

foreign direct investment net inflows as a share of GDP, 2006 or latest available data

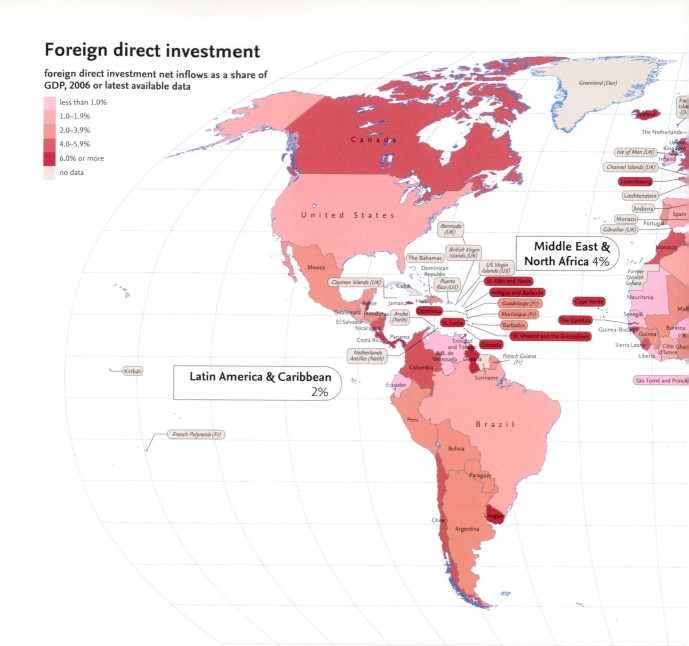

- less than 1.0%
- 1.0–1.9%
- 2.0–3.9%
- 4.0–5.9%
- 6.0% or more
- no data

Greenland (Den)

Iceland

Canada

United States

The Netherlands
United Kingdom
Ireland
Isle of Man (UK)
Channel Islands (UK)
Luxembourg
Liechtenstein
Andorra
Monaco
Gibraltar (UK)
Spain
Portugal
Morocco

Bermuda (UK)
British Virgin Islands (UK)
US Virgin Islands (US)
The Bahamas
Dominican Republic
Puerto Rico (US)
Cuba
Haiti
Jamaica
Cayman Islands (UK)

Middle East & North Africa 4%

Former Spanish Sahara
Mauritania
Mali
Senegal
Burkina
Guinea-Bissau
Guinea
Sierra Leone
Côte d'Ivoire
Liberia

Mexico
Belize
Guatemala
Honduras
El Salvador
Nicaragua
Costa Rica
Panama

St. Kitts and Nevis
Antigua and Barbuda
Guadeloupe (Fr)
Dominica
Martinique (Fr)
St. Lucia
Barbados
Aruba (Neth)
St. Vincent and the Grenadines
Grenada
Trinidad and Tobago
Netherlands Antilles (Neth)
R.B. de Venezuela
Guyana
French Guiana (Fr)
Suriname
Cape Verde
The Gambia

Kiribati

Latin America & Caribbean 2%

Colombia
Ecuador

São Tomé and Princ...

French Polynesia (Fr)

Peru

Brazil

Bolivia

Paraguay

Chile

Uruguay

Argentina

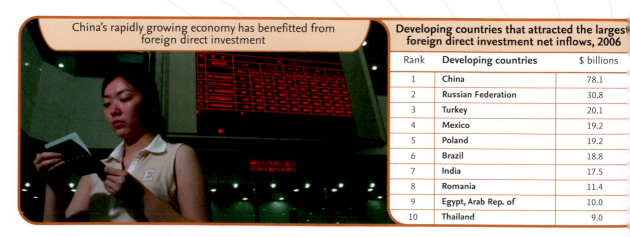

China's rapidly growing economy has benefitted from foreign direct investment

Developing countries that attracted the largest foreign direct investment net inflows, 2006

Rank	Developing countries	$ billions
1	China	78.1
2	Russian Federation	30.8
3	Turkey	20.1
4	Mexico	19.2
5	Poland	19.2
6	Brazil	18.8
7	India	17.5
8	Romania	11.4
9	Egypt, Arab Rep. of	10.0
10	Thailand	9.0

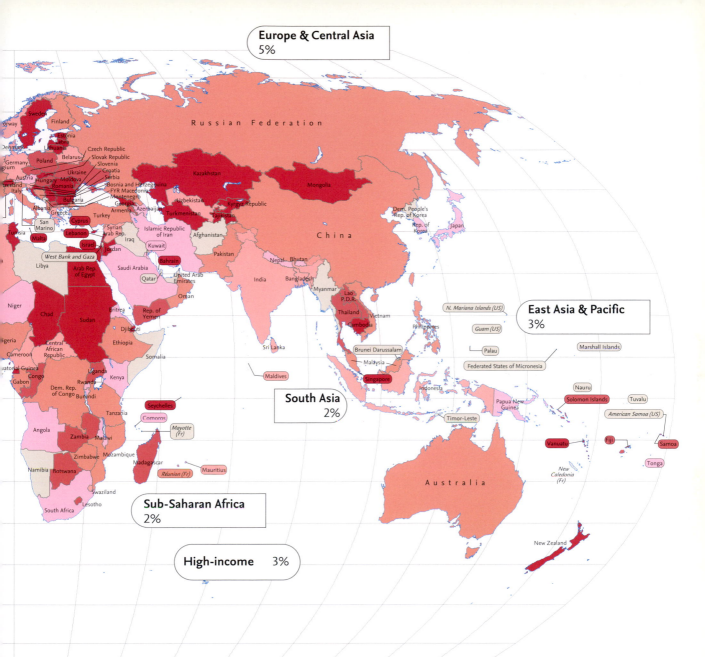

Europe & Central Asia 5%

East Asia & Pacific 3%

South Asia 2%

Sub-Saharan Africa 2%

High-income 3%

Facts	Internet links	
▶ Luxembourg's net outward direct investment in foreign economies in 2006 was nearly 2.7 times its GDP; Iceland's was 33 percent of its GDP.	▶ International Monetary Fund Balance of Payments Statistics	**www.imfstatistics.org/bop**
▶ East Asia and Pacific received the highest net flow of portfolio equity—$55 billion in 2006—accounting for more than half of the total for developing countries. China alone received 78 percent of this.	▶ World Bank	**www.worldbank.org/data**
▶ Turkey ($33 billion), Russian Federation ($27 billion), and Kazakhstan ($26 billion) raised the largest net amount of capital among all developing countries in 2006 through bond issuance and commercial borrowing.	▶ United Nations Conference on Trade and Development	**www.unctad.org** (go to Statistics, select Statistical databases online)
▶ Foreign direct investment net flows to high-income countries accounted for nearly 74 percent of the world total in 2006. Among developing regions, Europe and Central Asia received the highest amount, having grown by 83 percent in nominal terms in 2006 to $114.3 billion.	▶ Multilateral Investment Guarantee Agency, World Bank Group	**www.fdi.net**

The movement of people across national borders is a visible and increasingly important aspect of global integration. Three percent of the world's people—more than 190 million—now live in countries in which they were not born. The forces driving the flow of migrants from poor countries to rich countries are likely to grow stronger in the future.

Migration is on the rise, especially from poor countries to rich countries. One reason is the large wage gap. Demographic trends in both developed and developing countries may also encourage migration. In many high-income countries, the population is aging and growing slowly, while in many developing countries the population is young and growing rapidly. This imbalance creates a strong demand for developing-country workers, especially to provide services that can only be supplied locally. Immigrants in high-income countries have increased to 11 percent of the population, up from 8 percent two decades before.

One of the benefits of migration is an increasing flow of remittances—transfers of gifts and wages and salaries earned abroad—from migrants to their country of origin. Remittances have become an important source of foreign exchange for many developing countries. They have increased nearly five-fold since 1990, reaching almost $337 billion in 2007, with $251 billion going to developing countries. Already more than twice the size of foreign aid, remittances to developing countries are expected to continue growing. The largest share of remittances goes to a small number of middle-income economies in Latin America and Asia. However, the economies of Eastern Europe have also received a large part of the additional remittances.

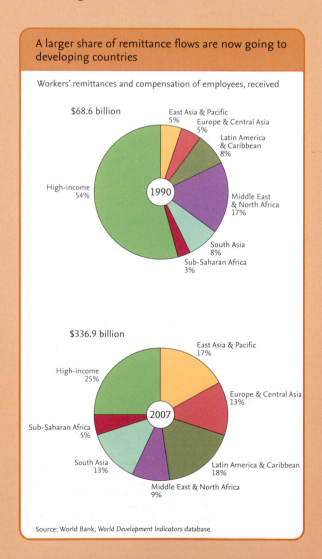

A larger share of remittance flows are now going to developing countries

Workers' remittances and compensation of employees, received

$68.6 billion

1990

- East Asia & Pacific 5%
- Europe & Central Asia 5%
- Latin America & Caribbean 8%
- Middle East & North Africa 17%
- South Asia 8%
- Sub-Saharan Africa 3%
- High-income 54%

$336.9 billion

2007

- East Asia & Pacific 17%
- Europe & Central Asia 13%
- Latin America & Caribbean 18%
- Middle East & North Africa 9%
- South Asia 13%
- Sub-Saharan Africa 5%
- High-income 25%

Source: World Bank, *World Development Indicators* database

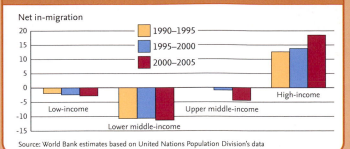

Migration from low- and middle-income countries to high-income countries is on the rise

Net in-migration

Legend:
- 1990–1995
- 1995–2000
- 2000–2005

Categories: Low-income, Lower middle-income, Upper middle-income, High-income

Source: World Bank estimates based on United Nations Population Division's data

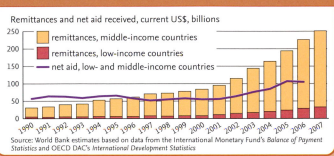

Remittances to developing countries, especially to middle-income countries, continue to increase

Remittances and net aid received, current US$, billions

Legend:
- remittances, middle-income countries
- remittances, low-income countries
- net aid, low- and middle-income countries

Years: 1990 through 2007

Source: World Bank estimates based on data from the International Monetary Fund's *Balance of Payment Statistics* and OECD DAC's *International Development Statistics*

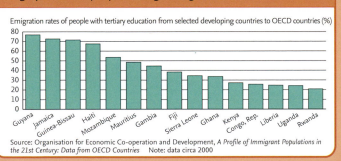

Small-island economies and Sub-Saharan African economies lose highly educated people through emigration

Emigration rates of people with tertiary education from selected developing countries to OECD countries (%)

Countries: Guyana, Jamaica, Guinea-Bissau, Haiti, Mozambique, Mauritius, Gambia, Fiji, Sierra Leone, Ghana, Kenya, Congo, Rep., Liberia, Uganda, Rwanda

Source: Organisation for Economic Co-operation and Development, *A Profile of Immigrant Populations in the 21st Century: Data from OECD Countries* Note: data circa 2000

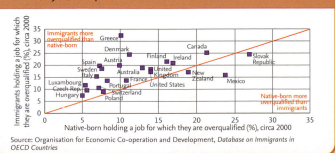

Immigrants in OECD countries are more likely to be overqualified for their job, compared to the native-born

Immigrants holding a job for which they are overqualified (%), circa 2000

Native-born holding a job for which they are overqualified (%), circa 2000

Immigrants more overqualified than native-born

Native-born more overqualified than immigrants

Countries: Greece, Denmark, Canada, Finland, Ireland, Austria, Spain, Sweden, Australia, United Kingdom, Slovak Republic, Italy, France, New Zealand, Luxembourg, Czech Rep., Portugal, United States, Mexico, Hungary, Switzerland, Poland

Source: Organisation for Economic Co-operation and Development, *Database on Immigrants in OECD Countries*

Empirical studies have found that remittances can raise income levels, especially among the poor. Evidence from some countries suggests that a large proportion of remittances received are invested, which may lead to improvements in the overall economy. Migration also encourages higher levels of educational attainment. Moreover, increases in income from remittances along with the transfer of knowledge through migrants result in better health outcomes for other household members.

Migration may also have negative effects. Among international migrants are millions of highly educated people who have moved to developed countries from developing countries. By migrating, they improve their own prospects and provide valuable services in high-income economies. But the loss of human capital, the so-called "brain drain," from developing countries may increase the concentration of poverty and reduce the social benefits of migration. The regions most affected by brain drain are small-island economies and Sub-Saharan Africa. For example, between 1995 and 2002, an estimated 69 percent of the medical officers trained in Ghana emigrated abroad, causing health services in the country to deteriorate.

Furthermore, highly skilled emigrants do not always find jobs that match their skills in the destination country. Immigrants in most countries in the Organisation for Economic Co-operation and Development (OECD) are more likely to be overqualified —working in occupations for which their skills are too high—compared to the native-born population.

Migration

international migrants as a share of population, 2005

- less than 1.0%
- 1.0–2.9%
- 3.0–5.9%
- 6.0–14.9%
- 15.0% or more
- no data

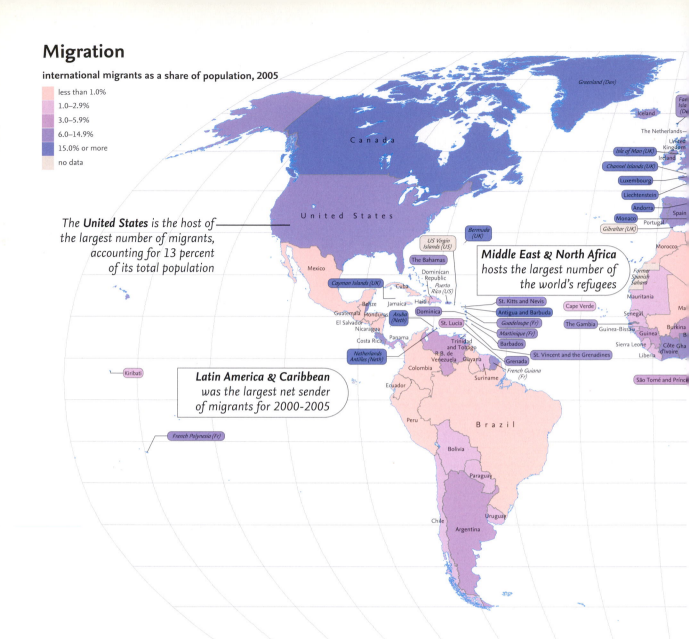

The **United States** is the host of the largest number of migrants, accounting for 13 percent of its total population

Middle East & North Africa hosts the largest number of the world's refugees

Latin America & Caribbean was the largest net sender of migrants for 2000-2005

Greenland (Den)

Iceland

Canada

United States

Mexico

Guatemala   Honduras
El Salvador
Nicaragua
Costa Rica   Panama

The Bahamas
Cuba
Jamaica   Haiti
Dominican Republic
Puerto Rico (US)
US Virgin Islands (US)
Cayman Islands (UK)
Bermuda (UK)
Belize
Dominica
St. Lucia
Aruba (Neth)
Netherlands Antilles (Neth)

St. Kitts and Nevis
Antigua and Barbuda
Guadeloupe (Fr)
Martinique (Fr)
Barbados
Grenada
St. Vincent and the Grenadines
Trinidad and Tobago
R.B. de Venezuela   Guyana
Colombia   Suriname
French Guiana (Fr)
Ecuador
Peru

Brazil

Bolivia
Paraguay
Chile
Uruguay
Argentina

Kiribati

French Polynesia (Fr)

Cape Verde

The Netherlands
United Kingdom
Isle of Man (UK)
Ireland
Channel Islands (UK)
Luxembourg
Liechtenstein
Andorra
Monaco
Spain
Portugal
Gibraltar (UK)

Faeroe Isla (De

Morocco
Former Spanish Sahara
Mauritania
Senegal
The Gambia
Guinea-Bissau   Guinea
Sierra Leone
Liberia
Côte Gha d'Ivoire
Mali
Burkina
B

São Tomé and Princ

Immigrants becoming US citizens at a swearing-in ceremony

Countries with highest migrations, 2000–2005

Rank	Country	net in-migration (thousar
1	United States	6,493
2	Spain	2,846
3	Italy	1,125
5	Canada	1,041
6	Germany	1,000

Rank	Country	net out-migration (thousar
1	Mexico	3,983
2	China	1,900
3	India	1,350
4	Iran, Islamic Rep. of	1,250
5	Pakistan	1,239

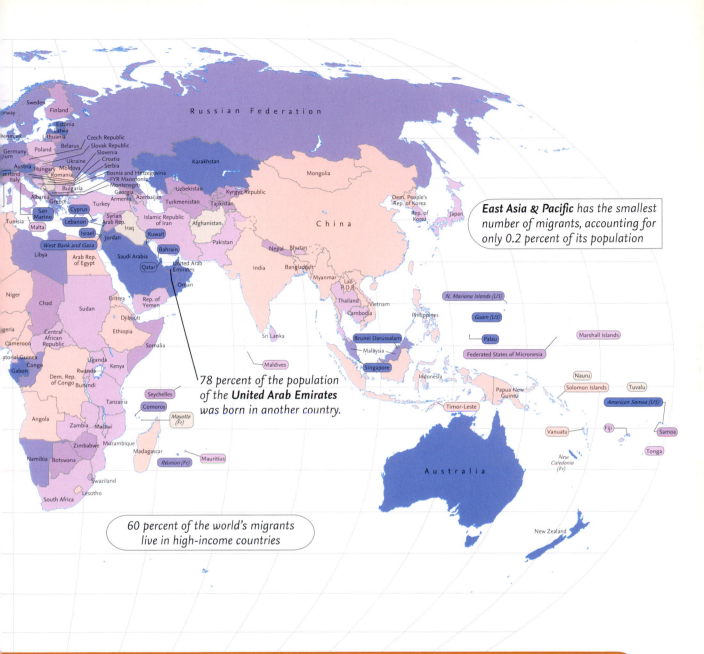

East Asia & Pacific has the smallest number of migrants, accounting for only 0.2 percent of its population

78 percent of the population of the **United Arab Emirates** was born in another country.

60 percent of the world's migrants live in high-income countries

Facts	Internet links	
▶ In the 1960s, the majority of migrants lived in developing countries. Today, the majority reside in high-income countries.	▶ United Nations Population Division	**www.un.org/esa/ population/migration**
▶ The number of migrants in the world grew from about 70 million in 1960, to more than 190 million in 2005. But this remained about 3 percent of the world's population.	▶ International Organization for Migration	**www.iom.int**
▶ As of 2005, 76 million migrants live in developing countries (about 1.4 percent of their population), compared to 114 million in high-income countries (about 11 percent of their population).	▶ United Nations Refugee Agency	**www.unhcr.org/ statistics.html**
▶ Refugees are an important component of the migrant stock. At the end of 2006, the number of refugees, including Palestinian refugees under the mandate of the United Nations Relief and Works Agency (UNRWA), stood at 14.3 million, accounting for approximately 7.5 percent of the migrants in the world.	▶ Organisation for Economic Co-operation and Development (OECD)	**www.oecd.org/migration**
▶ Out of 180 countries with migration estimates for 2000–2005, 82 are net migrant recipients and 98 are net migrant senders.	▶ International Labour Organization	**www.ilo.org** (go to Themes, select labour migration)

Remittances

remittances received as a share of GDP, 2007
or latest available data

- 5.0% or more
- 2.5–4.9%
- 1.0–2.4%
- 0.5–0.9%
- less than 0.5%
- no data

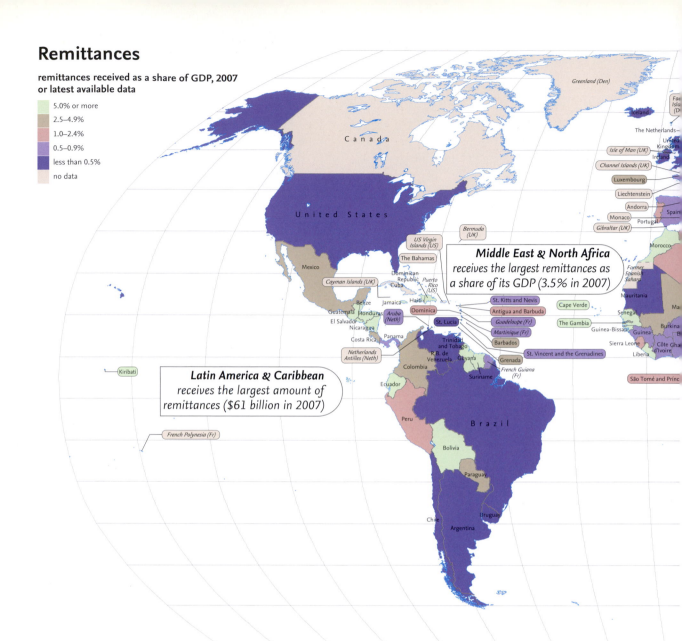

Middle East & North Africa
*receives the largest remittances as
a share of its GDP (3.5% in 2007)*

Latin America & Caribbean
*receives the largest amount of
remittances ($61 billion in 2007)*

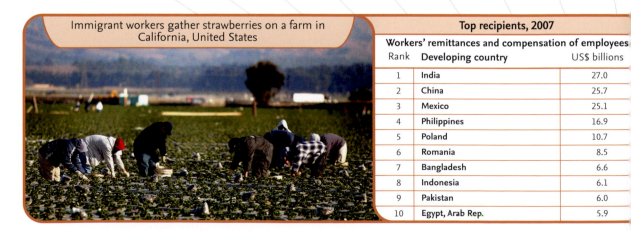

Immigrant workers gather strawberries on a farm in
California, United States

Top recipients, 2007		
Workers' remittances and compensation of employees		
Rank	Developing country	US$ billions
1	India	27.0
2	China	25.7
3	Mexico	25.1
4	Philippines	16.9
5	Poland	10.7
6	Romania	8.5
7	Bangladesh	6.6
8	Indonesia	6.1
9	Pakistan	6.0
10	Egypt, Arab Rep.	5.9

Outflows of remittances from **high-income economies** was $186 billion in 2007, up from $661 billion in 1990

Russian Federation

Sweden
Finland
Norway
Estonia
Latvia
Lithuania
Denmark
Czech Republic
Poland
Belarus
Slovak Republic
Slovenia
Germany
Ukraine
Moldova
Croatia
Belgium
Austria
Hungary
Romania
Serbia
Switzerland
Italy
Bulgaria
Bosnia and Herzegovina
FYR Macedonia
Montenegro
Georgia
Albania
Greece
Armenia
Azerbaijan
San Marino
Cyprus
Turkey
Tunisia
Malta
Lebanon
Syrian Arab Rep.
Iraq
Islamic Republic of Iran
Israel
Jordan
Kuwait
West Bank and Gaza
Libya
Arab Rep. of Egypt
Saudi Arabia
Bahrain
Qatar
United Arab Emirates
Oman
Rep. of Yemen

Kazakhstan
Uzbekistan
Kyrgyz Republic
Turkmenistan
Tajikistan
Afghanistan
Pakistan
Nepal
Bhutan
India
Bangladesh
Myanmar

Mongolia
China
Dem. People's Rep. of Korea
Rep. of Korea
Japan

Niger
Chad
Sudan
Eritrea
Djibouti
Central African Republic
Ethiopia
Cameroon
Somalia
Equatorial Guinea
Uganda
Kenya
Gabon
Congo
Rwanda
Dem. Rep. of Congo
Burundi
Tanzania
Angola
Zambia
Malawi
Zimbabwe
Mozambique
Madagascar
Namibia
Botswana
Swaziland
South Africa
Lesotho

Sri Lanka
Maldives
Lao P.D.R.
Thailand
Vietnam
Cambodia
Philippines
Brunei Darussalam
Malaysia
Singapore
Indonesia
Timor-Leste
Papua New Guinea

Seychelles
Comoros
Mayotte (Fr)
Réunion (Fr)
Mauritius

N. Mariana Islands (US)
Guam (US)
Palau
Marshall Islands
Federated States of Micronesia
Nauru
Solomon Islands
Tuvalu
American Samoa (US)
Vanuatu
Fiji
Samoa
Tonga
New Caledonia (Fr)

Australia

New Zealand

Sub-Saharan Africa receives the smallest amount of remittances ($16 billion in 2007), accounting for 2 percent of its GDP

Lao PDR ($1 million), **Malawi** ($1 million), **Samoa** ($0.8 million), and **Burundi** ($0.1 million) received the smallest amount of remittances in 2007

In 2007, **Estonia** received remittances more than 140 times the value in 2000. **Romania** and **Kyrgyz Republic** received remittances 88 and 78 times the value in 2000.

Facts

▶ As a share of GDP, countries such as Seychelles (675 percent), Liberia (94 percent), Moldova (34 percent), Tajikistan (34 percent), and Tonga (33 percent) had the largest receipt of remittances in 2007. Chile (0.002 percent), Burundi (0.01 percent), Slovak Republic (0.02 percent), United States (0.02 percent), and Lao PDR (0.03 percent) had the smallest.

▶ At the beginning of the 1990s, more than half of remittances went to high-income countries. In 2007, middle-income countries received nearly 65 percent of all remittances, and low-income countries received 10 percent.

▶ Remittances to developing countries increased from 1.2 percent of GDP in 1990 to 1.8 percent in 2007. In high-income countries it remained constant at 0.2 percent.

▶ High-income countries are the principal source of outward remittance flows. The United States is the largest, with $44 billion in outward flows. Russian Federation ($18 billion) is the second largest, followed by Saudi Arabia ($16 billion), Switzerland ($15 billion) and Spain ($15 billion).

Internet links

▶ World Bank Group	**www.worldbank.org/prospects/migrationandremittances**
▶ International Monetary Fund, Balance of Payments Statistics	**www.imfstatistics.org/bop**
▶ Development Research Centre on Migration, Globalisation and Poverty	**www.migrationdrc.org**
▶ Organisation for Economic Co-operation and Development (OECD)	**www.oecd.org/migration**
▶ Migration Information Source	**www.migrationinformation.org**

Aid for development

The global economy has become more integrated. More people are on the move. Countries are exchanging more goods and services, and international financial flows have increased. But even in an expanding world economy, many countries cannot finance their own development. Aid helps to fill the gap.

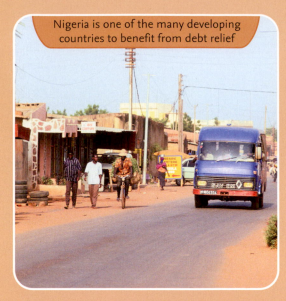

Nigeria is one of the many developing countries to benefit from debt relief

Development is a partnership between developing and donor countries. Donor countries help recipient countries build the capacity to foster change; recipient countries invest in their people and create an environment that sustains growth. Countries that have difficulty tapping financial markets must rely on aid flows from wealthier countries to fund development programs. After rising to a record $107 billion in 2005, official development assistance (ODA) to developing countries fell 1.9 percent in 2006 to $105 billion.

Who were the largest donors? According to the Organisation for Economic Co-operation and Development's Development Assistance Committee (DAC), the top 10 donors in 2007 contributed 83 percent of all aid provided by DAC members. The top four—the United States, Germany, France, and United Kingdom—contributed more than half.

Aid increased sharply in 2005, as donor countries followed through on promises made at the 2002 United Nations International Conference on Financing for Development, in Monterrey, Mexico, and reinforced at the 2005 Group of Eight (G8) summit at Gleneagles, Scotland. But a large part of this came as debt relief, not new aid flows. Aid in absolute terms and measured as a share of donors' gross national income has declined since 2005. A significant increase in donor commitment is required to meet the targets set at Gleneagles.

The form and purpose for which aid is given makes a difference. Technical co-operation is mainly spent in the donor economy. Debt-related aid provides relief from liabilities that recipient countries have

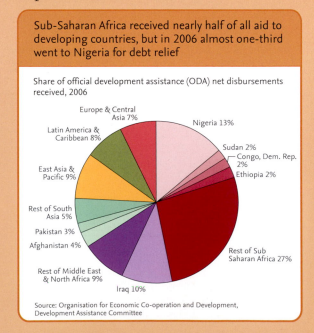

Sub-Saharan Africa received nearly half of all aid to developing countries, but in 2006 almost one-third went to Nigeria for debt relief

Share of official development assistance (ODA) net disbursements received, 2006

- Europe & Central Asia 7%
- Nigeria 13%
- Sudan 2%
- Congo, Dem. Rep. 2%
- Ethiopia 2%
- Rest of Sub Saharan Africa 27%
- Iraq 10%
- Rest of Middle East & North Africa 9%
- Afghanistan 4%
- Pakistan 3%
- Rest of South Asia 5%
- East Asia & Pacific 9%
- Latin America & Caribbean 8%

Source: Organisation for Economic Co-operation and Development, Development Assistance Committee

Aid for long-term development programs has not increased much since 1970s

Bilateral ODA net disbursements from DAC donors by purpose, constant 2006 $ (billions)

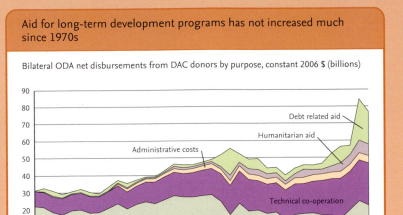

Source: Organisation for Economic Co-operation and Development, Development Assistance Committee

Significant increase in ODA from DAC members is required to meet the target for 2010

Net ODA from DAC donors, constant 2004 $ (billions)

Net ODA as a share of donors' GNI (%)

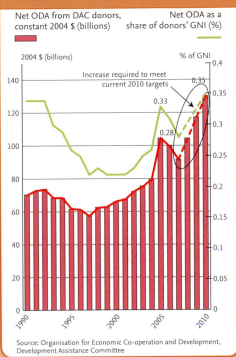

Source: Organisation for Economic Co-operation and Development, Development Assistance Committee

difficulty servicing and can free up public resources for other purposes, but it may not result in an equivalent expansion of development activities. Humanitarian assistance provides relief for sudden disasters and emergency situations, but it does not generally contribute to financing long-term development.

Aid is not the only source of development finance, or, for many countries, the most important. Remittances and private capital flows are a growing source of financing for some. But extremely poor countries, especially in Sub-Saharan Africa, still require substantial increases in aid to reach their developmental goals.

Different sources of finance for developing countries

Sources of net financial flows, 2006 ($ billions)

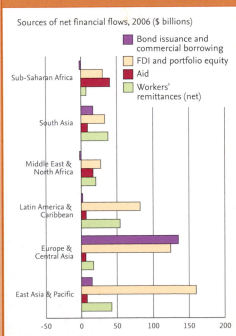

Source: World Bank, *Global Development Finance*, World Bank estimates based on data from the International Monetary Fund, *Balance of Payment Statistics*, OECD DAC, *International Development Stastistics*

Who were the largest donors in 2007?

Net aid disbursement from DAC donors, 2007

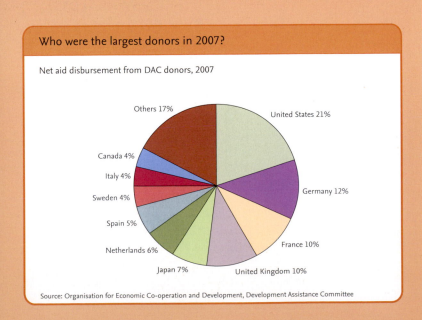

Source: Organisation for Economic Co-operation and Development, Development Assistance Committee

Aid

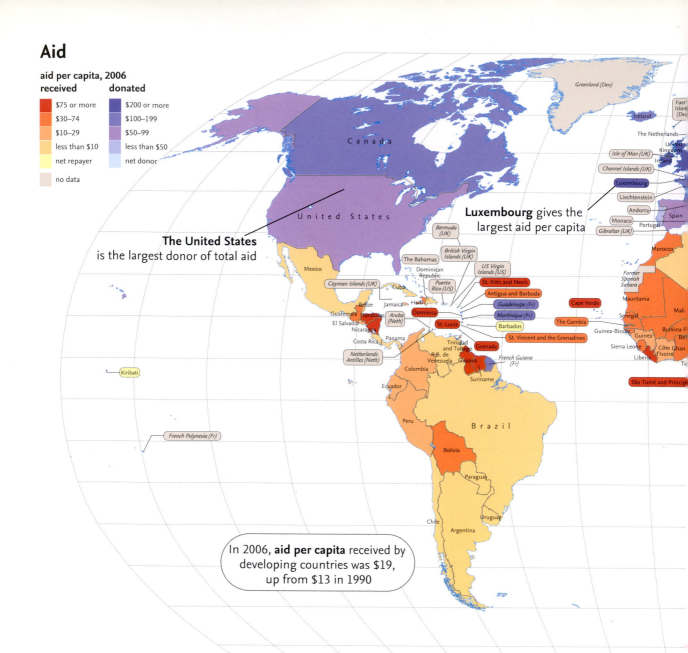

aid per capita, 2006

received
- ■ $75 or more
- ■ $30–74
- ■ $10–29
- ■ less than $10
- ■ net repayer

donated
- ■ $200 or more
- ■ $100–199
- ■ $50–99
- ■ less than $50
- ■ net donor

- ■ no data

The United States is the largest donor of total aid

Luxembourg gives the largest aid per capita

In 2006, **aid per capita** received by developing countries was $19, up from $13 in 1990

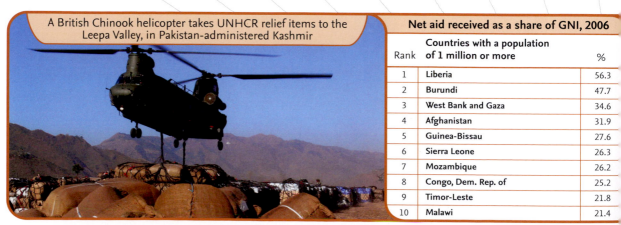

A British Chinook helicopter takes UNHCR relief items to the Leepa Valley, in Pakistan-administered Kashmir

Net aid received as a share of GNI, 2006

Rank	Countries with a population of 1 million or more	%
1	Liberia	56.3
2	Burundi	47.7
3	West Bank and Gaza	34.6
4	Afghanistan	31.9
5	Guinea-Bissau	27.6
6	Sierra Leone	26.3
7	Mozambique	26.2
8	Congo, Dem. Rep. of	25.2
9	Timor-Leste	21.8
10	Malawi	21.4

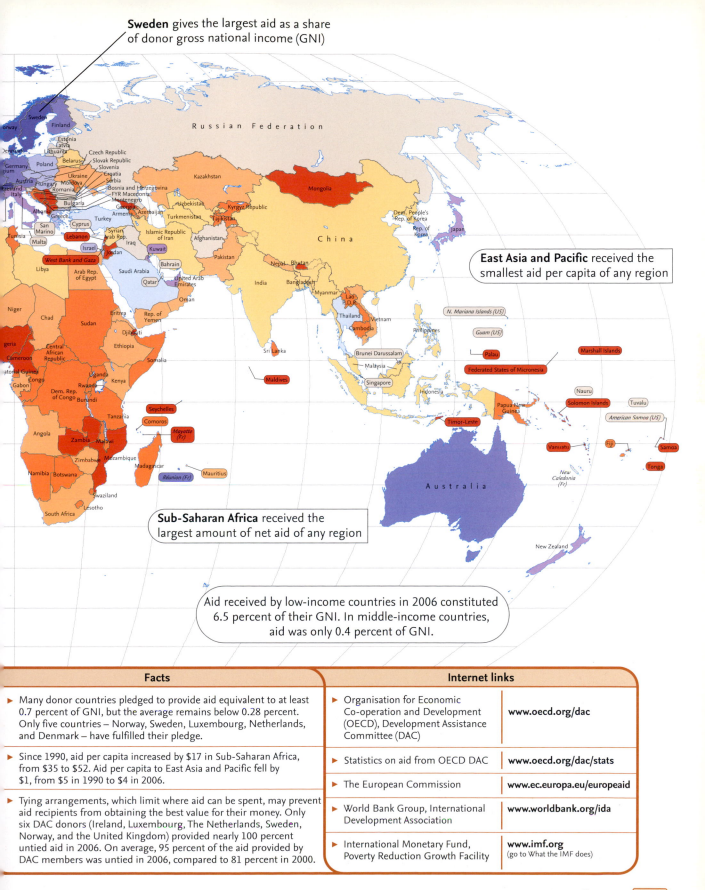

Sweden gives the largest aid as a share of donor gross national income (GNI)

East Asia and Pacific received the smallest aid per capita of any region

Sub-Saharan Africa received the largest amount of net aid of any region

Aid received by low-income countries in 2006 constituted 6.5 percent of their GNI. In middle-income countries, aid was only 0.4 percent of GNI.

Facts	Internet links	
▶ Many donor countries pledged to provide aid equivalent to at least 0.7 percent of GNI, but the average remains below 0.28 percent. Only five countries – Norway, Sweden, Luxembourg, Netherlands, and Denmark – have fulfilled their pledge.	▶ Organisation for Economic Co-operation and Development (OECD), Development Assistance Committee (DAC)	www.oecd.org/dac
▶ Since 1990, aid per capita increased by $17 in Sub-Saharan Africa, from $35 to $52. Aid per capita to East Asia and Pacific fell by $1, from $5 in 1990 to $4 in 2006.	▶ Statistics on aid from OECD DAC	www.oecd.org/dac/stats
	▶ The European Commission	www.ec.europa.eu/europeaid
▶ Tying arrangements, which limit where aid can be spent, may prevent aid recipients from obtaining the best value for their money. Only six DAC donors (Ireland, Luxembourg, The Netherlands, Sweden, Norway, and the United Kingdom) provided nearly 100 percent untied aid in 2006. On average, 95 percent of the aid provided by DAC members was untied in 2006, compared to 81 percent in 2000.	▶ World Bank Group, International Development Association	www.worldbank.org/ida
	▶ International Monetary Fund, Poverty Reduction Growth Facility	www.imf.org (go to What the IMF does)

Many countries borrow from abroad to finance development. However, when debt exceeds the capacity of a country to service it, the debt burden becomes unsustainable and hinders development. Making debt manageable for poor countries is central to their efforts to achieve the Millennium Development Goals.

A country's external debt burden affects its creditworthiness and vulnerability to financial shocks. In 2006, the external debt of developing countries was $2.8 trillion, with the 10 largest debtors owing 61 percent of the debt.

Debt has been increasing in most regions, with two exceptions—the Middle East and North Africa, where debt declined by 16 percent from the 1995 level, and Sub-Saharan Africa, where debt relief programs reduced total indebtedness by 27 percent. Private debt in other developing regions, especially in Europe and Central Asia, increased significantly between 1995 and 2006. This, in part, reflects improved creditworthiness and increased confidence of foreign lenders in the long-term growth of developing countries. Extensive private borrowing, however, increases the risk of financial downturns to developing countries and foreign investors.

Total debt service paid by developing countries was $538 billion in 2006. However, the debt burden measured by the ratio of debt service to exports fell from a high of 23 percent in 1999 to 12 percent in 2006. The

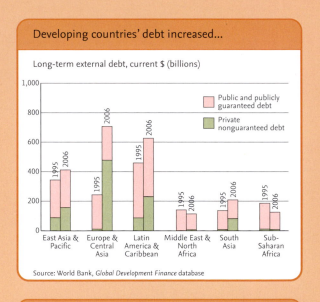

Developing countries' debt increased...

Long-term external debt, current $ (billions)

Source: World Bank, *Global Development Finance* database

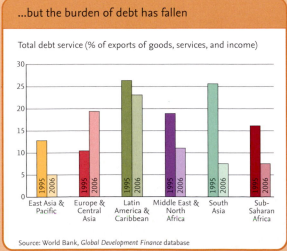

...but the burden of debt has fallen

Total debt service (% of exports of goods, services, and income)

Source: World Bank, *Global Development Finance* database

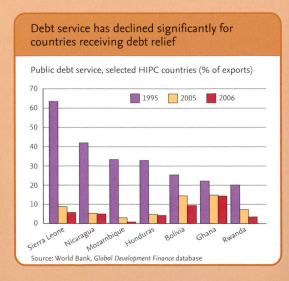

Debt service has declined significantly for countries receiving debt relief

Public debt service, selected HIPC countries (% of exports)

Source: World Bank, *Global Development Finance* database

ratio of total external debt to gross national income (GNI) declined from 43 percent to 26 percent.

The size of their debt and their ability to repay became a problem for some Latin American countries in the 1980s, as well as for many countries in Africa, East Asia, Latin America, and Russia in the 1990s. The debt crises of the 1980s and 1990s were the result of excessive borrowing with overly optimistic expectations of future growth. Cyclical global recession, declining agricultural commodity prices, poor governance and economic mismanagement, and internal and external conflicts left many poor countries unable to service their external debt. Some countries continued to borrow to meet their outstanding obligations, which only added to their burden in the absence of sustained output and export growth. Traditional debt relief, based on rescheduling and restructuring of payments, was insufficient to meet the needs of the poorest countries.

Special programs were started to address the problem of the poor countries with predominantly official creditors. In 1996, the World Bank and the International Monetary Fund (IMF) launched the Heavily Indebted Poor Countries (HIPC) initiative to provide relief to a group of mostly African countries with recurring debt repayment problems. The initiative aims to provide permanent relief from unsustainable debt by redirecting the resources going towards debt service to social expenditures directed to poverty reduction. The HIPC initiative will provide a nominal debt service relief of over $68 billion for 33 countries. Eight other countries are potentially eligible for HIPC debt relief, pending the agreement of macroeconomic reforms, poverty reduction strategies, and arrears clearance plans.

Furthermore, the International Development Association (IDA), the IMF, the African Development Fund (AfDF), and the Inter-American Development Bank (IaDB) will provide additional debt relief for all countries under the Multilateral Debt Relief Initiative (MDRI). As of September 2008, the four multilaterals have already cancelled more than $42 billion in nominal terms to 23 countries that have made progress in their economic and social reforms, as agreed to with the World Bank and IMF under the HIPC initiative. The IDA, IMF, AfDF, and IaDB have provided approximately 69, 9, 15, and 7 percent of the total MDRI debt relief, respectively.

HIPC Initiative and MDRI: Committed Debt Relief.

Status as of September 2008, in current $ (millions)

Country	Assistance under the HIPC Initiative	Assistance delivered under MDRI
* Afghanistan	1,272	...
Benin	460	1,098
Bolivia	2,060	2,801
Burkina Faso	930	1,161
* Burundi	1,465	...
Cameroon	4,917	1,266
* Central African Republic	697	...
* Chad	260	...
* Congo, Dem. Rep. of	10,389	...
* Congo, Rep. of	2,881	...
Ethiopia	3,275	3,208
Gambia, The	90	394
Ghana	3,500	3,801
* Guinea	800	...
* Guinea-Bissau	790	...
Guyana	1,354	705
* Haiti	213	...
Honduras	1,000	2,703
* Liberia	4,006	...
Madagascar	1,900	2,339
Malawi	1,600	1,526
Mali	895	1,914
Mauritania	1,100	855
Mozambique	4,300	1,990
Nicaragua	4,500	1,895
Niger	1,190	1,026
Rwanda	1,316	486
São Tomé and Príncipe	263	59
Senegal	850	2,408
Sierra Leone	994	644
Tanzania	3,000	3,743
Uganda	1,950	3,422
Zambia	3,900	2,699
Total	**68,116**	**42,143**

* Countries will receive MDRI assistance once they reach the HIPC completion point.
Source: World Bank

Internal conflict can add to a country's debt burden

External debt

external debt as a share of GNI, 2006

- 60% or more
- 45–59%
- 30–44%
- 15–29%
- less than 15%
- no data

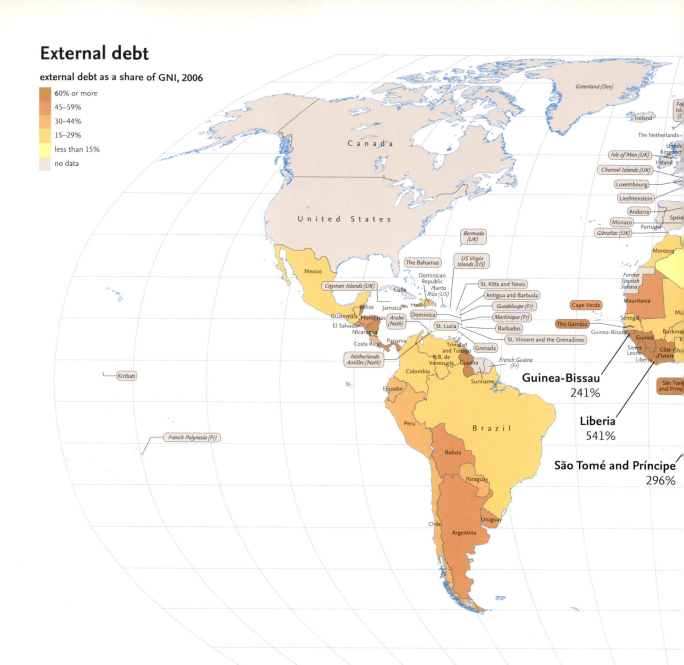

Guinea-Bissau
241%

Liberia
541%

São Tomé and Príncipe
296%

Turkey is one of the top ten debtor countries

Top 10 debtors in 2006

Rank	Developing countries	Total external debt ($ billions
1	China	323
2	Russian Federation	251
3	Turkey	208
4	Brazil	194
5	Mexico	161
6	India	153
7	Indonesia	131
8	Poland	126
9	Argentina	122
10	Kazakhstan	74

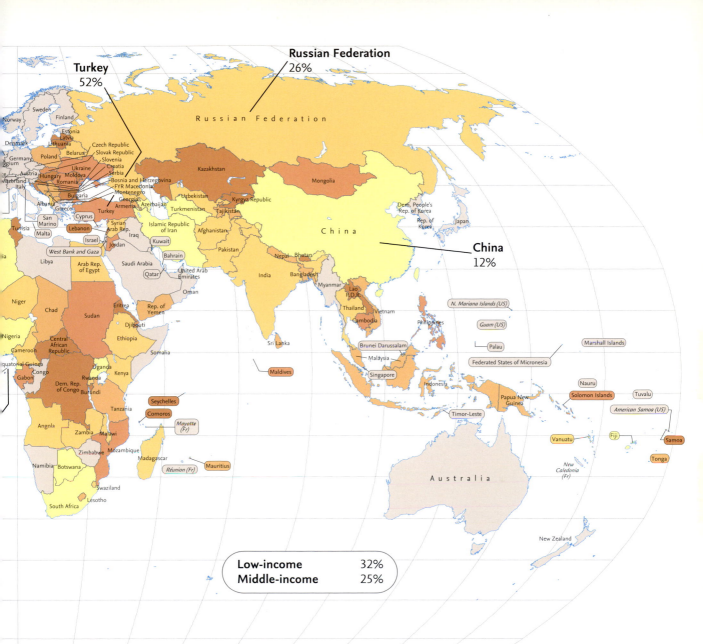

Turkey 52%

Russian Federation 26%

China 12%

Low-income 32%
Middle-income 25%

Facts		Internet links	
▶ In Sub-Saharan Africa, the ratio of debt to GNI fell from an average 65 percent in 2000–2002 to 26 percent in 2006.		▶ Bank for International Settlements	**www.bis.org** (go to statistics, select external debt)
▶ Out of 126 countries with available estimates, 86 lowered their external debt to GNI ratio between 1995 and 2006.		▶ World Bank	**www.worldbank.org/debt**
▶ For 41 Heavily Indebted Poor Countries (HIPC), the ratio of public debt service to exports fell from 13 percent in 2000 to 5 percent in 2006.		▶ Quarterly External Debt Statistics	**www.worldbank.org/qeds**
▶ It is projected that HIPC debt service ratios will fall to an average of 3.3 percent by 2011.		▶ Organisation for Economic Co-operation and Development	**www.oecd.org** (go to statistics, select finance)
▶ Short-term debt poses an immediate burden and is particularly important for monitoring financial vulnerability. Developing countries lowered their short-term debt to foreign exchange reserves ratio from 95 in 1990 to 23 in 2006.		▶ International Monetary Fund	**www.imf.org/external/np/sta/ed/ed.htm**
		▶ Joint External Debt Hub	**www.jedh.org**

Cities can be tremendously efficient, as it is easier to provide water and sanitation services to people living closer together in urban settings than in dispersed rural communities. Health care, education, and other social and cultural services are more accessible. But as cities grow, the cost of meeting basic needs increases, and so does the demand on the environment and natural resources.

Cities, now home to almost half of the world's people, are growing rapidly in size and number, especially in developing countries. People flock to cities for work, access to public services, and a higher standard of living. By 2050, the world's urban population is expected to double, from 3.2 billion in 2006 to 6.4 billion. Sub-Saharan Africa will experience a drastic urbanization as its urban population increases from 269 million to more than a billion in the next four decades. Among developing countries, urbanization has gone farthest in Latin America and the Caribbean, where 78 percent of people now live in urban areas; increasing to 89 percent by 2050 (definitions of urban areas vary by country and may not be fully comparable). By 2050, 70 percent of the world's population will live in urban

East Asia and Pacific has the largest urban population, surpassing the high-income countries; Middle East and North Africa has the smallest

Population living in urban areas (millions)

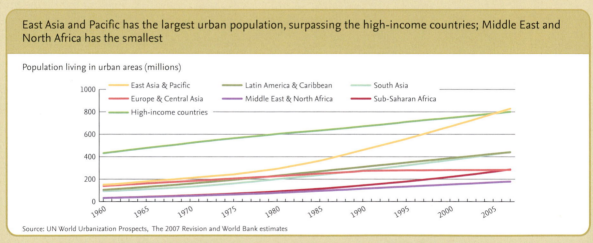

Source: UN World Urbanization Prospects, The 2007 Revision and World Bank estimates

Particulate matter concentration has been reduced in all regions

Urban-population-weighted particulate matter (PM10 per cubic meter)

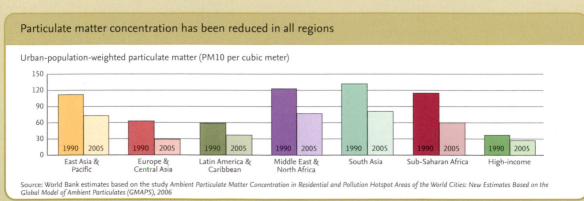

Source: World Bank estimates based on the study *Ambient Particulate Matter Concentration in Residential and Pollution Hotspot Areas of the World Cities: New Estimates Based on the Global Model of Ambient Particulates (GMAPS), 2006*

In slum areas, lack of hygiene and sanitation ensures that water-borne diseases are rife

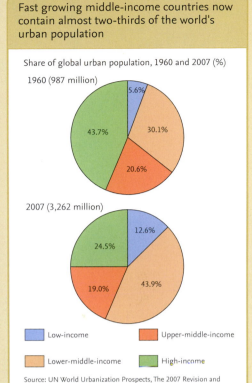

Fast growing middle-income countries now contain almost two-thirds of the world's urban population

Share of global urban population, 1960 and 2007 (%)

1960 (987 million)

5.6%
30.1%
20.6%
43.7%

2007 (3,262 million)

12.6%
24.5%
19.0%
43.9%

Low-income
Upper-middle-income
Lower-middle-income
High-income

Source: UN World Urbanization Prospects, The 2007 Revision and World Bank estimates

areas, in some countries placing tremendous pressure on the capacity of the natural and manmade environment to support them. The consequences are deteriorating living conditions, the growth of slums, the destruction of habitat, and air and water pollution.

Urbanization and the environment

Urbanization by itself is not an environmental issue, but environmental externalities are more frequent in cities. The cost of urbanization to human health comes from a variety of sources. Diarrheal diseases from inadequate sanitation account for an estimated 4 percent of the global burden of disease. The proximity to industrial works and roadways, and the use of inefficient and polluting sources of energy can result in exposure to high levels of soot and small particles (PM10—fine, suspended particulates less than 10 microns in diameter) and contribute to respiratory diseases, lung cancer, and heart disease.

Air and water pollution in many of the world's major cities cause moderate to severe sickness and death, and cost billions of dollars in lost productivity and damages. Although all the world's large cities share these problems, water pollution tends to be most serious in south, southeast, and central Asia. Air pollution has the biggest impact in China, Latin America and the Caribbean, and Eastern Europe. Not only are the human and financial costs of pollution high, they tend to fall disproportionately on poor people. So addressing pollution is justified on equity, economic, and environmental grounds.

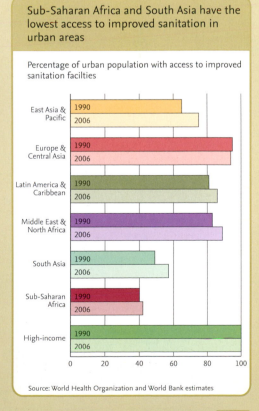

Sub-Saharan Africa and South Asia have the lowest access to improved sanitation in urban areas

Percentage of urban population with access to improved sanitation facilties

East Asia & Pacific — 1990, 2006
Europe & Central Asia — 1990, 2006
Latin America & Caribbean — 1990, 2006
Middle East & North Africa — 1990, 2006
South Asia — 1990, 2006
Sub-Saharan Africa — 1990, 2006
High-income — 1990, 2006

0   20   40   60   80   100

Source: World Health Organization and World Bank estimates

Urbanization

urban population as a share of total population, 2007

- less than 35%
- 35–49%
- 50–64%
- 65–79%
- 80% or more
- no data

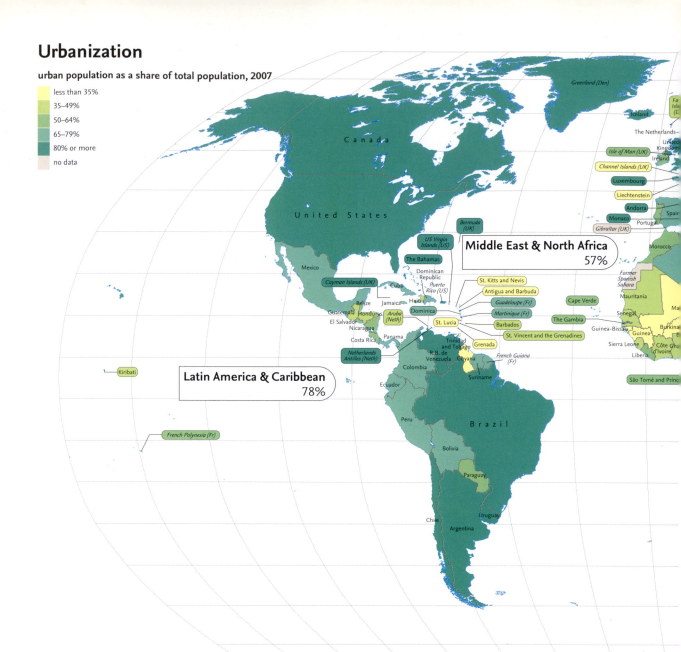

Greenland (Den)

Iceland

Fa
Isle
(C

The Netherlands

United
Kingdom

Isle of Man (UK)

Ireland

Channel Islands (UK)

Luxembourg

Liechtenstein

Andorra

Spain

Monaco

Portugal

Gibraltar (UK)

Morocco

Former
Spanish
Sahara

Canada

United States

Bermuda
(UK)

US Virgin
Islands (US)

Middle East & North Africa
57%

The Bahamas

Dominican
Republic

St. Kitts and Nevis

Mexico

Cayman Islands (UK)

Cuba

Puerto
Rico (US)

Antigua and Barbuda

Mauritania

Cape Verde

Mali

Belize

Jamaica

Haiti

Guadeloupe (Fr)

Senegal

Burkina

Guatemala

Honduras

Dominica

Martinique (Fr)

The Gambia

Guinea

El Salvador

Aruba
(Neth)

St. Lucia

Guinea-Bissau

Côte Gha
d'Ivoire

Nicaragua

Barbados

Sierra Leone

Costa Rica

Panama

St. Vincent and the Grenadines

Liberia

Netherlands
Antilles (Neth)

Trinidad
and Tobago

Grenada

Kiribati

R.B. de
Venezuela

Guyana

French Guiana
(Fr)

São Tomé and Princ

Latin America & Caribbean
78%

Colombia

Suriname

Ecuador

Peru

Brazil

French Polynesia (Fr)

Bolivia

Paraguay

Chile

Uruguay

Argentina

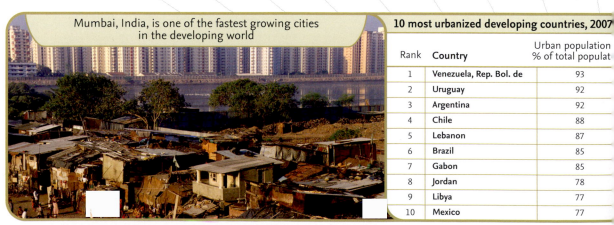

Mumbai, India, is one of the fastest growing cities in the developing world

Rank	Country	Urban population % of total populat
		10 most urbanized developing countries, 2007
1	Venezuela, Rep. Bol. de	93
2	Uruguay	92
3	Argentina	92
4	Chile	88
5	Lebanon	87
6	Brazil	85
7	Gabon	85
8	Jordan	78
9	Libya	77
10	Mexico	77

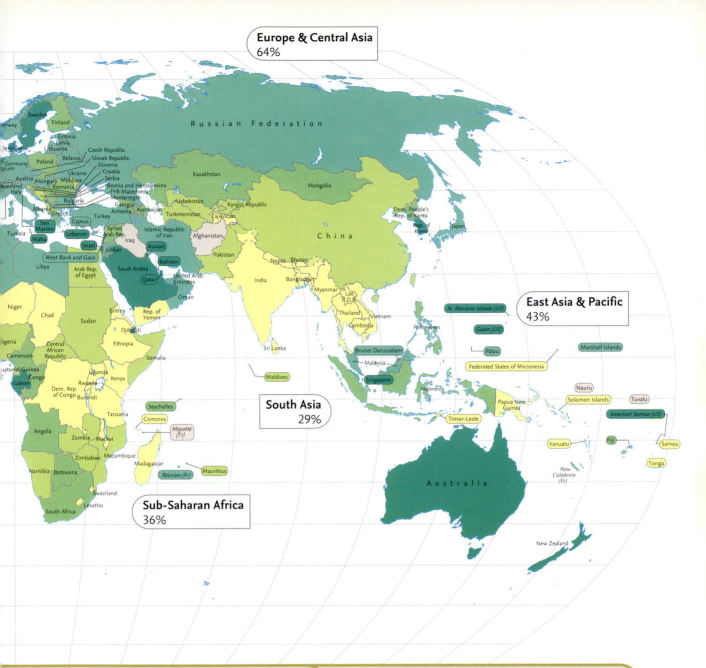

Europe & Central Asia
64%

East Asia & Pacific
43%

South Asia
29%

Sub-Saharan Africa
36%

Facts	Internet links	
▶ In most developed countries, the onset of urbanization coincided with the Industrial Revolution of the 19th century, when farm workers, displaced by the mechanization of agriculture, flooded into the cities.	▶ United Nations Population Information Network	www.un.org/popin
▶ In 2001, 924 million people were living in slums worldwide; the present trend indicates that about 2 billion people will be living in slums in 2030.	▶ Population Reference Bureau	www.prb.org
▶ Latin America and the Caribbean has a higher percentage of urban population than high-income countries.	▶ World Bank Urban Development	www.worldbank.org/urban
▶ Urban areas cover only about 3 percent of the world's land area.	▶ United Nations World Urbanization Prospects, The 2007 Revision	http://esa.un.org/unup/
▶ There is a great disparity in the world's concentration of urban population: 75 percent live in 25 countries, and 55 percent live in 10 countries.		

Agricultural output has grown more rapidly than population, but so has the demand for agricultural products. Malnutrition and food shortages take a pervasive toll in developing countries, especially in Sub-Saharan Africa. Meeting the growing demand for food and improving the quality of life of those who produce it requires increasing the productivity of farmers and their land.

By 2050, there will be 9 billion people living on Earth, almost 3 billion more than today. Most will live in cities, but all will depend on rural areas to feed them. Since 2000, the world's food supply has grown by 1.2 percent annually. Production in the developing regions of Asia and Latin America and the Caribbean has grown even faster, at around 2 percent. But in Africa, with some of the highest rates of under-nourishment, food production has barely kept pace with the population increase.

The demand for food will continue to grow because of population growth, increasing income and changes in dietary habits, and industrial demand for commodities such as corn and soybean. Food consumption patterns in developing countries are changing as incomes rise. Traditional meals, based on cereals and vegetables, are being replaced by more input-intensive and higher-priced meat products.

Producing more food requires more efficient use of the agricultural inputs—land, water, and soil fertility. Intensified cultivation through the use of fertilizers, pesticides, irrigation, and new plant varieties can make limited land more productive. Such practices,

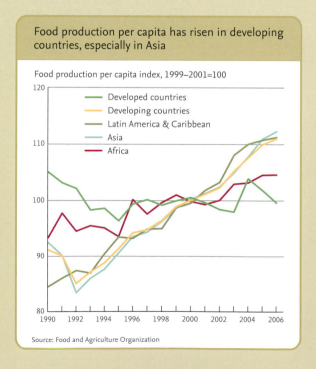

Food production per capita has risen in developing countries, especially in Asia

Food production per capita index, 1999–2001=100

- Developed countries
- Developing countries
- Latin America & Caribbean
- Asia
- Africa

Source: Food and Agriculture Organization

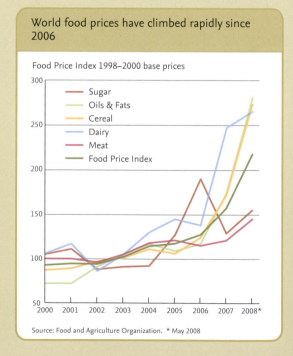

World food prices have climbed rapidly since 2006

Food Price Index 1998–2000 base prices

- Sugar
- Oils & Fats
- Cereal
- Dairy
- Meat
- Food Price Index

Source: Food and Agriculture Organization. * May 2008

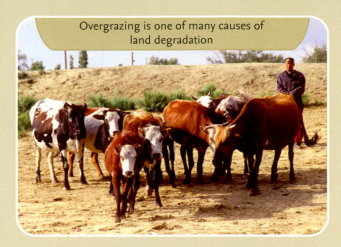
Overgrazing is one of many causes of land degradation

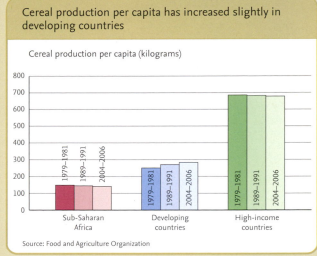
Cereal production per capita has increased slightly in developing countries

Cereal production per capita (kilograms)

Sub-Saharan Africa: 1979–1981, 1989–1991, 2004–2006
Developing countries: 1979–1981, 1989–1991, 2004–2006
High-income countries: 1979–1981, 1989–1991, 2004–2006

Source: Food and Agriculture Organization

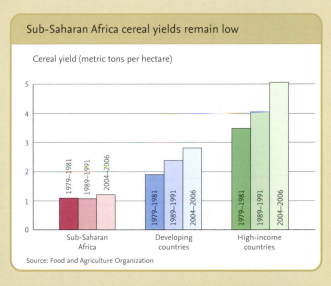
Sub-Saharan Africa cereal yields remain low

Cereal yield (metric tons per hectare)

Sub-Saharan Africa: 1979–1981, 1989–1991, 2004–2006
Developing countries: 1979–1981, 1989–1991, 2004–2006
High-income countries: 1979–1981, 1989–1991, 2004–2006

Source: Food and Agriculture Organization

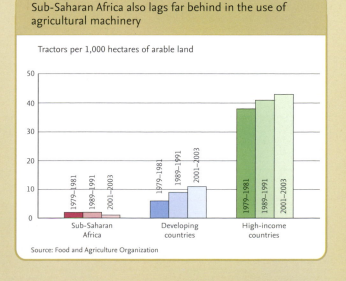
Sub-Saharan Africa also lags far behind in the use of agricultural machinery

Tractors per 1,000 hectares of arable land

Sub-Saharan Africa: 1979–1981, 1989–1991, 2001–2003
Developing countries: 1979–1981, 1989–1991, 2001–2003
High-income countries: 1979–1981, 1989–1991, 2001–2003

Source: Food and Agriculture Organization

however, may also cause further environmental degradation. The effects of climate change represent a further challenge to efforts to raise the productivity of plants and animals.

Many poor farmers subsist on fragile lands, poorly suited to intensive farming. They lack access to fertilizers, farm equipment, irrigation systems, high-yielding plant varieties, and markets for their produce. Overgrazing, deforestation, improper crop rotation, and poor soil and water management contribute to land degradation. The degradation of land reduces its productivity, encouraging growing populations to move on to new and poorer land, converting forests and fragile, semi-arid areas into low-productivity cultivated areas.

In 2002, almost 1.4 billion people were living on fragile lands, more than three-quarters of them in Asia and Africa. On these lands, the yields are low, the risks of crop failure are high, and a large portion of the population is undernourished. Many, especially in Africa, are vulnerable to climate variability and associated floods and droughts that are likely to become more pronounced as a result of climate change, leading to local famines and increased levels of malnutrition. Sustainable production methods, based on environmentally sound practices, along with the development of more efficient markets for farm inputs and outputs and off-farm activities, are the keys to improving rural livelihoods and expanding the global food supply.

Undernourishment

prevalence of undernourishment,
share of population, 2004

- ███ 40% or more
- ███ 25–39%
- ███ 10–24%
- ███ 5–9%
- ███ less than 5%
- ███ no data

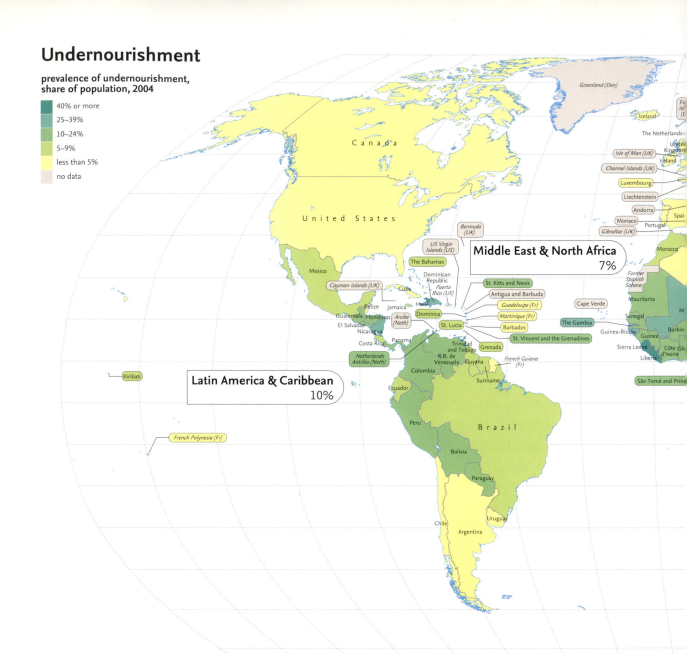

Greenland (Den)

Iceland

The Netherlands

Isle of Man (UK) United Kingdom

Channel Islands (UK) Ireland

Luxembourg

Liechtenstein

Andorra

Monaco Spai

Gibraltar (UK) Portugal

Morocco

C a n a d a

U n i t e d   S t a t e s

Bermuda (UK)

Middle East & North Africa
7%

Former Spanish Sahara

Mexico

Cayman Islands (UK)

US Virgin Islands (US)

The Bahamas

Dominican Republic

Puerto Rico (US)

Cuba

Haiti

St. Kitts and Nevis

Antigua and Barbuda

Cape Verde

Mauritania

Belize Jamaica

Guadeloupe (Fr)

Guatemala Honduras

Dominica

Aruba (Neth)

Martinique (Fr)

Senegal

El Salvador

St. Lucia

Barbados

The Gambia

Guinea-Bissau Guinea Burkin

Nicaragua

Costa Rica Panama

Grenada

St. Vincent and the Grenadines

Sierra Leone Côte Gh d'Ivoire

Netherlands Antilles (Neth)

Trinidad and Tobago

R.B. de Venezuela

Guyana

French Guiana (Fr)

Liberia

Colombia

Suriname

São Tomé and Prín

Ecuador

Latin America & Caribbean
10%

Kiribati

Peru

B r a z i l

French Polynesia (Fr)

Bolivia

Paraguay

Uruguay

Chile

Argentina

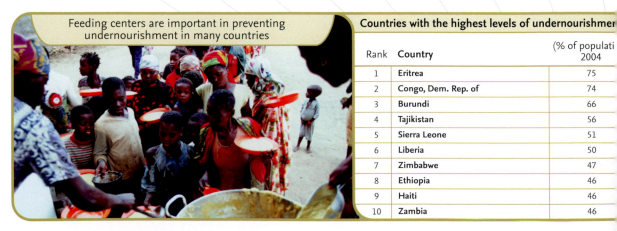

Feeding centers are important in preventing
undernourishment in many countries

Countries with the highest levels of undernourishmen

Rank	Country	(% of populati 2004
1	Eritrea	75
2	Congo, Dem. Rep. of	74
3	Burundi	66
4	Tajikistan	56
5	Sierra Leone	51
6	Liberia	50
7	Zimbabwe	47
8	Ethiopia	46
9	Haiti	46
10	Zambia	46

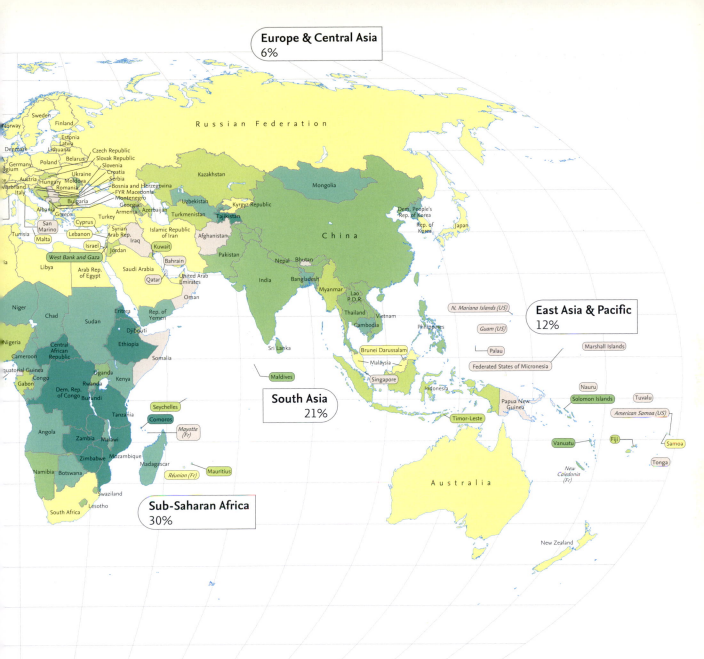

Europe & Central Asia
6%

R u s s i a n   F e d e r a t i o n

Sweden
Norway
Finland
Denmark
Estonia
Latvia
Lithuania
Germany
Belgium
Poland
Belarus
Czech Republic
Slovak Republic
Slovenia
Croatia
Serbia
Austria
Hungary
Moldova
Ukraine
Switzerland
Italy
Romania
Bosnia and Herzegovina
FYR Macedonia
Montenegro
Georgia
Armenia
Azerbaijan
Albania
Bulgaria
Greece
Turkey
San Marino
Cyprus
Syrian Arab Rep.
Tunisia
Malta
Lebanon
Israel
Jordan
West Bank and Gaza
Libya
Arab Rep. of Egypt
Saudi Arabia
Qatar
Kuwait
Bahrain
United Arab Emirates
Oman
Rep. of Yemen

Kazakhstan
Mongolia
Uzbekistan
Kyrgyz Republic
Turkmenistan
Tajikistan
Islamic Republic of Iran
Afghanistan
China
Pakistan
Nepal
Bhutan
India
Bangladesh
Myanmar
Lao P.D.R.
Thailand
Vietnam
Cambodia
Sri Lanka
Dem. People's Rep. of Korea
Rep. of Korea
Japan

Niger
Chad
Sudan
Eritrea
Djibouti
Ethiopia
Somalia
Nigeria
Central African Republic
Cameroon
Equatorial Guinea
Congo
Gabon
Dem. Rep. of Congo
Uganda
Rwanda
Burundi
Kenya
Tanzania
Angola
Zambia
Malawi
Zimbabwe
Mozambique
Namibia
Botswana
Madagascar
Swaziland
South Africa
Lesotho

Seychelles
Comoros
Mayotte (Fr)
Réunion (Fr)
Mauritius
Maldives

East Asia & Pacific
12%

N. Mariana Islands (US)
Guam (US)
Palau
Marshall Islands
Federated States of Micronesia
Philippines
Brunei Darussalam
Malaysia
Singapore
Indonesia
Papua New Guinea
Timor-Leste
Nauru
Solomon Islands
Tuvalu
American Samoa (US)
Vanuatu
Fiji
Samoa
Tonga
New Caledonia (Fr)

South Asia
21%

Sub-Saharan Africa
30%

A u s t r a l i a

New Zealand

Facts	Internet links
▶ Among developing regions, East Asia and Pacific has had the fastest reduction in the prevalence of undernourishment since 1990.	▶ Food and Agriculture Organization — **www.fao.org/faostat/ foodsecurity/index_en.htm**
▶ In Sub-Saharan Africa, the number of undernourished people has increased from 150 million in 1990 to 222 million in 2004.	▶ Consultative Group on International Agricultural Research — **www.cgiar.org**
▶ Rural poor people make up an estimated 80 percent of the world's 800 million hungry people.	▶ World Food Programme — **www.wfp.org/english**
▶ A large proportion of the hungry is concentrated in areas vulnerable to environmental degradation and climate change.	▶ International Fund for Agricultural Development — **www.ifad.org**

Food production

**food production per capita index,
average annual growth, 1990–2006**

- ▮ less than -1.0%
- ▮ -1.0–0.0%
- ▮ 0.1–0.9%
- ▮ 1.0–1.9%
- ▮ 2.0% or more
- ▮ no data

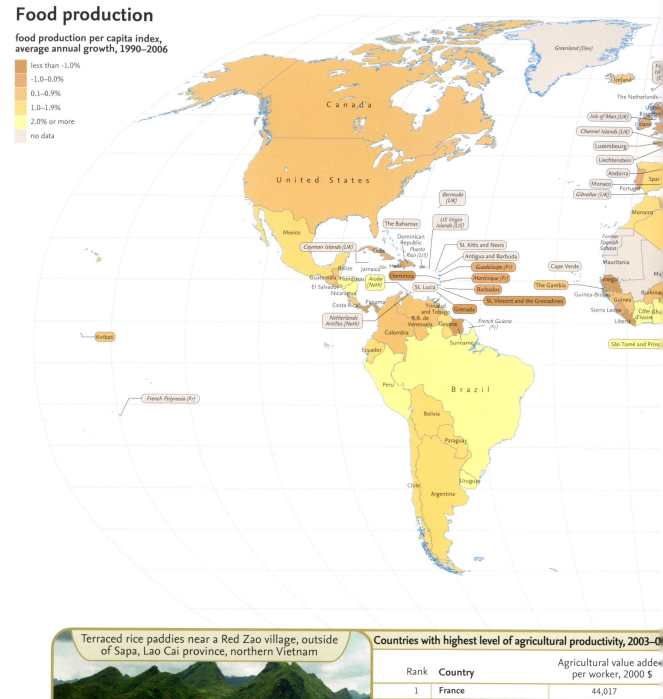

Greenland (Den)

Iceland

The Netherlands

Isle of Man (UK)

Channel Islands (UK)

Luxembourg

Liechtenstein

Andorra

Monaco

Gibraltar (UK)

United Kingdom

Ireland

Spain

Portugal

Morocco

Former Spanish Sahara

Mauritania

Cape Verde

The Gambia

Senegal

Guinea-Bissau

Guinea

Sierra Leone

Liberia

Burkina

Côte Gh.
d'Ivoire

São Tomé and Princ.

C a n a d a

United States

Bermuda (UK)

Mexico

Cayman Islands (UK)

The Bahamas

US Virgin Islands (US)

Dominican Republic
Puerto Rico (US)

Cuba

Haiti

Jamaica

Belize

Guatemala

Honduras

Aruba (Neth)

Dominica

El Salvador

Nicaragua

Costa Rica

Panama

St. Kitts and Nevis

Antigua and Barbuda

Guadeloupe (Fr)

Martinique (Fr)

St. Lucia

Barbados

St. Vincent and the Grenadines

Grenada

Trinidad and Tobago

R.B. de Venezuela

Netherlands Antilles (Neth)

Colombia

Guyana

Suriname

French Guiana (Fr)

Ecuador

Kiribati

Peru

B r a z i l

French Polynesia (Fr)

Bolivia

Paraguay

Chile

Uruguay

Argentina

Terraced rice paddies near a Red Zao village, outside
of Sapa, Lao Cai province, northern Vietnam

Countries with highest level of agricultural productivity, 2003–0

Rank	Country	Agricultural value adde[d] per worker, 2000 $
1	France	44,017
2	Canada	43,055
3	Netherlands	42,198
4	United States	41,797
5	Belgium	41,631
6	Denmark	40,780
7	Singapore	40,419
8	Norway	37,776
9	Japan	35,517
10	Sweden	33,023

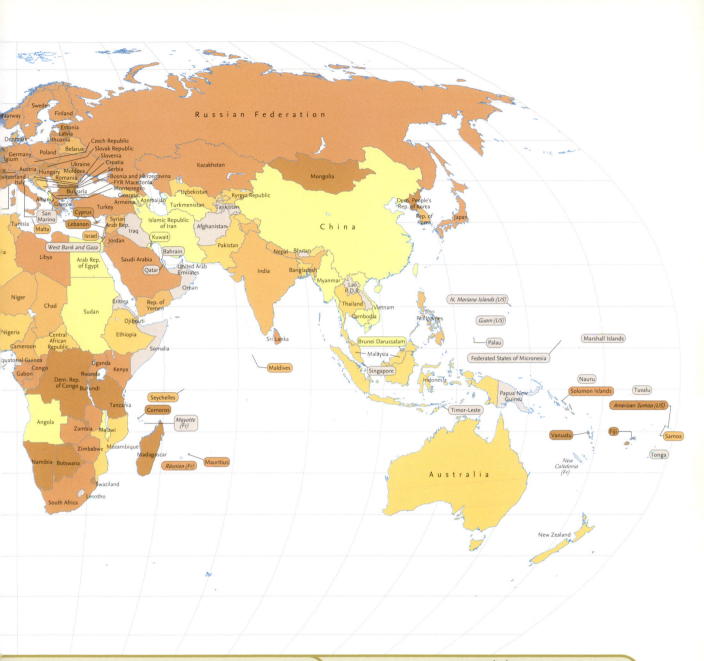

Facts	Internet links	
▶ Worldwide, agriculture accounts for 3 percent of Gross Domestic Product (GDP), but 26 percent of GDP in low-income economies.	▶ Food and Agriculture Organization	**www.fao.org**
▶ World food production per capita grew by 1.2 percent a year between 2000 and 2006.	▶ International Food Policy Research Institute	**www.ifpri.org**
▶ Over the last 30 years, Africa experienced at least one major drought each year.	▶ Consultative Group on International Agricultural Research	**www.cgiar.org**
	▶ World Food Programme	**www.wfp.org/english**
▶ The Sub-Saharan African cereal yield is about 1,100 kilograms per hectare, one-third of the world average.	▶ African Green Revolution	**www.africagreenrevolution.com/en/index.html**

A thirsty planet gets thirstier

Water is crucial to economic growth and development—and to the survival of both terrestrial and aquatic ecosystems. 700 million people worldwide, living in 43 countries, currently suffer from water shortage, and more than 900 million people lack access to safe drinking water.

Freshwater supplies are declining. With the projected growth in population and economic activity, the share of the world's population facing water shortages will increase more than fivefold by 2050. Human needs for water in daily life compete with demand from agriculture for irrigation, energy production, and other industrial uses. Urbanization and changes in lifestyle also lead to higher per capita use. Climate change is also expected to influence the availability and distribution of freshwater supplies. These trends pose a significant challenge for meeting the Millennium Development Goals and sustaining the growth of developing countries.

Although the Earth's water resources are estimated at about 1.4 billion cubic kilometers, only a fraction is available for human needs. Freshwater makes up only 2.5 percent of total water resources, or about 35 million cubic kilometers. Most freshwater occurs in the form of permanent ice or snow, locked up in Antarctica and Greenland, or in deep groundwater aquifers. The principal sources of water for human use are lakes,

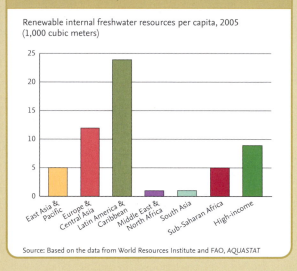

South Asia, and Middle East and North Africa face severe water scarcity

Renewable internal freshwater resources per capita, 2005 (1,000 cubic meters)

Source: Based on the data from World Resources Institute and FAO, AQUASTAT

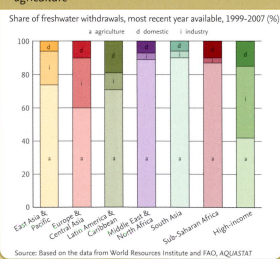

Most freshwater in developing countries is used for agriculture

Share of freshwater withdrawals, most recent year available, 1999-2007 (%)

a agriculture   d domestic   i industry

Source: Based on the data from World Resources Institute and FAO, AQUASTAT

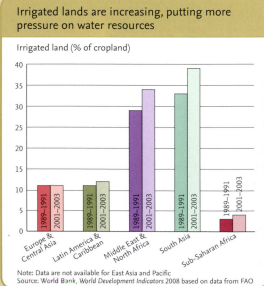

Irrigated lands are increasing, putting more pressure on water resources

Irrigated land (% of cropland)

Note: Data are not available for East Asia and Pacific
Source: World Bank, *World Development Indicators* 2008 based on data from FAO

The diversion of water for irrigation has resulted in the Aral Sea shrinking, causing health problems and destroying the fishing industry

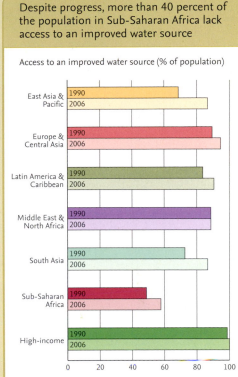

Despite progress, more than 40 percent of the population in Sub-Saharan Africa lack access to an improved water source

Access to an improved water source (% of population)

Source: World Health Organization and World Bank estimates

rivers, soil moisture, and relatively shallow groundwater basins. The usable portion is less than 1 percent of all freshwater and only 0.03 percent of all water on Earth. Much of that is located far from human populations.

Humans compete with ecosystems for the use of freshwater. Extraction of water for human needs diminishes the amount available to maintain the ecosystem's integrity. Pollution of water bodies leads to the further degradation of natural systems. The three major factors leading to increased water demand over the past century have been population growth, industrial development, and the expansion of irrigated land for agriculture. Agriculture accounts for 70 percent of freshwater withdrawals— 90 percent in low-income countries. Most is used for irrigation to provide about 40 percent of world food production.

Although domestic use of water for drinking and washing is the smallest part of demand, providing safe water for human consumption is of great importance for health and wellbeing. Water supplies should be free of chemical and biological contaminants, delivered in such a way that their cleanliness is protected. They should also be regularly and conveniently available. To meet the water supply MDG target by 2015, more than 500 million people need to gain access to improved water sources.

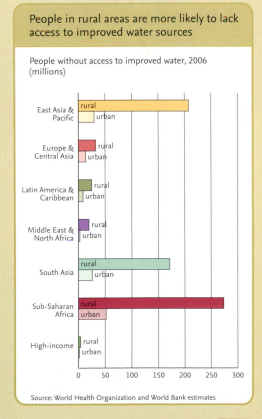

People in rural areas are more likely to lack access to improved water sources

People without access to improved water, 2006 (millions)

Source: World Health Organization and World Bank estimates

Freshwater resources

renewable internal freshwater resources
per capita (cubic meters), 2005

- less than 1,000
- 1,000–1,999
- 2,000–4,999
- 5,000–19,999
- 20,000 or more
- no data

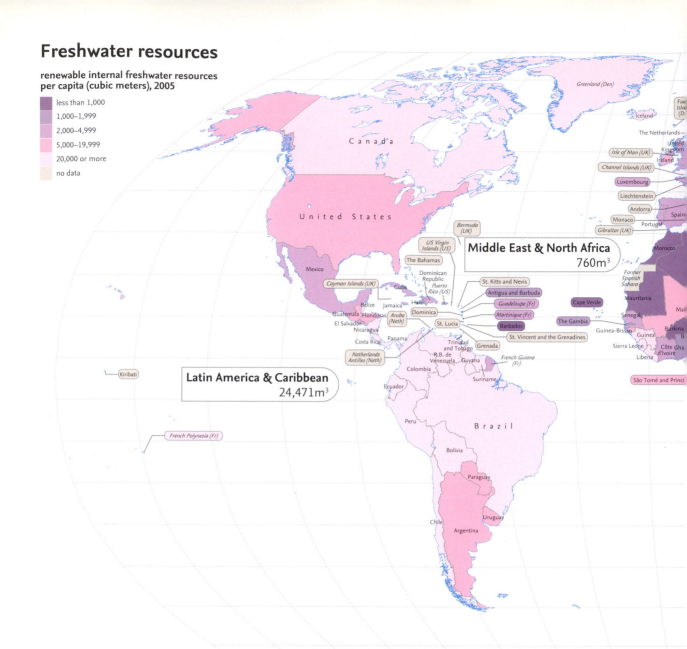

Greenland (Den)

Iceland

The Netherlands

Canada

Isle of Man (UK)

Channel Islands (UK)

Luxembourg

Liechtenstein

Andorra

Monaco

Gibraltar (UK)

Faeroe Islands (D)

United Kingdom

Ireland

Spain

Portugal

United States

Middle East & North Africa
760m³

Bermuda (UK)

US Virgin Islands (US)

The Bahamas

Mexico

Cayman Islands (UK)

Cuba

Dominican Republic

Puerto Rico (US)

St. Kitts and Nevis

Antigua and Barbuda

Guadeloupe (Fr)

Martinique (Fr)

Dominica

St. Lucia

Barbados

St. Vincent and the Grenadines

Grenada

Morocco

Former Spanish Sahara

Mauritania

Cape Verde

The Gambia

Senegal

Guinea-Bissau

Sierra Leone

Liberia

Guinea

Côte d'Ivoire

Mali

Burkina

São Tomé and Príncipe

Belize

Jamaica

Haiti

Guatemala

Honduras

Aruba (Neth)

El Salvador

Nicaragua

Costa Rica

Panama

Netherlands Antilles (Neth)

Trinidad and Tobago

R.B. de Venezuela

Guyana

Colombia

Suriname

French Guiana (Fr)

Ecuador

Latin America & Caribbean
24,471m³

Kiribati

Peru

Brazil

French Polynesia (Fr)

Bolivia

Paraguay

Chile

Uruguay

Argentina

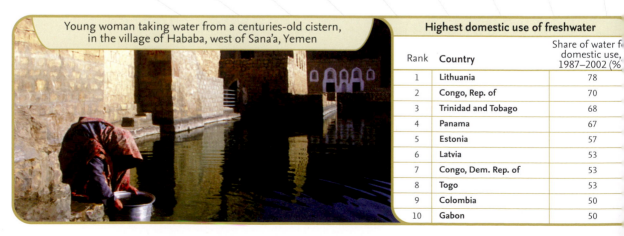

Young woman taking water from a centuries-old cistern,
in the village of Hababa, west of Sana'a, Yemen

Highest domestic use of freshwater

Rank	Country	Share of water for domestic use, 1987–2002 (%
1	Lithuania	78
2	Congo, Rep. of	70
3	Trinidad and Tobago	68
4	Panama	67
5	Estonia	57
6	Latvia	53
7	Congo, Dem. Rep. of	53
8	Togo	53
9	Colombia	50
10	Gabon	50

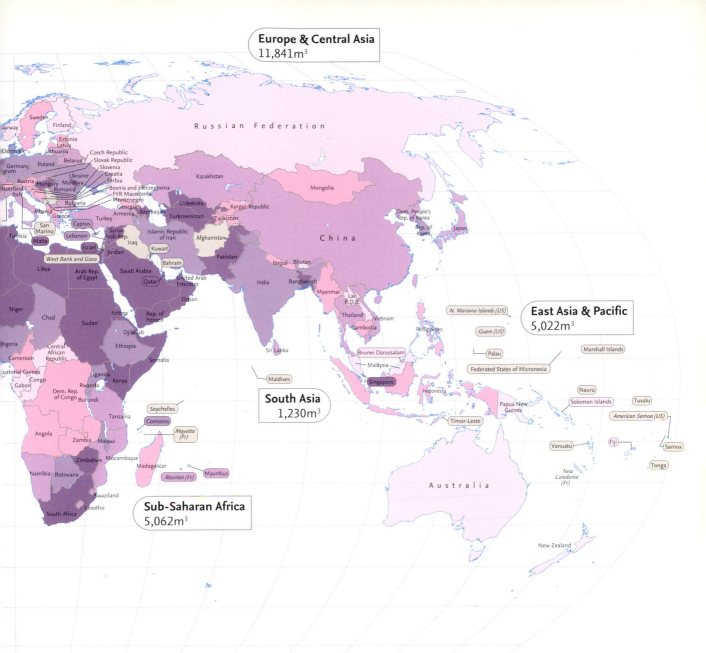

Europe & Central Asia
11,841m³

East Asia & Pacific
5,022m³

South Asia
1,230m³

Sub-Saharan Africa
5,062m³

Facts	Internet links	
► The world's use of freshwater exceeds 3,800 billion cubic meters a year.	► *AQUASTAT*, Food and Agriculture Organization of the United Nations	**www.fao.org** (click on 'statistical databases')
► Latin America, with 31 percent, and East Asia, with 22 percent, have more than half of the world's freshwater resources.		
► The Middle East and North Africa region has the least per capita freshwater resources: less than 760 cubic meters per person.	► UN Environment Programme	**www.unep.org**
► South Asia uses 90 percent of total freshwater withdrawals for agricultural use.		
► Since the 1900s freshwater withdrawals have increased sixfold, almost twice the rate of population growth.	► World Resource Institute	**www.wri.org**

Access to water

share of population with access to improved
water source, 2006

- less than 50%
- 50–69%
- 70–89%
- 90–99%
- 100%
- no data

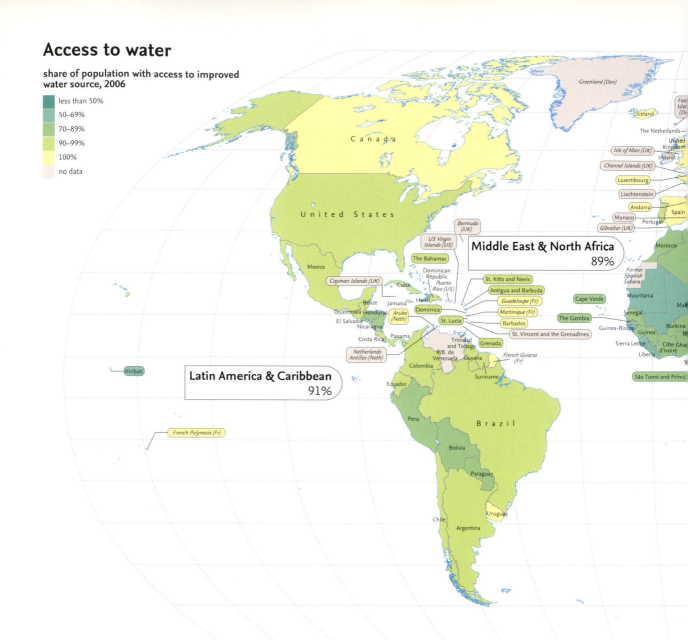

Middle East & North Africa
89%

Latin America & Caribbean
91%

A standpipe is often the only freshwater supply
to communities in the developing world

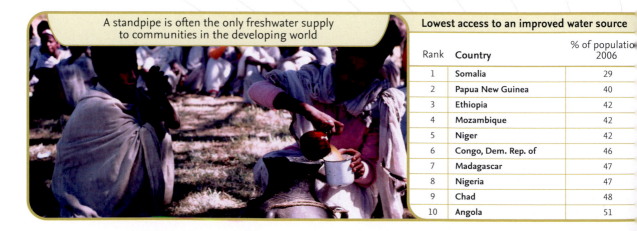

Lowest access to an improved water source

Rank	Country	% of populatio 2006
1	Somalia	29
2	Papua New Guinea	40
3	Ethiopia	42
4	Mozambique	42
5	Niger	42
6	Congo, Dem. Rep. of	46
7	Madagascar	47
8	Nigeria	47
9	Chad	48
10	Angola	51

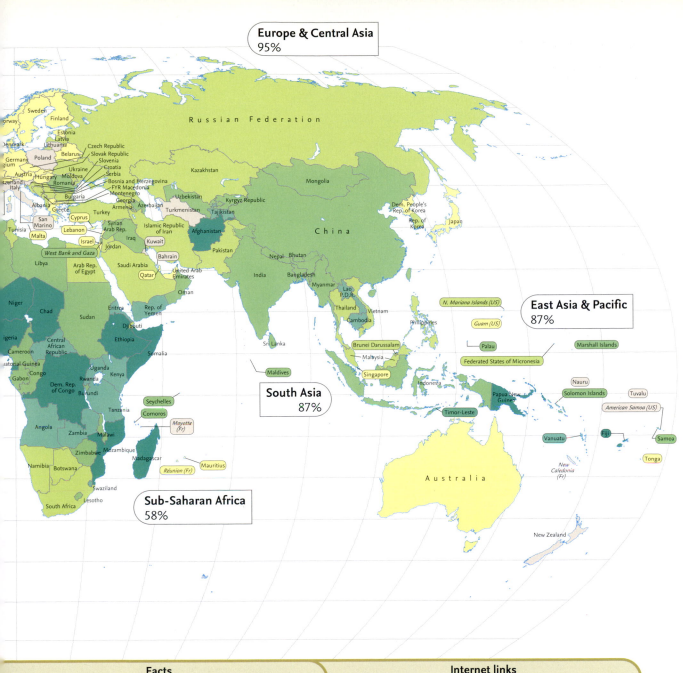

Europe & Central Asia 95%

East Asia & Pacific 87%

South Asia 87%

Sub-Saharan Africa 58%

Facts	Internet links	
▶ Globally, around 900 million people do not have access to improved water sources. Of those, 36 percent, or about 325 million, live in Sub-Saharan Africa.	▶ WHO/UNICEF Joint Monitoring Programme (JMP) for Water Supply and Sanitation	**www.wssinfo.org/en/ welcome.html**
▶ In developing countries about 16 percent of the population do not have access to an improved source of water.	▶ WHO Water Sanitation and Health (WSH)	**www.who.int/ water_sanitation_health/en**
▶ In Sub-Saharan Africa, about 54 percent of the rural population do not have access to an improved source of water.	▶ UNICEF ChildInfo	**www.childinfo.org**
▶ The world needs to increase food production by 50 percent by the year 2030, indicating more demand on the agricultural share of freshwater consumption.	▶ UN Development Programme	**www.undp.org**
▶ About 36 countries use more than 90 percent of their freshwater for agricultural purposes.		

Forests directly contribute to the livelihood of poor people. In addition, they nourish the natural systems on which many more people depend. They also account for as much as 90 percent of terrestrial biodiversity. In most countries, however, forests are shrinking.

Forests meet many people's basic, everyday needs, providing food, fuel, building materials, and clean water. Forests also provide essential public goods of global value. They facilitate the hydrological and nutrient cycles and act as carbon sinks, helping reduce greenhouse gas accumulation in the atmosphere. Many of the world's rural poor people directly depend on forest products for their livelihoods.

Forest loss is taking a terrible toll on both the natural and economic resources of many countries. Deforestation is the main cause of

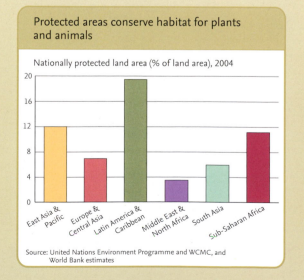

Forests cover over 30 percent of all land

Forest coverage (% of land area), 1990 and 2005

Source: FAO, *Global Forest Resources Assessment 2005*

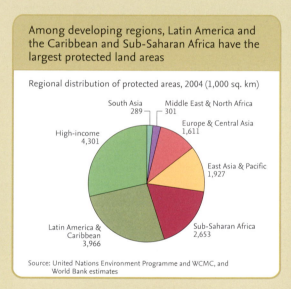

Among developing regions, Latin America and the Caribbean and Sub-Saharan Africa have the largest protected land areas

Regional distribution of protected areas, 2004 (1,000 sq. km)

Source: United Nations Environment Programme and WCMC, and World Bank estimates

Protected areas conserve habitat for plants and animals

Nationally protected land area (% of land area), 2004

Source: United Nations Environment Programme and WCMC, and World Bank estimates

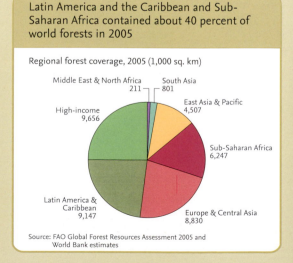

Latin America and the Caribbean and Sub-Saharan Africa contained about 40 percent of world forests in 2005

Regional forest coverage, 2005 (1,000 sq. km)

Source: FAO Global Forest Resources Assessment 2005 and World Bank estimates

Burned out forest in Amazonia, Para, Brazil

biodiversity loss. *Biodiversity* refers to the variety of plants and animal species on earth, the genetic variability within each species, and the variety of ecosystems in which they live. Tropical forests are particularly rich in diversity of life. In addition, forest loss in the tropics is responsible for 10 to 30 percent of global greenhouse gas emissions.

Deforestation is largely driven by human action and economic development. Because many services provided by forests are not valued, they are subject to destructive and unsustainable exploitation that is not economically or environmentally justified. Forests are cleared to expand agricultural land or allow the exploitation of minerals. Timber is used to provide fuel and raw material for manufacturing and construction. In many cases, proper accounting would show that forests are more valuable than these destructive uses.

New incentives and careful regulation are needed to stop deforestation. Particularly valuable forest areas may be designated as protected areas to safeguard them from illegal and unsustainable exploitation. The total area of terrestrial and marine protected sites has increased steadily in the past three decades. It is estimated that about 12 percent of forest areas worldwide have come under protection. However, designating land as protected is not sufficient. Enforcement is needed to ensure protection.

Rainforest protected from destruction within the Argentinian sector of Iguazú National Park

Forest lost and gained

average annual change in forest area, between
1990 and 2005

- Decrease of 1.0% or more
- Decrease of 0.1–0.9%
- No significant change
- Increase of 0.1–0.9%
- Increase of 1.0% or more
- no data

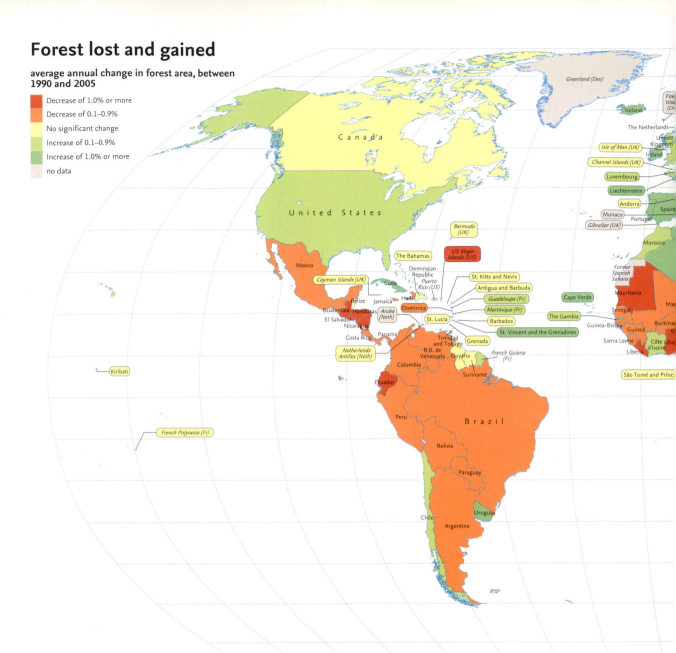

Greenland (Den)

Canada

United States

Mexico

The Bahamas

Cuba

Jamaica

Haiti

Dominican
Republic

Puerto
Rico (US)

Bermuda
(UK)

US Virgin
Islands (US)

St. Kitts and Nevis

Antigua and Barbuda

Guadeloupe (Fr)

Martinique (Fr)

Barbados

St. Vincent and the Grenadines

Cayman Islands (UK)

Belize

Guatemala

Honduras

El Salvador

Nicaragua

Costa Rica

Panama

Aruba
(Neth)

Dominica

St. Lucia

Grenada

Netherlands
Antilles (Neth)

Trinidad
and Tobago

R.B. de
Venezuela

Guyana

Suriname

French Guiana
(Fr)

Colombia

Ecuador

Peru

Brazil

Bolivia

Paraguay

Uruguay

Chile

Argentina

Kiribati

French Polynesia (Fr)

Iceland

Faer
Isla
(D

The Netherlands

United
Kingdom

Ireland

Isle of Man (UK)

Channel Islands (UK)

Luxembourg

Liechtenstein

Andorra

Spain

Monaco

Portugal

Gibraltar (UK)

Morocco

Former
Spanish
Sahara

Mauritania

Mal

Senegal

Cape Verde

The Gambia

Guinea-Bissau

Guinea

Sierra Leone

Liberia

Burkina

Côte
d'Ivoire

Gha

São Tomé and Prínc

Tropical rainforest cleared to make way for an airstrip in Sarawak, Borneo

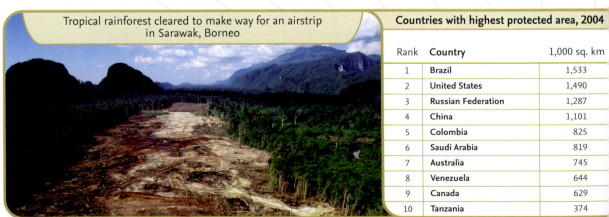

Countries with highest protected area, 2004

Rank	Country	1,000 sq. km
1	Brazil	1,533
2	United States	1,490
3	Russian Federation	1,287
4	China	1,101
5	Colombia	825
6	Saudi Arabia	819
7	Australia	745
8	Venezuela	644
9	Canada	629
10	Tanzania	374

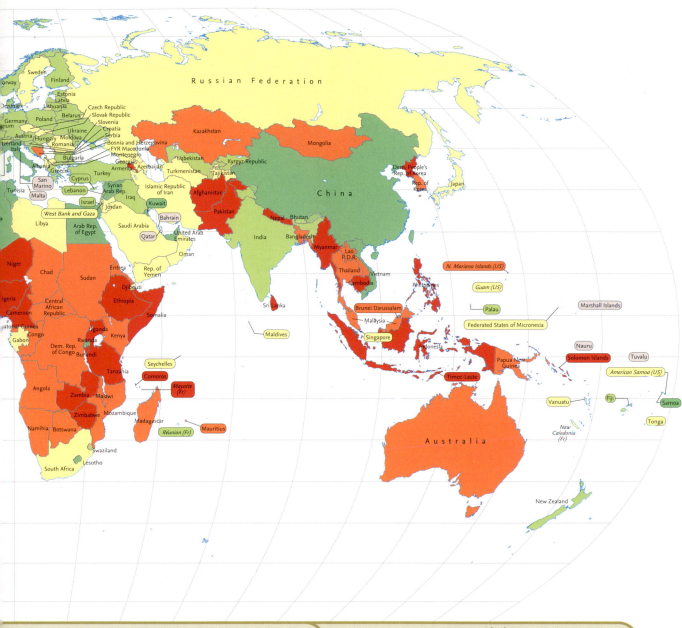

Facts	Internet links	
▶ Between 1990 and 2005, the world lost more than 125 million hectares of forest, about 8 million hectares per year.	▶ United Nations Food and Agriculture Organization (FAO)	**www.fao.org** (click on forestry)
▶ China added about 4 million hectares of forest each year from 2000 to 2005.	▶ International Union for Conservation of Nature	**www.iucn.org**
▶ The forest area in Brazil decreased by more than 15 million hectares, over 40 percent of the world's forest loss between 2000 and 2005.	▶ World Wide Fund for Nature	**www.wwf.org**
▶ At the global level, deforestation seems to be slowing; the estimate of forest cover change indicates an annual loss of 7.3 million hectares during the years 2000 to 2005, compared with 8.8 million hectares annually between 1990 and 2000.	▶ Food and Agriculture Organization's Global Forest Resources Assessment 2005	**www.fao.org/forestry/fra2005/en**

Protected areas

nationally protected areas as a share of
total land area, 2004

- less than 2%
- 2–4%
- 5–9%
- 10–19%
- 20% or more
- no data

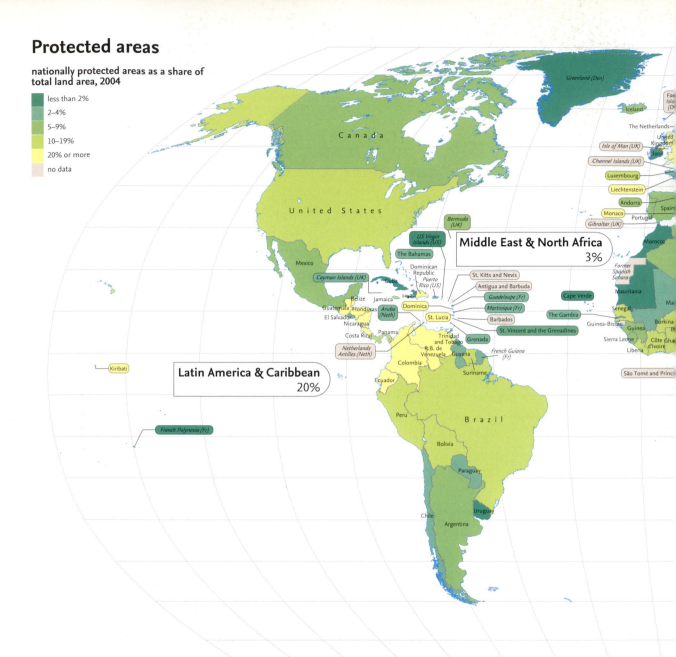

Greenland (Den)

Foe Islo (D

Iceland

The Netherlands—

United Kingdom

Isle of Man (UK)

Ireland

Channel Islands (UK)

Luxembourg

Liechtenstein

Andorra

Spain

Monaco

Portugal

Gibraltar (UK)

Morocco

C a n a d a

U n i t e d   S t a t e s

Bermuda (UK)

US Virgin Islands (US)

The Bahamas

Mexico

Cayman Islands (UK)

Cuba

Dominican Republic

Puerto Rico (US)

Haiti

Jamaica

Belize

Guatemala

Honduras

El Salvador

Nicaragua

Costa Rica

Panama

Aruba (Neth)

Dominica

St. Lucia

St. Kitts and Nevis

Antigua and Barbuda

Guadeloupe (Fr)

Martinique (Fr)

Barbados

St. Vincent and the Grenadines

Grenada

Trinidad and Tobago

Netherlands Antilles (Neth)

R.B. de Venezuela

Colombia

Guyana

Suriname

French Guiana (Fr)

Ecuador

Peru

B r a z i l

Bolivia

Paraguay

Chile

Argentina

Uruguay

Cape Verde

The Gambia

Mauritania

Senegal

Guinea-Bissau

Guinea

Sierra Leone

Liberia

Côte d'Ivoire

Burkina

Ma

São Tomé and Príncip

Kiribati

French Polynesia (Fr)

Middle East & North Africa
3%

Latin America & Caribbean
20%

Virgin tropical rainforest, northern Brazil

Greatest marine protected areas, 2004

Rank	Country	% of surface area
1	Jamaica	75
2	Ecuador	50
3	Cuba	29
4	Hong Kong, China	26
5	Puerto Rico	19
6	Dominican Republic	18
7	Chile	15
8	Panama	13
9	Denmark	12
10	Oman	10

Europe & Central Asia 7%

East Asia & Pacific 12%

South Asia 6%

Sub-Saharan Africa 11%

Facts	Internet links	
▶ The world's nationally protected areas are about 15 million square kilometers or 12 percent of the total land area.	▶ United Nations Environment Programme World Conservation Monitoring Centre	**www.unep_wcmc.org/ protected_areas**
▶ Marine surface areas are about 4 million square kilometers or 3 percent of the world's total surface area.	▶ International Union for Conservation of Nature	**www.iucn.org**
▶ About 71,000 protected areas are registered with the International Union for Conservation of Nature, an increase from 1,000 in 1962.	▶ World Wide Fund for Nature	**www.wwf.org**
▶ More than 10 percent, or about 400 million hectares, of the world's forest area has been declared protected.	▶ Food and Agriculture Organization's Global Forest Resources Assessment 2005	**www.fao.org/forestry**

World demand for energy is surging, and fossil fuels are the primary energy source. The share of the world's clean energy production has increased slightly since 1990, but fossil fuels supplied more than 80 percent of the world's total energy production in 2005. Fossil fuels are also the primary source of carbon dioxide emissions, which, along with the other greenhouse gases, are believed to be the principal cause of global climate change. Producing the energy needed for growth while mitigating its effects on the world's climate is a global challenge for everyone.

Developing countries use about half of the world's energy, but their demand is growing faster than richer countries. In 2005, global energy production increased by about 3 percent, but in fast-growing East Asia and Pacific, production grew by 7.5 percent.

As economies grow, two forces are at work: technological progress and a shift away from energy-intensive activities help to increase energy efficiency, but rising incomes and growing populations increase the demand for energy. As a result, between 1990 and 2005 worldwide energy use increased by about 30 percent, while the population rose by only 23 percent.

Carbon dioxide (CO_2) emissions are highest in high-income economies, and still growing

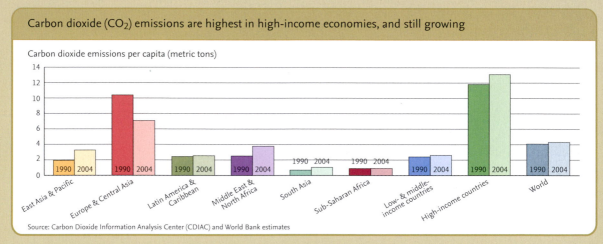

Carbon dioxide emissions per capita (metric tons)

Source: Carbon Dioxide Information Analysis Center (CDIAC) and World Bank estimates

The five largest emitters account for more than half of all carbon dioxide produced each year, but average emissions per person in China and India are still quite low

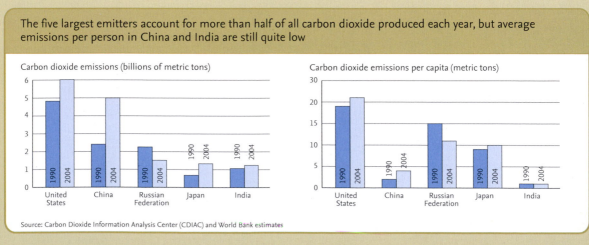

Carbon dioxide emissions (billions of metric tons)

Carbon dioxide emissions per capita (metric tons)

Source: Carbon Dioxide Information Analysis Center (CDIAC) and World Bank estimates

The way energy is generated determines its environmental consequences. The extensive use of fossil fuels in recent decades has boosted emissions of carbon dioxide (CO_2), the principal greenhouse gas that traps heat in the atmosphere. Burning coal releases twice as much carbon dioxide as burning the equivalent amount of natural gas. The amount of carbon released each year by human activities is estimated to be 6 to 7 billion tons. Some 2 billion tons are absorbed by oceans, and another 1.5 to 2.5 billion by plants; the rest is released into the atmosphere. Clearing of forests has reduced their ability to trap carbon dioxide.

The level of carbon dioxide in the atmosphere has increased by more than 30 percent since the beginning of the industrial revolution. According to the Intergovernmental Panel on Climate Change, the rate and duration of global warming in the 20th century are unprecedented in the past thousand years. The global average surface temperature has increased by about 0.6 degrees Celsius since 1861 when instrument records became available, with the 1990s as the warmest decade. Increases in the maximum temperature and the number of hot days have been observed over nearly all regions. Warming is expected to continue, with increases in the range of 1.4 to 5.8 degrees Celsius over the next 100 years.

Global warming shrinks glaciers, changes the frequency and intensity of rainfall, shifts growing seasons, advances the flowering of trees and emergence of insects, and causes the sea level to rise. The magnitude and effect of climate change vary across regions, but developing countries are likely to suffer most because of their dependence on climate-sensitive activities such as agriculture and fishing. They also have a more limited capacity to respond to the effects of climate change.

Deserts are advancing and rainfall is becoming less predictable as a result of global warming

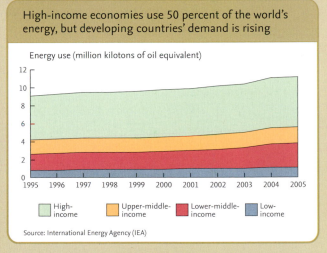
High-income economies use 50 percent of the world's energy, but developing countries' demand is rising

Energy use (million kilotons of oil equivalent)

Legend: High-income | Upper-middle-income | Lower-middle-income | Low-income

Source: International Energy Agency (IEA)

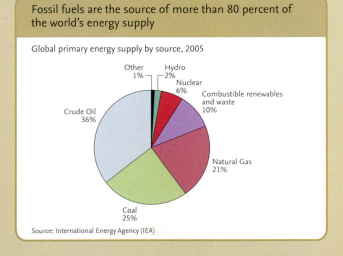
Fossil fuels are the source of more than 80 percent of the world's energy supply

Global primary energy supply by source, 2005

Other 1%
Hydro 2%
Nuclear 6%
Combustible renewables and waste 10%
Crude Oil 36%
Natural Gas 21%
Coal 25%

Source: International Energy Agency (IEA)

Energy flows

million tons of oil equivalent, 2005

net importers **net exporters**

	net importers		net exporters
■	200 or more	■	200 or more
■	100–199	■	100–199
■	50–99	■	50–99
■	less than 50	■	less than 50
■	no data		

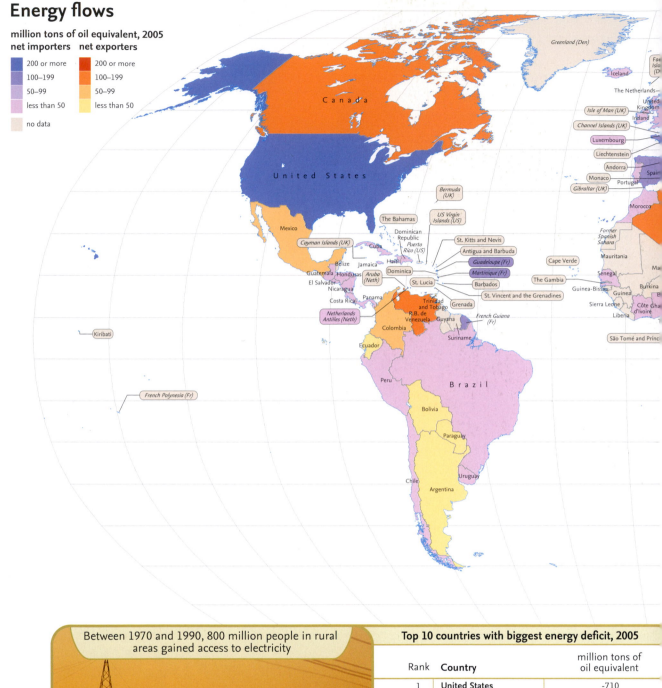

Between 1970 and 1990, 800 million people in rural areas gained access to electricity

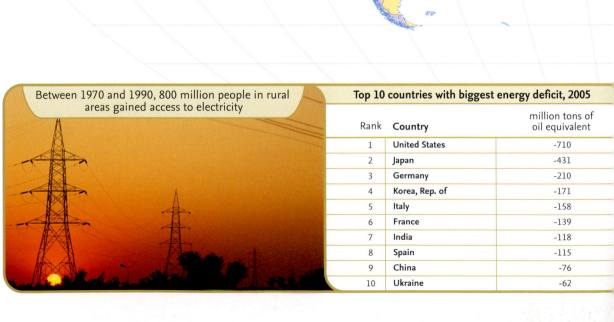

Top 10 countries with biggest energy deficit, 2005

Rank	Country	million tons of oil equivalent
1	United States	-710
2	Japan	-431
3	Germany	-210
4	Korea, Rep. of	-171
5	Italy	-158
6	France	-139
7	India	-118
8	Spain	-115
9	China	-76
10	Ukraine	-62

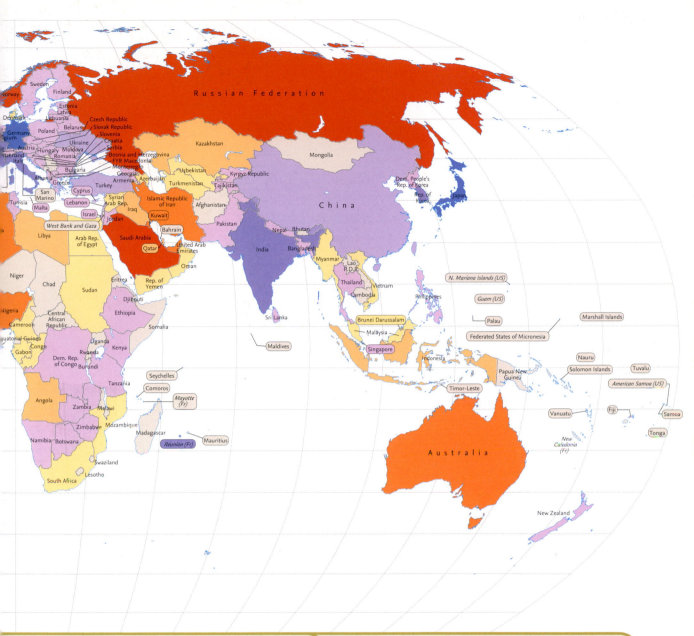

Facts	Internet links	
▶ In the developing world, more than 2 billion people do not have access to modern energy services, and 2.4 billion people rely on traditional biomass for their basic energy needs.	▶ Intergovernmental Panel on Climate Change	**www.ipcc.ch**
▶ The indoor air pollution caused by the use of biomass in inefficient stoves is responsible for 1.5 million deaths per year—mostly of mothers and young children.	▶ International Energy Agency	**www.iea.org**
▶ Brazil, Canada, China, and the United States produce about half of the world's hydropower energy.	▶ United Nations Statistics Division	**unstats.un.org/unsd/ default.htm**
▶ Less than 10 percent of the world's energy use is from renewable sources.	▶ The World Bank Group Energy Program	**www.worldbank.org/energy**
▶ Petroleum is the source of more than 35 percent of the world's total energy production.	▶ Energy Information Administration	**www.eia.doe.gov**

Greenhouse gases

carbon dioxide emissions per capita, 2004 or latest available data

- 15.0 metric tons or more
- 10.0–14.9 metric tons
- 5.0–9.9 metric tons
- 1.0–4.9 metric tons
- less than 1.0 metric tons
- no data

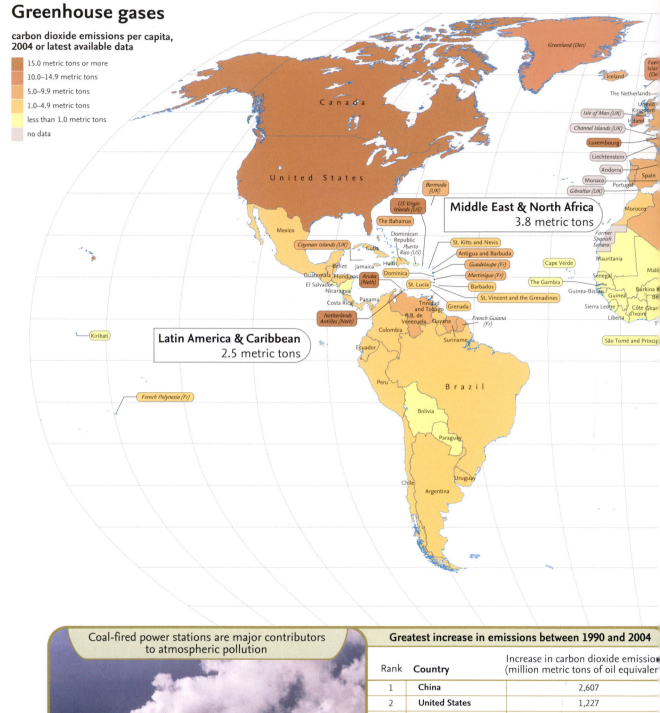

Greenland (Den)

Faeroe Islands (De)

Iceland

The Netherlands

United Kingdom

Isle of Man (UK)

Ireland

Channel Islands (UK)

Luxembourg

Liechtenstein

Andorra

Spain

Monaco

Portugal

Gibraltar (UK)

Morocco

Canada

United States

Bermuda (UK)

US Virgin Islands (US)

The Bahamas

Mexico

Cayman Islands (UK)

Cuba

Dominican Republic

Puerto Rico (US)

Haiti

Jamaica

Belize

Guatemala

Honduras

El Salvador

Nicaragua

Costa Rica

Panama

Aruba (Neth)

St. Kitts and Nevis

Antigua and Barbuda

Dominica

St. Lucia

Guadeloupe (Fr)

Martinique (Fr)

Barbados

St. Vincent and the Grenadines

Grenada

Trinidad and Tobago

R.B. de Venezuela

Guyana

Colombia

Suriname

French Guiana (Fr)

Ecuador

Netherlands Antilles (Neth)

Cape Verde

The Gambia

Guinea-Bissau

Senegal

Mali

Mauritania

Former Spanish Sahara

Burkina

Guinea

Sierra Leone

Côte d'Ivoire

Liberia

São Tomé and Príncipe

Kiribati

French Polynesia (Fr)

Peru

Brazil

Bolivia

Paraguay

Chile

Argentina

Uruguay

Middle East & North Africa
3.8 metric tons

Latin America & Caribbean
2.5 metric tons

Coal-fired power stations are major contributors to atmospheric pollution

Greatest increase in emissions between 1990 and 2004

Rank	Country	Increase in carbon dioxide emission (million metric tons of oil equivalen
1	China	2,607
2	United States	1,227
3	India	660
4	Korea, Rep. of	224
5	Canada	223
6	Iran, Islamic Rep. of	215
7	Japan	186
8	Thailand	172
9	Indonesia	164
10	Malaysia	122

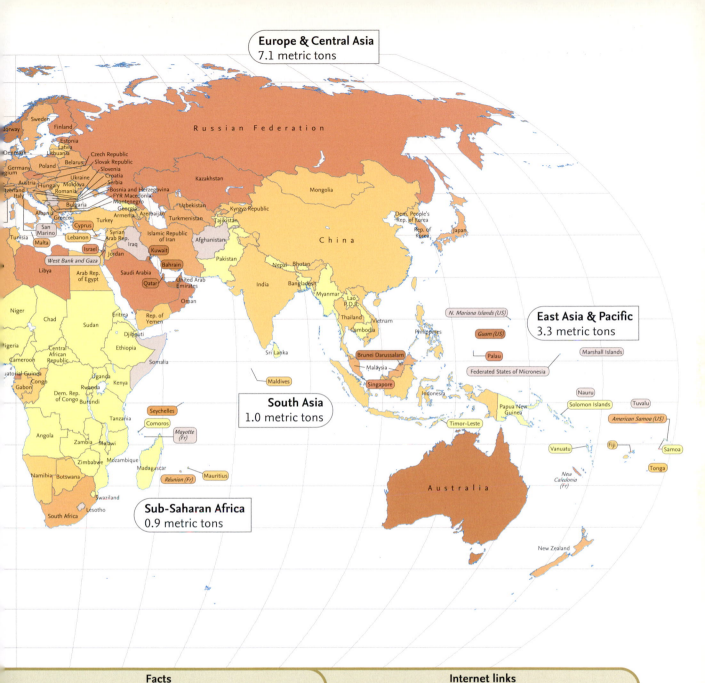

Europe & Central Asia
7.1 metric tons

East Asia & Pacific
3.3 metric tons

South Asia
1.0 metric tons

Sub-Saharan Africa
0.9 metric tons

Facts	Internet links	
▶ Between 1990 and 2004, the world's carbon dioxide emissions rose by almost 28 percent, to 29 billion metric tons.	▶ Intergovernmental Panel on Climate Change	**www.ipcc.ch**
▶ Of the 29 billion metric tons of carbon dioxide released in 2004, almost half came from high-income economies.	▶ Carbon Dioxide Information Analysis Center (CDIAC)	**cdiac.ornl.gov**
▶ High-income economies emit five times as much carbon dioxide per person as developing economies.	▶ World Resources Institute	**www.wri.org**
▶ As well as contributing to global warming, regional climate changes, and accelerated sea-level rise, atmospheric carbon dioxide directly affects plant photosynthesis and water use, potentially altering vegetation and ecosystems.	▶ World Bank Prototype Carbon Fund	**www.prototypecarbonfund.org**

Economy	Total population millions 2007	Life expectancy at birth years 2006	Under five mortality rate per 1,000 2006	Access to an improved water source % of population 2006	Gross national income (GNI)[a] $ billions 2007	per capita $ 2007
Afghanistan	..				10.1	.. d
Albania	3.18	76	17	97	10.5	3,290
Algeria	33.85	72	38	85	122.5	3,620
American Samoa	0.06	..	..		..	.. e
Andorra	0.07	..	3	100	..	..
Angola	17.02	42	260	51	43.6	2,560
Antigua and Barbuda	0.08	75	11	..	1.0	11,520
Argentina	39.50	75	16	96	238.9	6,050
Armenia	3.00	72	24	98	7.9	2,640
Aruba	0.10	..	..	100	..	.. f
Australia	21.02	81	6	100	755.8	35,960
Austria	8.32	80	5	100	355.1	42,700
Azerbaijan	8.57	72	88	78	21.9	2,550
Bahamas, The	0.33	73	14	..	..	.. f
Bahrain	0.75	76	10	..	14.0	19,350
Bangladesh	158.57	64	69	80	75.0	470
Barbados	0.29	77	12	100	..	.. f
Belarus	9.70	69	13	100	40.9	4,220
Belgium	10.63	79	4	..	432.5	40,710
Belize	0.30	72	16	..	1.2	3,800
Benin	9.03	56	148	65	5.1	570
Bermuda	0.06	79	..	..	..	.. f
Bhutan	0.66	65	70	81	1.2	1,770
Bolivia	9.52	65	61	86	12.0	1,260
Bosnia and Herzegovina	3.77	75	15	99	14.3	3,790
Botswana	1.88	50	124	96	11.0	5,840
Brazil	191.60	72	20	91	1,133.0	5,910
Brunei Darussalam	0.39	77	9	99	10.3	26,930
Bulgaria	7.64	73	14	99	35.1	4,590
Burkina Faso	14.78	52	204	72	6.4	430
Burundi	8.50	49	181	71	0.9	110
Cambodia	14.45	59	82	65	7.9	540
Cameroon	18.53	50	149	70	19.4	1,050
Canada	32.98	80	6	100	1,300.0	39,420
Cape Verde	0.53	71	34	..	1.3	2,430
Cayman Islands	0.05	..	..	..	..	.. f
Central African Republic	4.34	44	175	66	1.7	380
Chad	10.76	51	209	48	5.8	540
Channel Islands	0.15	79	..	..	..	.. f
Chile	16.59	78	9	95	138.6	8,350
China	1,319.98	72	24	88	3,120.9	2,360
Hong Kong, China	6.93	82	..	..	218.9	31,610
Macao, China	0.48	80	..	..	..	..
Colombia	46.12	73	21	93	149.9	3,250
Comoros	0.63	63	68	85	0.4	680
Congo, Dem. Rep. of	62.40	46	205	46	8.6	140
Congo, Rep.	3.77	55	126	71	5.8	1,540
Costa Rica	4.46	79	12	98	24.8	5,560
Côte d'Ivoire	19.27	48	127	81	17.5	910
Croatia	4.44	76	6	99	46.4	10,460
Cuba	11.26	78	7	91	..	.. e
Cyprus	0.79	79	4	100	19.6	24,940
Czech Republic	10.33	76	4	100	149.4	14,450
Denmark	5.46	78	5	100	299.8	54,910
Djibouti	0.83	54	130	92	0.9	1,090
Dominica	0.07	77	15	..	0.3	4,250
Dominican Republic	9.75	72	29	95	34.6	3,550
Ecuador	13.34	75	24	95	41.1	3,080
Egypt, Arab Rep. of	75.47	71	35	98	119.4	1,580
El Salvador	6.85	72	25	84	19.5	2,850
Equatorial Guinea	0.51	51	206	43	6.5	12,860
Eritrea	4.84	57	74	60	1.1	230
Estonia	1.34	73	7	100	17.7	13,200
Ethiopia	79.09	52	123	42	17.6	220
Faeroe Islands	0.05	79	..	..	..	.. f
Fiji	0.84	69	18	47	3.2	3,800
Finland	5.29	79	4	100	234.8	44,400
France	61.71	81	4	100	2,447.1 g	38,500 g
French Polynesia	0.26	74	..	100	..	..
Gabon	1.33	57	91	87	8.9	6,670
Gambia, The	1.71	59	113	86	0.5	320
Georgia	4.40	71	32	99	9.3	2,120
Germany	82.27	79	4	100	3,197.0	38,860
Ghana	23.46	60	120	80	13.9	590
Greece	11.19	79	4	100	331.7	29,630
Greenland	0.06	69			..	.. f
Grenada	0.11	73	20	..	0.5	4,670
Guam	0.17	75	..	100	..	.. f
Guatemala	13.35	70	41	96	32.6	2,440

Total debt service % of exports of goods, services and income[b] 2006	Merchandise trade % of GDP 2007	Foreign direct investment net inflows, % of GDP 2006	Starting a business time required in days June 2007	Internet users[c] per 100 people 2007	Carbon dioxide emissions per capita metric tons 2004	Economy
..	29.5	..	9	2.1	..	Afghanistan
3.5	49.8	3.6	36	14.9	1.2	Albania
..	64.3	1.5	24	10.3	6.0	Algeria
..	..	..	..	..	5.1	American Samoa
..	..	..	..	87.6	..	Andorra
12.8	84.5	-0.1	119	0.6	0.5	Angola
..	80.6	13.3	21	70.7	5.1	Antigua and Barbuda
31.6	38.4	2.3	31	23.6	3.7	Argentina
7.6	49.0	5.4	18	5.7	1.2	Armenia
..	..	..	..	23.8	21.8	Aruba
..	37.3	3.7	2	53.3	16.2	Australia
..	85.9	0.0	28	51.4	8.5	Austria
1.6	49.1	-2.8	30	12.1	3.8	Azerbaijan
..	..	..	..	36.2	6.3	Bahamas, The
..	122.4	6.5	..	33.2	23.8	Bahrain
3.7	45.5	1.1	74	0.3	0.2	Bangladesh
..	60.3	2.0	..	95.3	4.4	Barbados
3.3	118.4	1.0	48	61.8	6.6	Belarus
..	189.1	15.7	4	49.1	9.7	Belgium
15.9	74.2	6.0	44	10.5	2.8	Belize
..	31.3	1.4	31	1.7	0.3	Benin
..	..	..	..	75.0	8.7	Bermuda
..	98.5	0.6	48	6.1	0.7	Bhutan
8.5	60.5	2.1	50	2.1	0.8	Bolivia
8.7	91.7	3.5	54	28.0	4.1	Bosnia and Herzegovina
0.9	80.4	4.4	108	4.3	2.4	Botswana
37.3	21.9	1.8	152	26.1	1.8	Brazil
..	80.5	..	116	41.7	24.1	Brunei Darussalam
12.4	122.6	16.3	32	52.3	5.5	Bulgaria
..	34.9	0.4	18	0.6	0.1	Burkina Faso
40.4	41.6	0.0	43	0.7	0.0	Burundi
0.6	112.4	6.7	86	0.5	0.0	Cambodia
..	36.4	1.7	37	2.1	0.2	Cameroon
..	60.9	5.4	3	84.9	20.0	Canada
4.7	53.6	10.4	52	7.0	0.6	Cape Verde
..	..	..	..	47.0	7.1	Cayman Islands
..	24.8	1.6	14	0.3	0.1	Central African Republic
..	69.9	11.1	75	0.6	0.0	Chad
..	..	..	..	..	..	Channel Islands
20.0	69.8	5.4	27	33.6	3.9	Chile
2.5	66.3	2.9	35	15.9	3.9	China
..	348.5	22.6	11	57.2	5.5	Hong Kong, China
..	50.1	18.7	..	49.6	4.7	Macao, China
31.3	36.2	4.8	42	26.2	1.2	Colombia
..	28.6	0.2	23	3.4	0.1	Comoros
..	62.0	2.1	155	0.4	0.0	Congo, Dem. Rep. of
..	117.7	4.5	37	1.9	1.0	Congo, Rep.
5.0	88.5	6.6	77	33.6	1.5	Costa Rica
1.4	74.1	1.8	40	1.6	0.3	Côte d'Ivoire
33.1	74.5	7.9	40	45.0	5.3	Croatia
..	..	..	..	11.6	2.3	Cuba
..	46.3	8.3	..	48.3	9.1	Cyprus
..	143.0	4.2	17	42.6	11.5	Czech Republic
..	65.8	1.2	6	64.1	9.8	Denmark
6.4	56.6	14.1	37	1.3	0.5	Djibouti
..	70.0	10.5	19	36.6	1.5	Dominica
9.6	54.0	3.7	22	17.2	2.1	Dominican Republic
24.1	61.8	0.7	65	11.7	2.3	Ecuador
4.9	33.8	9.3	9	11.4	2.2	Egypt, Arab Rep. of
13.1	62.6	1.1	26	10.4	0.9	El Salvador
..	133.0	19.3	136	1.6	11.5	Equatorial Guinea
..	44.1	0.3	84	2.5	0.2	Eritrea
..	122.7	9.6	7	58.1	14.0	Estonia
6.8	34.1	2.4	16	0.4	0.1	Ethiopia
..	..	..	..	70.4	13.7	Faeroe Islands
1.0	73.8	5.0	46	9.6	1.3	Fiji
..	69.4	2.5	14	68.1	12.6	Finland
..	45.5	3.6	7	49.1	6.2	France
..	..	..	..	28.6	2.7	French Polynesia
..	76.5	2.8	58	10.9	1.1	Gabon
12.4	49.4	16.1	32	5.9	0.2	Gambia, The
8.8	63.5	13.7	11	8.2	0.9	Georgia
..	72.4	1.5	18	51.7	9.8	Germany
4.9	80.7	3.4	42	2.8	0.3	Ghana
..	27.5	1.8	38	22.7	8.7	Greece
..	..	..	..	91.6	10.0	Greenland
..	73.1	22.7	20	21.3	2.0	Grenada
..	..	..	..	38.6	25.0	Guam
4.8	61.3	1.2	26	10.1	1.0	Guatemala

Economy	Total population millions 2007	Life expectancy at birth years 2006	Under five mortality rate per 1,000 2006	Access to an improved water source % of population 2006	Gross national income (GNI)[a] $ billions 2007	per capita $ 2007
Guinea	9.38	56	161	70	3.7	400
Guinea-Bissau	1.69	46	200	57	0.3	200
Guyana	0.74	66	62	93	1.0	1,300
Haiti	9.61	60	80	58	5.4	560
Honduras	7.09	70	27	84	11.3	1,600
Hungary	10.06	73	7	100	116.3	11,570
Iceland	0.31	81	3	100	16.8	54,100
India	1,123.32	64	76	89	1,069.4	950
Indonesia	225.63	68	34	80	373.1	1,650
Iran, Islamic Rep. of	71.02	71	34	..	246.5	3,470
Iraq	..	..	..	..	..	.. [h]
Ireland	4.37	79	5	..	210.2	48,140
Isle of Man	0.08	78	..	..	3.1	40,600
Israel	7.17	80	5	100	157.1	21,900
Italy	59.37	81	4	..	1,991.3	33,540
Jamaica	2.68	71	31	93	9.9	3,710
Japan	127.77	82	4	100	4,813.3	37,670
Jordan	5.72	72	25	98	16.3	2,850
Kazakhstan	15.48	66	29	96	78.3	5,060
Kenya	37.53	53	121	57	25.6	680
Kiribati	0.10	63	64	65	0.1	1,170
Korea, Dem. Rep. of	23.78	67	55	100	..	.. [d]
Korea, Rep.	48.53	78	5	..	955.8	19,690
Kuwait	2.66	78	11	..	80.2	31,640
Kyrgyz Republic	5.24	68	41	89	3.1	590
Lao PDR	5.86	64	75	60	3.4	580
Latvia	2.28	71	9	99	22.6	9,930
Lebanon	4.10	72	30	100	23.7	5,770
Lesotho	2.01	43	132	78	2.0	1,000
Liberia	3.75	45	235	64	0.6	150
Libya	6.16	74	18	..	55.5	9,010
Liechtenstein	0.04	..	3	..	..	.. [f]
Lithuania	3.38	71	8	..	33.5	9,920
Luxembourg	0.48	79	4	100	36.4	75,880
Macedonia, FYR	2.04	74	17	100	7.1	3,460
Madagascar	19.67	59	115	47	6.3	320
Malawi	13.92	48	120	76	3.5	250
Malaysia	26.55	74	12	99	173.7	6,540
Maldives	0.31	68	30	83	1.0	3,200
Mali	12.33	54	217	60	6.1	500
Malta	0.41	79	6	100	6.2	15,310
Marshall Islands	0.07	65	56	..	0.2	3,070
Mauritania	3.12	64	125	60	2.6	840
Mauritius	1.26	73	14	100	6.9	5,450
Mayotte	0.19	..	..	..	..	.. [e]
Mexico	105.28	74	35	95	878.0	8,340
Micronesia, Fed. Sts. of	0.11	68	41	94	0.3	2,470
Moldova	3.79	69	19	90	4.3 [i]	1,260 [i]
Monaco	0.03	..	4	..	..	.. [f]
Mongolia	2.61	67	43	72	3.4	1,290
Montenegro	0.60	74	10	98	3.1	5,180
Morocco	30.86	71	37	83	69.4	2,250
Mozambique	21.37	42	138	42	6.8	320
Myanmar	48.78	62	104	80	..	.. [d]
Namibia	2.07	52	61	93	7.0	3,360
Nepal	28.11	63	59	89	9.7	340
Netherlands Antilles	0.19	75	..	..	..	.. [f]
Netherlands	16.38	80	5	100	750.5	45,820
New Caledonia	0.24	75	..	..	..	.. [f]
New Zealand	4.23	80	6	..	121.7	28,780
Nicaragua	5.60	72	36	79	5.5	980
Niger	14.20	56	253	42	4.0	280
Nigeria	147.98	47	191	47	137.1	930
Northern Mariana Islands	0.08	..	..	98	..	.. [f]
Norway	4.71	80	4	100	360.0	76,450
Oman	2.60	76	12	..	27.9	11,120
Pakistan	162.39	65	97	90	141.0	870
Palau	0.02	..	11	89	0.2	8,210
Panama	3.34	75	23	92	18.4	5,510
Papua New Guinea	6.32	57	73	40	5.4	850
Paraguay	6.12	72	22	77	10.2	1,670
Peru	27.90	71	25	84	96.2	3,450
Philippines	87.89	71	32	93	142.6	1,620
Poland	38.06	75	7	..	374.6	9,840
Portugal	10.61	78	5	99	201.1	18,950
Puerto Rico	3.94	78	..	..	..	.. [f]
Qatar	0.84	75	21	100	..	.. [f]
Romania	21.55	72	18	88	132.5	6,150
Russian Federation	141.64	66	16	97	1,071.0	7,560

Total debt service % of exports of goods, services and income[b] 2006	Merchandise trade % of GDP 2007	Foreign direct investment net inflows, % of GDP 2006	Starting a business time required in days June 2007	Internet users[c] per 100 people 2007	Carbon dioxide emissions per capita metric tons 2004	Economy
..	50.2	3.4	41	0.5	0.2	Guinea
..	50.4	13.7	233	2.2	0.2	Guinea-Bissau
3.4	166.7	11.3	44	25.7	2.0	Guyana
3.2	34.2	3.2	202	10.4	0.2	Haiti
5.1	72.6	3.6	21	4.9	1.1	Honduras
33.1	136.7	5.4	16	41.8	5.7	Hungary
..	56.7	24.9	5	65.0	7.6	Iceland
7.7	30.9	1.9	33	17.8	1.2	India
16.6	48.5	1.5	105	5.8	1.7	Indonesia
..	47.2	0.4	47	32.4	6.4	Iran, Islamic Rep. of
..	..	..	77	..	..	Iraq
..	79.5	-0.4	13	39.1	10.4	Ireland
..	..	..	..	..	..	Isle of Man
..	69.8	10.1	34	27.9	10.5	Israel
..	47.3	2.1	13	53.9	7.7	Italy
11.9	77.5	8.8	8	56.0	4.0	Jamaica
..	30.5	-0.2	23	73.6	9.8	Japan
6.1	120.4	22.8	14	19.7	3.1	Jordan
33.7	76.5	7.6	21	12.3	13.3	Kazakhstan
6.5	45.2	0.2	44	8.0	0.3	Kenya
..	117.9	..	21	2.0	0.3	Kiribati
..	..	..	..	..	3.4	Korea, Dem. Rep. of
..	75.1	0.4	17	71.7	9.7	Korea, Rep.
..	70.2	0.1	35	33.8	40.4	Kuwait
5.7	102.2	6.5	21	14.3	1.1	Kyrgyz Republic
..	59.4	5.5	103	1.7	0.2	Lao PDR
33.3	86.1	8.3	16	51.7	3.1	Latvia
21.0	65.9	12.3	46	23.4	4.1	Lebanon
4.0	158.8	5.2	73	3.5	0.1	Lesotho
..	89.2	-13.3	99	0.0	0.1	Liberia
..	91.9	..	..	4.3	10.3	Libya
..	..	..	..	65.3	..	Liechtenstein
22.1	107.7	6.1	26	39.5	3.9	Lithuania
..	104.5	304.9	26	71.9	24.9	Luxembourg
15.7	113.1	5.5	15	33.6	5.1	Macedonia, FYR
..	51.6	4.2	7	0.6	0.2	Madagascar
..	57.7	0.9	37	1.0	0.1	Malawi
4.0	178.8	3.9	24	56.5	7.0	Malaysia
4.9	126.3	1.5	9	10.8	2.5	Maldives
..	52.8	3.2	26	0.8	0.1	Mali
..	104.2	28.1	..	38.6	6.1	Malta
..	104.4	..	17	3.4	..	Marshall Islands
..	108.6	-0.1	65	1.0	0.9	Mauritania
7.1	98.1	1.7	7	26.9	2.6	Mauritius
..	..	..	..	..	..	Mayotte
18.9	63.6	2.3	27	21.7	4.3	Mexico
..	51.0	..	16	14.5	..	Micronesia, Fed. Sts. of
12.2	115.8	7.1	23	18.5	2.0	Moldova
..	..	..	..	61.2	..	Monaco
2.2	102.9	10.8	20	12.2	3.4	Mongolia
..	104.0	..	24	46.6	..	Montenegro
12.2	62.9	4.1	12	23.7	1.4	Morocco
1.9	75.6	2.2	29	0.9	0.1	Mozambique
1.7	..	..	..	0.1	0.2	Myanmar
..	93.9	..	99	4.9	1.2	Namibia
5.1	37.2	-0.1	31	1.2	0.1	Nepal
..	..	..	..	..	22.2	Netherlands Antilles
..	138.1	1.1	10	91.6	8.7	Netherlands
..	..	..	..	33.6	11.2	New Caledonia
..	44.7	7.5	12	79.5	7.7	New Zealand
4.1	83.2	5.3	39	2.8	0.7	Nicaragua
..	38.8	0.6	23	0.3	0.1	Niger
..	56.7	3.7	34	6.8	0.8	Nigeria
..	..	..	..	..	..	Northern Mariana Islands
..	57.5	1.4	10	80.7	19.1	Norway
1.3	91.4	2.7	34	11.5	12.5	Oman
8.6	34.9	3.4	24	10.8	0.8	Pakistan
..	79.1	..	28	27.0	11.9	Palau
24.7	41.6	15.1	19	15.7	1.8	Panama
..	120.7	0.6	56	1.8	0.4	Papua New Guinea
6.8	88.8	2.0	35	4.6	0.7	Paraguay
12.9	44.1	3.7	72	27.4	1.2	Peru
19.6	74.5	2.0	52	6.0	1.0	Philippines
24.7	71.0	5.6	31	42.0	8.0	Poland
..	58.1	3.8	7	33.5	5.6	Portugal
..	..	..	7	25.4	0.5	Puerto Rico
..	84.4	..	..	42.0	69.2	Qatar
18.4	66.3	9.4	14	55.7	4.2	Romania
13.8	44.8	3.1	29	21.2	10.6	Russian Federation

Economy	Total population millions 2007	Life expectancy at birth years 2006	Under five mortality rate per 1,000 2006	Access to an improved water source % of population 2006	Gross national income (GNI)[a] $ billions 2007	per capita $ 2007
Rwanda	9.74	46	160	65	3.1	320
Samoa	0.19	71	28	88	0.5	2,430
San Marino	0.03	82	3	..	1.3	45,130
São Tomé and Príncipe	0.16	65	96	86	0.1	870
Saudi Arabia	24.20	73	25	96	373.5	15,440
Senegal	12.41	63	116	77	10.2	820
Serbia	7.39 j	73	8	99	35.0 j	4,730 j
Seychelles	0.09	72	13	..	0.8	8,960
Sierra Leone	5.85	42	270	53	1.5	260
Singapore	4.59	80	3	100	149.0	32,470
Slovak Republic	5.40	74	8	100	63.3	11,730
Slovenia	2.02	78	4	..	42.3	20,960
Solomon Islands	0.50	63	73	70	0.4	730
Somalia	8.70	48	145	29	..	.. d
South Africa	47.59	51	69	93	274.0	5,760
Spain	44.88	81	4	100	1,321.8	29,450
Sri Lanka	19.94	75	13	82	30.8	1,540
St. Kitts and Nevis	0.05	71	19	99	0.5	9,630
St. Lucia	0.17	74	14	98	0.9	5,530
St. Vincent and the Grenadines	0.12	71	20	..	0.5	4,210
Sudan	38.56	58	89	70	37.0	960
Suriname	0.46	70	39	92	2.2	4,730
Swaziland	1.14	41	164	60	3.0	2,580
Sweden	9.15	81	3	100	421.3	46,060
Switzerland	7.55	82	5	100	452.1	59,880
Syrian Arab Republic	19.89	74	14	89	35.0	1,760
Tajikistan	6.74	67	68	67	3.1	460
Tanzania	40.43	52	118	55	16.3 k	400 k
Thailand	63.83	70	8	98	217.3	3,400
Timor-Leste	1.07	57	55	62	1.6	1,510
Togo	6.58	58	108	59	2.4	360
Tonga	0.10	73	24	100	0.2	2,320
Trinidad and Tobago	1.33	70	38	94	18.8	14,100
Tunisia	10.25	74	23	94	32.8	3,200
Turkey	73.89	71	26	97	592.9	8,020
Turkmenistan	4.96	63	51	..	..	.. h
Uganda	30.93	51	134	64	10.5	340
Ukraine	46.38	68	24	97	118.4	2,550
United Arab Emirates	4.36	79	8	100	..	.. f
United Kingdom	61.03	79	6	100	2,608.5	42,740
United States	301.62	78	8	99	13,886.5	46,040
Uruguay	3.32	76	12	100	21.2	6,380
Uzbekistan	26.87	67	43	88	19.7	730
Vanuatu	0.23	70	36	..	0.4	1,840
Venezuela, RB de	27.47	74	21	..	201.1	7,320
Vietnam	85.14	71	17	92	67.2	790
Virgin Islands (U.S.)	0.11	79	..	..	..	.. f
West Bank and Gaza	3.87	73	22	89	4.5	1,230
Yemen, Rep. of	22.38	62	100	66	19.4	870
Zambia	11.92	42	182	58	9.5	800
Zimbabwe	13.40	43	105	81	4.5	340
World	6,612.0 s	68 w	72 w	86 w	52,621.4 t	7,958 w
Low-income	1,295.7	57	135	68	748.8	578
Middle-income	4,260.0	69	49	89	12,234.7	2,872
Lower-middle-income	3,437.1	69	54	88	6,485.0	1,887
Upper-middle-income	822.9	70	26	95	5,749.6	6,987
Low- and middle-income	5,555.7	66	79	84	12,985.9	2,337
East Asia & Pacific	1,914.1	71	29	87	4,173.5	2,180
Europe & Central Asia	445.1	69	26	95	2,693.7	6,051
Latin America & the Caribbean	562.8	73	26	91	3,118.0	5,540
Middle East & North Africa	313.4	70	42	89	875.6	2,794
South Asia	1,520.4	64	83	87	1,338.6	880
Sub-Saharan Africa	799.8	50	157	58	761.6	952
High-income	1,056.3	79	7	100	39,682.1	37,566
Euro area	318.7	80	4	100	11,578.0	36,329

See page 142 for explanation of symbols.

Notes: Figures in italics are for years other than those specified.
a. Calculated using the World Bank Atlas method.
b. Exports include workers' remittances.
c. Data are from the International Telecommunication Union's (ITU) *World Telecommunication Development Report* database. Please cite ITU for third-party use of these data.
d. Estimated to be low-income ($935 or less).
e. Estimated to be upper-middle-income ($3,706-$11,455).

Total debt service % of exports of goods, services and income[b] 2006	Merchandise trade % of GDP 2007	Foreign direct investment net inflows, % of GDP 2006	Starting a business time required in days June 2007	Internet users[c] per 100 people 2007	Carbon dioxide emissions per capita metric tons 2004	Economy
9.6	23.0	0.4	16	1.1	0.1	Rwanda
19.9	50.4	4.8	35	4.3	0.8	Samoa
..	..	..	..	54.0	..	San Marino
..	48.4	-0.3	144	14.6	0.6	São Tomé and Príncipe
..	84.6	0.2	15	25.6	13.7	Saudi Arabia
..	52.9	0.6	58	6.6	0.4	Senegal
..	65.1	16.1	23	20.3	..	Serbia
20.6	155.9	18.8	38	37.6	6.6	Seychelles
9.6	40.7	4.1	26	0.2	0.2	Sierra Leone
..	348.6	17.7	5	58.8	12.5	Singapore
..	157.7	7.5	25	43.5	6.7	Slovak Republic
..	135.2	1.7	60	64.4	8.1	Slovenia
2.0	113.8	5.6	57	1.7	0.4	Solomon Islands
..	..	..	..	1.1	..	Somalia
6.7	57.9	0.0	31	8.3	9.4	South Africa
..	43.1	1.6	47	43.9	7.7	Spain
8.6	57.5	1.7	39	3.9	0.6	Sri Lanka
..	59.9	40.9	46	30.7	2.7	St. Kitts and Nevis
..	74.3	12.8	40	65.5	2.3	St. Lucia
..	65.1	17.2	12	47.4	1.7	St. Vincent and the Grenadines
4.1	34.9	9.7	39	9.9	0.3	Sudan
..	100.4	..	694	9.6	5.1	Suriname
1.8	173.3	1.3	61	3.7	0.9	Swaziland
..	71.6	7.1	15	76.5	5.9	Sweden
..	80.0	7.1	20	61.1	5.5	Switzerland
1.3	68.7	1.8	43	17.4	3.7	Syrian Arab Republic
5.1	105.7	12.0	49	0.3	0.8	Tajikistan
3.4	45.4	3.3	29	1.0	0.1	Tanzania
9.4	119.5	4.4	33	21.0	4.3	Thailand
..	..	..	82	0.1	0.2	Timor-Leste
..	85.8	2.6	53	5.0	0.4	Togo
2.7	62.5	-0.7	32	8.3	1.2	Tonga
..	110.9	6.2	43	16.9	24.7	Trinidad and Tobago
14.4	97.1	10.6	11	16.8	2.3	Tunisia
33.2	42.2	3.8	6	18.0	3.2	Turkey
..	103.5	7.0	..	1.4	8.7	Turkmenistan
4.8	43.5	4.1	28	6.5	0.1	Uganda
18.1	78.0	5.2	27	21.6	6.9	Ukraine
..	155.7	..	62	52.7	37.8	United Arab Emirates
..	38.6	5.9	13	65.9	9.8	United Kingdom
..	23.0	1.4	6	72.9	20.6	United States
87.8	43.1	7.0	44	29.2	1.7	Uruguay
..	56.1	1.0	15	4.5	5.3	Uzbekistan
1.7	55.3	10.5	39	3.5	0.4	Vanuatu
13.3	51.6	-0.3	141	20.8	6.6	Venezuela, RB de
..	153.4	3.8	50	21.0	1.2	Vietnam
..	..	..	..	27.7	124.3	Virgin Islands (U.S.)
..	..	..	92	9.2	..	West Bank and Gaza
2.4	57.9	5.9	63	1.4	1.0	Yemen, Rep. of
3.6	78.2	5.3	33	4.2	0.2	Zambia
..	122.0	3.0	96	10.1	0.8	Zimbabwe
.. w	51.0 w	2.8 w	44 u	22.7 w	4.3 w	World
5.4	61.0	3.1	55	5.2	0.6	Low-income
12.7	56.3	3.1	47	17.7	3.2	Middle-income
7.0	59.2	2.9	41	15.8	2.6	Lower-middle-income
19.7	53.1	3.3	57	26.5	5.5	Upper-middle-income
12.3	56.5	3.1	50	15.0	2.6	Low- and middle-income
5.0	74.0	2.9	47	14.4	3.3	East Asia & Pacific
19.3	56.4	4.6	26	25.8	7.1	Europe & Central Asia
23.0	43.1	2.4	73	23.7	2.5	Latin America & the Caribbean
11.0	58.2	4.2	40	16.4	3.8	Middle East & North Africa
7.5	32.7	2.0	33	14.5	1.0	South Asia
7.5	59.3	2.1	55	4.4	0.9	Sub-Saharan Africa
..	49.1	2.7	25	63.5	13.1	High-income
..	66.5	3.8	22	51.5	8.2	Euro area

f. Estimated to be high-income ($11,456 or more).
g. Data include the French overseas departments of French Guiana, Guadeloupe, Martinique, and Réunion.
h. Estimated to be lower-middle-income ($936–$3,705).
i. Data exclude Transnistria.
j. Data exclude Kosovo and Metohija.
k. Data refer to mainland Tanzania only.

Ranking of economies by GNI per capita

Rank	Economy	Atlas methodology $	Purchasing power parity international $	PPP rank
1	Liechtenstein	.. a	..	..
2	Bermuda	.. a	..	..
3	Norway	76,450	53,320	5
4	Luxembourg	75,880	63,590	1
5	Qatar	.. a	..	..
6	Switzerland	59,880	43,870	13
7	Denmark	54,910	36,300	24
8	Iceland	54,100	33,960	30
9	Channel Islands	.. a	..	..
10	Andorra	.. a	..	..
11	Cayman Islands	.. a	..	..
12	Ireland	48,140	37,090	19
13	San Marino	45,130 a	..	..
14	Sweden	46,060	36,590	23
15	United States	46,040	45,850	10
16	Netherlands	45,820	39,310	17
17	Finland	44,400	34,550	29
18	Isle of Man	40,600 a		
19	United Kingdom	42,740	33,800	31
20	Austria	42,700	38,140	18
21	Belgium	40,710	34,790	27
22	Canada	39,420	35,310	26
23	Germany	38,860	33,530	33
24	France	38,500 c	33,600	32
25	Japan	37,670	34,600	28
28	Australia	35,960	33,340	34
29	Kuwait	31,640 a	49,970 a	4
30	Italy	33,540	29,850	39
31	Singapore	32,470	48,520	9
33	Hong Kong, China	31,610	44,050	12
35	Greece	29,630	32,330	36
36	Spain	29,450	30,820	38
38	New Zealand	28,780	26,340	47
39	Brunei Darussalam	26,930 a	49,900 a	6
41	Cyprus	24,940	26,370	46
45	Israel	21,900	25,930	48
46	Slovenia	20,960	26,640	45
47	Bahrain	19,350 a	34,310 a	20
49	Korea, Rep. of	19,690	24,750	51
51	Portugal	18,950	20,890	60
53	Malta	15,310 a	20,990 a	57
54	Saudi Arabia	15,440	22,910	52
56	Czech Republic	14,450	22,020	56
58	Trinidad and Tobago	14,100	22,490 b	54
59	Estonia	13,200	19,810	61
60	Equatorial Guinea	12,860	21,230	58
61	Oman	11,120 a	19,740 a	59
62	Slovak Republic	11,730	19,340	62
64	Hungary	11,570	17,210	65
65	Antigua and Barbuda	11,520	17,620 b	63
66	Croatia	10,460	15,050	70
68	Latvia	9,930	16,890	67
69	Lithuania	9,920	17,180	66
70	Poland	9,840	15,330	69
71	St. Kitts and Nevis	9,630	13,320 b	75
72	Libya	9,010	14,710 b	72
73	Seychelles	8,960	15,450 b	68
74	Chile	8,350	12,590	78
75	Mexico	8,340	12,580	79
76	Palau	8,210	..	..
77	Turkey	8,020	12,350	81
78	Russian Federation	7,560	14,400	73
79	Venezuela, RB de	7,320	11,920	83
80	Gabon	6,670	13,080	76
81	Malaysia	6,540	13,570	74
82	Uruguay	6,380	11,040	86
83	Romania	6,150	10,980	87
84	Argentina	6,050	12,990	77
85	Brazil	5,910	9,370	98
86	Botswana	5,840	12,420	80
87	Lebanon	5,770	10,050	94
88	South Africa	5,760	9,560	96
89	Costa Rica	5,560	10,700 b	90
90	St. Lucia	5,530	9,430 b	97
91	Panama	5,510	10,610 b	91
92	Mauritius	5,450	11,390	84
93	Montenegro	5,180	10,290	92
94	Kazakhstan	5,060	9,700	95
95	Serbia	4,730 d	10,220	93
95	Suriname	4,730	7,640 b	103
98	Grenada	4,670	6,910 b	111
99	Bulgaria	4,590	11,180	85
101	Dominica	4,250	7,410 b	106
102	Belarus	4,220	10,740	89
103	St. Vincent and the Grenadines	4,210	7,170 b	108
104	Belize	3,800	6,200 b	118
104	Fiji	3,800	4,370	134
106	Bosnia and Herzegovina	3,790	7,700	102
107	Jamaica	3,710	6,210 b	117
108	Algeria	3,620	7,640 b	103
109	Dominican Republic	3,550	6,340 b	115
110	Iran, Islamic Rep. of	3,470	10,800	88
111	Macedonia, FYR	3,460	8,510	100
112	Peru	3,450	7,240	107
113	Thailand	3,400	7,880	101
114	Namibia	3,360	5,120	125
115	Albania	3,290	6,580	114
116	Colombia	3,250	6,640	113
117	Maldives	3,200	5,040	126
117	Tunisia	3,200	7,130	109
119	Ecuador	3,080	7,040	110
120	Marshall Islands	3,070	..	..
121	El Salvador	2,850	5,640 b	120
121	Jordan	2,850	5,160	124
123	Armenia	2,640	5,900	119
124	Swaziland	2,580	4,930	128
125	Angola	2,560	4,400	132
126	Azerbaijan	2,550	6,260	116
126	Ukraine	2,550	6,810	112
128	Micronesia, Fed. Sts. of	2,470	3,270 b	146
129	Guatemala	2,440	4,520 b	131
130	Cape Verde	2,430	2,940	149
130	Samoa	2,430	3,930 b	139
132	China	2,360	5,370	122
133	Tonga	2,320	3,650 b	142
134	Morocco	2,250	3,990	138
135	Georgia	2,120	4,770	129
136	Vanuatu	1,840	3,410 b	145
137	Bhutan	1,770	4,980	127
138	Syrian Arab Republic	1,760	4,370	134
140	Paraguay	1,670	4,380	133
141	Indonesia	1,650	3,580	144
142	Philippines	1,620	3,730	141
143	Honduras	1,600	3,620 b	143

Rank	Economy	Atlas methodology $	Purchasing power parity international $	PPP rank
144	Egypt, Arab Rep. of	1,580	5,400	121
145	Congo, Rep.	1,540	2,750 a	153
145	Sri Lanka	1,540	4,210	136
147	Timor-Leste	1,510	3,080 b	148
148	West Bank and Gaza	1,230 a	..	..
149	Guyana	1,300	2,880 b	151
150	Mongolia	1,290	3,160	147
152	Bolivia	1,260	4,140	137
152	Moldova	1,260 e	2,930	150
154	Kiribati	1,170	2,240 b	160
155	Djibouti	1,090	2,260	159
156	Cameroon	1,050	2,120	162
157	Lesotho	1,000	1,890	166
158	Nicaragua	980	2,520 b	157
159	Sudan	960	1,880	167
160	India	950	2,740	154
161	Nigeria	930	1,770	169
162	Côte d'Ivoire	910	1,590	175
163	Pakistan	870	2,570	155
163	São Tomé and Príncipe	870	1,630	174
163	Yemen, Rep. of	870	2,200	161
166	Papua New Guinea	850	1,870 b	168
167	Mauritania	840	2,010	163
168	Senegal	820	1,640	173
169	Zambia	800	1,220	182
170	Vietnam	790	2,550	156
171	Solomon Islands	730	1,680 b	172
171	Uzbekistan	730	2,430 b	158
173	Comoros	680	1,150	184
173	Kenya	680	1,540	176
175	Ghana	590	1,330	178
175	Kyrgyz Republic	590	1,950	164
177	Lao PDR	580	1,940	165
178	Benin	570	1,310	179
179	Haiti	560	1,150 b	184
180	Cambodia	540	1,690	171
180	Chad	540	1,280	181
183	Mali	500	1,040	189
184	Bangladesh	470	1,340	177
185	Tajikistan	460	1,710	170
186	Burkina Faso	430	1,120	187
187	Guinea	400	1,120	187
187	Tanzania	400 f	1,200	183
189	Central African Republic	380	740	198
191	Togo	360	800	195
191	Zimbabwe	340 a	..	..
193	Nepal	340	1,040	189
193	Uganda	340	920	192
195	Gambia, The	320	1,140	186
195	Madagascar	320	920	192
195	Mozambique	320	690	200
195	Rwanda	320	860	194
200	Niger	280	630	203
202	Sierra Leone	260	660	201
203	Malawi	250	750	197
204	Eritrea	230	520 b	204
205	Ethiopia	220	780	196
206	Guinea-Bissau	200	470	205
207	Liberia	150	290	207
208	Congo, Dem. Rep. of	140	290	207
209	Burundi	110	330	206

Note: Rankings include all 209 economies presented in the key indicators table, but only those that have confirmed World Bank Atlas GNI per capita estimates or rank in the top twenty are shown.

Estimated ranges for economies that do not have confirmed World Bank Atlas GNI per capita figures are:

High-income ($11,456 and above):
- Aruba
- Bahamas, The
- Barbados
- Faeroe Islands
- French Polynesia
- Greenland
- Guam
- Macao, China
- Monaco
- Netherlands Antilles
- New Caledonia
- Northern Mariana Islands
- Puerto Rico
- United Arab Emirates
- Virgin Islands (U.S.)

Upper-middle-income ($3,706 – $11,455):
- American Samoa
- Cuba
- Mayotte

Lower-middle-income ($936 – $3,705):
- Iraq
- Turkmenistan

Low-income ($935 or less):
- Afghanistan
- Korea, Dem. Rep. of
- Myanmar
- Somalia

.. Not available. Figures in italics are for an earlier year.

a. 2007 data not available; ranking is approximate.

b. Estimate is based on regression; other PPP figures are extrapolated from the 2005 International Comparison Program benchmark estimates.

c. Data include the French overseas departments of French Guiana, Guadeloupe, Martinique, and Réunion.

d. Data exclude Kosovo and Metohija.

e. Data exclude Transnistria.

f. Data refer to mainland Tanzania only.

The need for statistics

When the United Nations met in September 2000 to set goals for the new millennium, the goals for social and economic development were defined by specific, quantifiable, time-bound targets—reducing poverty by half, ensuring that all children complete primary school, achieving gender equality in education, reducing child mortality rates by two-thirds, cutting maternal mortality rates by three-quarters, and increasing access to safe water and sanitation, all by 2015. These are ambitious goals. They are intended to draw public attention to the need for faster progress and firmer commitments to achieve results. Reliable statistics are needed to monitor progress toward the Millennium Development Goals and encourage greater effort.

The use of statistics to inform policy is not new. In a well-documented case over a century ago, Charles Booth produced detailed maps illustrating well-being and social class differences in London, using data gathered over a period of 20 years. These maps informed a famous policy debate that contributed to the development of radically new programs to alleviate poverty in London. Earlier in the 19th century, John Snow, a London doctor, discovered a statistical pattern among cholera cases that led to the removal of the source of the contamination of the water supply.

Official statistics—published and distributed in many forms—are now routinely used by governments, non-governmental organizations, and the private sector to guide decision making. Although statisticians rarely hit the headlines, the statistics they produce often do. The growth of the economy, the rates of inflation and unemployment, the prevalence of diseases—these and many other statistical indicators regularly make the front pages in countries around the world.

Statistics make possible the detailed analysis of complex social and economic problems, helping policy makers to choose the best interventions and then to monitor the results. Rates of poverty, economic growth, mortality, literacy, and employment are all affected by the actions of governments. Good quality statistics, produced by professionals free from political interference, using sound methods and reliable data sources, provide information to citizens about the successes and failures of public policy and promote debate. Official statistics help those in the private sector to make investment decisions, and they promote the efficient functioning of markets—for example, by providing information about levels of supply and demand. Rates of inflation, estimated from price surveys, are used in wage and salary negotiations and to adjust pensions.

In this book, statistics are used to describe the social and economic conditions of people, how they have changed over time, and how they compare to other countries. This would not be possible without the efforts of statisticians, who conduct surveys and collect data from administrative systems, and use them to compile the statistics that form the basis for the estimates of the indicators shown here.

Most of these statisticians work for governments or other public authorities and share their data through a network of international agencies working together to assemble a global database that describes the state of the world. The resulting statistics are a public good; once they have been produced, they can be used for many purposes.

Even though official statistics have many important uses, including helping to allocate scarce resources efficiently, the quality of statistics produced by governments of many of the world's poorest countries can often be improved. In over 50 countries, policy makers do not have access to estimates of the number of people living in poverty. In over 100 countries, they cannot determine whether the number is shrinking or growing. A common problem in the poorest countries is that the data systems providing the basis for many useful statistics are very fragile. Record-keeping is not always given a high priority in places where governments lack resources and struggle to provide the most basic services. Surveys and censuses are carried out irregularly. Professional statisticians, who manage statistical processes and provide the technical know-how needed to produce good quality statistics, are often underpaid and in short supply. When statistics are unreliable or missing, policy makers cannot make use of them, and the result may be poor decisions and outcomes.

Recent innovations have helped improve statistics at relatively low cost. Combining the extensive information collected on households from sample surveys with the finer spatial disaggregation obtained from population censuses provides a method of estimating poverty levels for small areas. When information about the location of public facilities is added, this technique has been very useful for policy makers and program managers, because it helps them identify vulnerable and underserved populations. It does not require additional data collection activities because it combines existing sources. Another way in which some countries have expanded the use of statistics is by providing researchers with access to survey and census datasets, under controlled conditions to protect the confidentiality of survey respondents. Electronic dissemination tools have also dramatically reduced the costs of publishing statistical data and enabled them to reach far wider audiences.

The international community increasingly recognizes the role that good data and statistics play in development, as well as the importance of encouraging their use. A global effort is underway to improve the capacity of developing countries to produce and analyze statistical data, with the key aims of improving the data to monitor and manage development policy, and of monitoring progress toward the Millennium Development Goals. A sustained effort is needed to put statistical capacity at the center of development policy; to increase investment in data collection, dissemination, and technical capacity; and to improve the use of existing datasets.

Millennium Development Goals

Goals and targets from the Millennium Declaration | Indicators for monitoring progress

---

Goal 1 **Eradicate extreme poverty and hunger**

Target 1.A: Halve, between 1990 and 2015, the proportion of people whose income is less than $1 a day

1.1 Proportion of population below $1 (PPP) per day[a]
1.2 Poverty gap ratio
1.3 Share of poorest quintile in national consumption

Target 1.B: Achieve full and productive employment and decent work for all, including women and young people

1.4 Growth rate of GDP per person employed
1.5 Employment-to-population ratio
1.6 Proportion of employed people living below $1 (PPP) per day
1.7 Proportion of own-account and contributing family workers in total employment

---

Target 1.C: Halve, between 1990 and 2015, the proportion of people who suffer from hunger

1.8 Prevalence of underweight children under 5 years of age
1.9 Proportion of population below minimum level of dietary energy consumption

---

Goal 2 **Achieve universal primary education**

Target 2.A: Ensure that, by 2015, children everywhere, boys and girls alike, will be able to complete a full course of primary schooling

2.1 Net enrollment ratio in primary education
2.2 Proportion of pupils starting grade 1 who reach last grade of primary education
2.3 Literacy rate of 15–24 year-olds, women and men

Goal 3 **Promote gender equality and empower women**

Target 3.A: Eliminate gender disparity in primary and secondary education, preferably by 2005, and in all levels of education no later than 2015

3.1 Ratios of girls to boys in primary, secondary, and tertiary education
3.2 Share of women in wage employment in the nonagricultural sector
3.3 Proportion of seats held by women in national parliament

Goal 4 **Reduce child mortality**

Target 4.A: Reduce by two-thirds, between 1990 and 2015, the under-5 mortality rate

4.1 Under-5 mortality rate
4.2 Infant mortality rate
4.3 Proportion of 1-year-old children immunized against measles

---

Goal 5 **Improve maternal health**

Target 5.A: Reduce by three-quarters, between 1990 and 2015, the maternal mortality ratio

5.1 Maternal mortality ratio
5.2 Proportion of births attended by skilled health personnel

Goals and targets from the Millennium Declaration	Indicators for monitoring progress
Target 5.B: Achieve, by 2015, universal access to reproductive health	5.3 Contraceptive prevalence rate 5.4 Adolescent birth rate 5.5 Antenatal care coverage (at least one visit and at least four visits) 5.6 Unmet need for family planning
Goal 6 **Combat HIV/AIDS, malaria, and other diseases**	
Target 6.A: Have halted by 2015 and begun to reverse the spread of HIV/AIDS	6.1 HIV prevalence among population aged 15–24 years 6.2 Condom use at last high-risk sex 6.3 Proportion of population aged 15–24 years with comprehensive correct knowledge of HIV/AIDS 6.4 Ratio of school attendance of orphans to school attendance of nonorphans aged 10–14 years
Target 6.B: Achieve, by 2010, universal access to treatment for HIV/AIDS for all those who need it	6.5 Proportion of population with advanced HIV infection with access to antiretroviral drugs
Target 6.C: Have halted by 2015 and begun to reverse the incidence of malaria and other major diseases	6.6 Incidence and death rates associated with malaria 6.7 Proportion of children under-5 sleeping under insecticide-treated bednets 6.8 Proportion of children under-5 with fever who are treated with appropriate anti-malarial drugs 6.9 Incidence, prevalence, and death rates associated with tuberculosis 6.10 Proportion of tuberculosis cases detected and cured under directly observed treatment short course
Goal 7 **Ensure environmental sustainability**	
Target 7.A: Integrate the principles of sustainable development into country policies and programs and reverse the loss of environmental resources	7.1 Proportion of land area covered by forest 7.2 CO_2 emissions, total, per capita and per \$1 GDP (PPP) 7.3 Consumption of ozone-depleting substances 7.4 Proportion of fish stocks within safe biological limits 7.5 Proportion of total water resources used
Target 7.B: Reduce biodiversity loss, achieving, by 2010, a significant reduction in the rate of loss	7.6 Proportion of terrestrial and marine areas protected 7.7 Proportion of species threatened with extinction
Target 7.C: Halve, by 2015, the proportion of people without sustainable access to safe drinking water and basic sanitation	7.8 Proportion of population using an improved drinking water source 7.9 Proportion of population using an improved sanitation facility
Target 7.D: By 2020, achieve a significant improvement in the lives of at least 100 million slum dwellers	7.10 Proportion of urban population living in slums[b]

Millennium Development Goals

Goals and targets from the Millennium Declaration   **Indicators for monitoring progress**

Goal 8	Develop a global partnership for development

Some of the indicators listed below are monitored separately for the least developed countries (LDCs), Africa, landlocked developing countries, and small island developing states.

Target 8.A: Develop further an open, rule-based, predictable, non-discriminatory trading and financial system

Includes a commitment to good governance, development, and poverty reduction—both nationally and internationally

Official development assistance (ODA)

8.1 Net ODA, total and to the least developed countries, as percentage of OECD/DAC donors' gross national income

8.2 Proportion of total bilateral, sector-allocable ODA of OECD/DAC donors to basic social services (basic education, primary health care, nutrition, safe water and sanitation)

Target 8.B: Address the special needs of the least-developed countries

Includes: tariff and quota-free access for the least-developed countries' exports; enhanced program of debt relief for heavily indebted poor countries (HIPC) and cancellation of official bilateral debt; and more generous official development assistance (ODA) for countries committed to poverty reduction

8.3 Proportion of bilateral official development assistance of OECD/DAC donors that is untied

8.4 ODA received in landlocked developing countries as a proportion of their gross national incomes

8.5 ODA received in small island developing states as a proportion of their gross national incomes

Market access

8.6 Proportion of total developed country imports (by value and excluding arms) from developing countries and least developed countries, admitted free of duty

8.7 Average tariffs imposed by developed countries on agricultural products and textiles and clothing from developing countries

Target 8.C: Address the special needs of landlocked developing countries and small island developing states (through the Programme of Action for the Sustainable Development of Small Island Developing States and the outcome of the 22nd special session of the General Assembly)

8.8 Agricultural support estimate for OECD countries as a percentage of their gross domestic product

8.9 Proportion of ODA provided to help build trade capacity

Debt sustainability

8.10 Total number of countries that have reached their HIPC decision points and number that have reached their HIPC completion points (cumulative)

Target 8.D: Deal comprehensively with the debt problems of developing countries through national and international measures in order to make debt sustainable in the long term

8.11 Debt relief committed under HIPC and MDRI Initiatives

8.12 Debt service as a percentage of exports of goods and services

Target 8.E: In cooperation with pharmaceutical companies, provide access to affordable essential drugs in developing countries

8.13 Proportion of population with access to affordable essential drugs on a sustainable basis

Target 8.F: In cooperation with the private sector, make available the benefits of new technologies, especially information and communications

8.14 Telephone lines per 100 population

8.15 Cellular subscribers per 100 population

8.16 Internet users per 100 population

The Millennium Development Goals and targets come from the Millennium Declaration, signed by 189 countries, including 147 heads of state and government, in September 2000 (http://www.un.org/millennium/declaration/ares552e.htm), as updated by the 60th United Nations General Assembly in September 2005. The goals and targets are interrelated and should be seen as a whole. They represent a partnership between the developed countries and the developing countries "to create an environment—at the national and global levels alike—which is conducive to development and the elimination of poverty."

All indicators should be disaggregated by sex and urban/rural location as far as possible.

[a] For monitoring country poverty trends, indicators based on national poverty lines should be used, where available.

[b] The actual proportion of people living in slums is measured by a proxy, represented by the urban population living in households with at least one of the four characteristics: (a) lack of access to improved water supply; (b) lack of access to improved sanitation; (c) overcrowding (3 or more persons per room); and (d) dwellings made of non-durable material.

Definitions, sources, notes, and abbreviations

Access to an all-season road The proportion of rural people who live within 2 km (typically equivalent to a 20-minute walk) of an all-season road. An "all-season road" is a road that is motorable all year by the prevailing means of rural transport. Predictable interruptions of short duration during inclement weather (for example, heavy rainfall) are accepted, particularly on low-volume roads. (World Bank)

Access to improved sanitation facilities The proportion of the urban or rural population with access to at least adequate excreta disposal facilities (private or shared, but not public) that can effectively prevent human, animal, or insect contact with excreta. (WHO)

Agricultural machinery Wheel and crawler tractors (excluding garden tractors) in use in agriculture at the end of the calendar year specified, or during the first quarter of the following year. (FAO)

Agricultural productivity The ratio of agricultural value added, measured in constant 2000 U.S. dollars, to the number of workers in agriculture. (FAO)

Agriculture Economic activity corresponding to International Standard Industrial Classification (ISIC) division 1–5 (ISIC Revision) or tabulation categories A–B (ISIC Revision 3)

Aid dependency ratios Net official development assistance, expressed as a share of gross national income and in per capita terms, provides a measure of the recipient country's dependency on aid. Calculated using values in U.S. dollars converted at official exchange rates. (OECD)

Aid, net Aid flows classified as official development assistance, net of repayments. (OECD)

Aid, debt-related Net disbursement of official development assistance provided for all actions relating to debt, including forgiveness, swaps, buybacks, rescheduling, and refinancing. (OECD)

Aid, development programs, projects, and other resource provisions Net disbursement of official development assistance provided as cash transfers, aid in kind, development food aid, and the financing of capital projects; intended to increase or improve the recipient's stock of physical capital, and to support the recipient's development plans and other activities with finance and commodity supply. (OECD)

Aid, humanitarian Net disbursement of official development assistance provided for emergency and distress relief, including aid to refugees and assistance for disaster preparedness. (OECD)

Aid, technical cooperation Net disbursement of official development assistance whose main aim is to augment the stock of human intellectual capital, such as the level of knowledge, skills, and technical know-how in the recipient country (including the cost of associated equipment). Contributions take the form mainly of the supply of human resources from donors or action directed to human resources (such as training or advice). Also included is aid for promoting development awareness and aid provided to refugees in the donor economy. Assistance specifically to facilitate a capital project is not included. (OECD)

Aid, untied Bilateral official development assistance commitment not subject to restrictions by donors on procurement sources. (OECD)

Births attended by skilled health staff The proportion of deliveries attended by personnel trained to give the necessary supervision, care, and advice to women during pregnancy, labor, and the postpartum period, to conduct deliveries on their own and to care for newborns. (UNICEF)

Bonds Securities issued with a fixed rate of interest for a period of more than one year. They include net flows through cross-border public and publicly guaranteed and private nonguaranteed bond issues. (World Bank)

Business, time to start up The time, in calendar days, needed to complete all the procedures required to legally operate a business. If a procedure can be speeded up at additional cost, the fastest procedure, regardless of cost, is chosen. Time spent gathering information about the registration process is excluded. (World Bank)

Carbon dioxide emissions Emissions from the burning of fossil fuels (including the consumption of solid, liquid, and gas fuels and gas flaring) and the manufacture of cement. (CDIAC)

Cereal yield The production of wheat, rice, maize, barley, oats, rye, millet, sorghum, buckwheat, and mixed grains, measured in kilograms per hectare of harvested land. Refers to crops harvested for dry grain only. Cereal crops harvested for hay or harvested green for food, feed, or silage, and those used for grazing, are excluded. The FAO allocates production data to the calendar year in which the bulk of the harvest took place. Most of a crop harvested near the end of the year will be used in the following year. (FAO)

Children out of school, primary school-age children The number of children of primary school age who are not enrolled in primary or secondary school. (UNESCO Institute for Statistics)

Commercial bank and other lending Net flows of commercial bank lending (public and publicly guaranteed and private nonguaranteed) and other private credits. (World Bank)

Contraceptive prevalence rate The percentage of women married or in-union ages 15–49 who are practicing, or whose sexual partners are practicing, any form of contraception. (UNICEF)

Control of corruption Measures the perceptions of corruption, conventionally defined as the abuse of public office for private gain and an outcome of poor governance, reflecting the breakdown of accountability. (World Bank)

Country Policy and Institutional Assessment CPIA index rates countries against a set of 16 criteria grouped in four clusters: (a) economic management; (b) structural policies; (c) policies for social inclusion and equity; and (d) public sector management and institutions. The CPIA measures the extent to which a country's policy and institutional framework supports sustainable growth and poverty reduction and, consequently, the effective use of development assistance.

Crop production index Agricultural production for each period relative to the base period 1999–2001; includes all crops except fodder crops. (FAO)

Debt, private nonguaranteed The long-term external obligations of private debtors that are not guaranteed for repayment by a public entity. (World Bank)

Debt, public and publicly guaranteed The long-term external obligations of public debtors, including the national governments and political subdivisions (or an agency of either) and autonomous public bodies, and the external obligations of private debtors that are guaranteed for repayment by a public entity. (World Bank)

Debt, short term All debt having an original maturity of one year or less and interest in arrears on long-term debt. (World Bank)

Debt, total external Debt owed to nonresidents repayable in foreign currency, goods, or services. It is the sum of public, publicly guaranteed, and private nonguaranteed long-term debt, use of International Monetary Fund credit, and short-term debt. (World Bank)

Debt service, public The sum of principal repayments and interest actually paid in foreign currency, goods, or services for long-term public and publicly guaranteed debt and repayments (repurchases and charges) to the International Monetary Fund. (World Bank)

Debt service, total The sum of principal repayments and interest actually paid in foreign currency, goods, or services on long-term debt, interest paid on short-term debt, and repayments (repurchases and charges) to the International Monetary Fund. (World Bank)

Deforestation The permanent conversion of natural forest area to other uses, including shifting cultivation, permanent agriculture, ranching, settlements, and infrastructure development. Deforested areas do not include areas logged but intended for regeneration, or areas degraded by fuelwood gathering, acid precipitation, or forest fires. Negative numbers indicate an increase in forest area. (FAO)

Dependency ratio The ratio of dependents—people younger than 15 and older than 64—to the working-age population. (World Bank)

Economically active children Children ages 7–14 who are involved in economic activity for at least one hour in the reference week of the survey. (UCW)

Economically active children, agriculture Children ages 7–14 who are involved in economic activity in the agricultural sector. Agriculture corresponds to division 1 (ISIC revision 2) or categories A and B (ISIC revision 3), and includes agriculture, hunting, forestry and logging, and fishing. (UCW)

Economically active children, manufacturing Children ages 7–14 who are involved in economic activity in the manufacturing sector. Manufacturing corresponds to division 3 (ISIC revision 2) or category D (ISIC revision 3). (UCW)

Economically active children, service Children ages 7–14 who are involved in economic activity in the service sector. Services correspond to divisions 6–9 (ISIC revision 2) or categories G–P (ISIC revision 3), and include wholesale and retail trade, hotels and restaurants, transport, financial intermediation, real estate, public administration, education, health and social work, other community services, and private household activity. (UCW)

Economically active children, work only Children ages 7–14 who are involved in economic activity and do not attend school. (UCW)

Economically active children, study and work Children ages 7–14 who are involved in economic activity and attend school. (UCW)

Economically active children, wage and salary workers Children ages 7–14 who are involved in economic activity and hold the type of jobs defined as "paid employment jobs." (UCW)

Economically active children, self-employed workers Children ages 7–14 who are involved in economic activity and hold the type of jobs defined as a "self-employment jobs," working on their own account or with one or a few partners. (UCW)

Economically active children, unpaid family workers Children ages 7–14 who are involved in economic activity and work without pay in a market-oriented establishment or activity operated by a related person living in the same household. (UCW)

Education, primary The level of education that provides children with basic reading, writing, and mathematics skills, along with an elementary understanding of such subjects as history, geography, natural science, social science, art, and music. (UNESCO Institute for Statistics)

Education, secondary The level of education that completes the provision of basic education aimed at laying the foundations for lifelong learning and human development by offering more subject or skill-oriented instruction using more specialized teachers. (UNESCO Institute for Statistics)

Education, tertiary The level of education, leading to an advanced research qualification that normally requires, as a minimum condition of admission, the successful completion of education at the secondary level. (UNESCO Institute for Statistics)

Electric power consumption The output of power plants and combined heat and power plants minus the transmission, distribution, and transformation losses and own-use by heat and power plants. (IEA)

Energy flows Estimated as energy uses less production, both measured in oil equivalents. (IEA)

Emigration rate of people with tertiary education The stock of emigrants with at least tertiary education as a share of the total tertiary educated people (residents and emigrants) in the country. Tertiary education refers to International Standard Classification of Education (ISCED) level 5 or above. (OECD)

Energy use, commercial The apparent consumption of commercial energy equals domestic production plus imports and stock changes, minus exports and fuels supplied to ships and aircraft engaged in international transport. (IEA)

Enrollment rate, gross The ratio of children who are enrolled in an education level, regardless of age, to the population of the corresponding official school age, as defined by the International Standard Classification of Education 1997 (ISCED97). (UNESCO Institute for Statistics)

Enrollment rate, net The ratio of children of official school age, as defined by the International Standard Classification of Education 1997 (ISCED97), who are enrolled in school, to the population of the corresponding official school age.
(UNESCO Institute for Statistics)

Exchange rate, official The exchange rate (local currency units relative to the U.S. dollar) determined by national authorities or the rate determined in the legally sanctioned exchange market. It is calculated as an annual average based on monthly averages. (IMF)

Exports of goods, services, and income International transactions involving a change in ownership of general merchandise, goods sent for processing and repairs, nonmonetary gold, services, receipts of employee compensation for nonresident workers, and investment income. (IMF)

Female-to-male enrollments in primary and secondary schools The ratio of female-to-male gross enrollment rates in primary and secondary schools.
(UNESCO Institute for Statistics)

Fertility rate, total The number of children that would be born to a woman if she were to live to the end of her childbearing years, and bear children in accordance with current age-specific fertility rates. (World Bank)

Fertilizer consumption The plant nutrients used per unit of arable land. Nitrogenous, potash, and phosphate fertilizers (including ground rock phosphate) are included; traditional nutrients, animal, and plant manures are not included. The time reference for fertilizer consumption is the crop year (July through June). (FAO)

Financing from abroad (obtained from nonresidents) and domestic financing (obtained from residents) The means by which a government provides financial resources to cover a budget deficit, or allocates financial resources arising from a budget surplus. Includes all government liabilities—other than those for currency issues or demand, time, or savings deposits with government—or claims on others held by government, and changes in government holdings of cash and deposits. Excludes government guarantees of the debt of others. (IMF)

Food production index The average of commodity group price indices of meat, dairy, cereal, oil and fats, and sugar weighted with the average export shares of each of the groups for 1999–2001. (FAO)

Food production per capita Covers food crops that are considered edible and that contain nutrients. To construct the index, production quantities of each commodity are weighted by international prices with the base period of 1999–2001. This method assigns a single price to each commodity so that, for example, one metric ton of wheat has the same price, regardless of where it is produced. Coffee and tea are excluded because, although edible, they have no nutritive value. (FAO)

Foreign direct investment, net inflows Net inflows of investment to acquire a lasting interest in or a management control over (10 percent or more of voting stock) an enterprise operating in an economy other than that of the investor. It is the sum of equity capital, reinvestment of earnings, other long-term capital, and short-term capital as shown in the balance of payments. (IMF)

Forest area Land under natural or planted stands of trees, whether productive or not. (FAO)

Freshwater resources Total internal renewable resources (internal river flows and groundwater from rainfall). (World Resources Institute)

Freshwater withdrawals, annual Total water withdrawals, not counting evaporation losses from storage basins, but including water from desalination plants in countries where they are a significant source. Withdrawals also include water from desalination sources. Withdrawals for agriculture and industry are total withdrawals for irrigation and livestock production and for direct industrial use (including for cooling thermoelectric plants). Withdrawals for domestic uses include drinking water, municipal use or supply, and use for public services, commercial establishments, and home. (WRI)

Gross capital formation (commonly called investment) Outlays on additions to the fixed assets of the economy, net of changes in the level of inventories, and net acquisitions of valuables. Fixed assets include land improvements (such as fences, ditches, and drains); plant, machinery, and equipment purchases; and the construction of roads, railways, and dwellings.
(World Bank, OECD, UN)

Gross domestic product (GDP) The sum of gross value added by all resident producers in the economy plus any product taxes (less subsidies) not included in the value of the products. It is calculated using purchaser prices and without deductions for the depreciation of fabricated assets, or for the depletion and degradation of natural resources. (World Bank)

Gross domestic product (GDP) per capita Gross domestic product divided by midyear population. (World Bank)

Gross national income (GNI) Gross domestic product plus net receipts of primary income (compensation of employees and property income) from abroad. Data are converted to dollars using the World Bank Atlas method. (World Bank)

Gross national income (GNI) per capita Gross national income divided by midyear population. (World Bank)

Gross national income (GNI), PPP Gross national income converted to international dollars using purchasing power parity rates. An international dollar has the same purchasing power over GNI as a U.S. dollar has in the United States. (World Bank)

Heavily Indebted Poor Countries (HIPC) Initiative A program of official creditors designed to relieve the poorest and most heavily indebted countries of their debt to certain multilateral creditors, including the World Bank and International Monetary Fund. (World Bank)

High-income economies Those with a gross national income (GNI) per capita of $11,456 or more in 2007. (World Bank)

HIV, adults and children living with All people with HIV infection, whether or not they have developed symptoms of AIDS. Adults are defined as those ages 15 and over, and children as ages 0–14. (UNAIDS)

HIV, adult prevalence of The proportion of people ages 15–49 who are infected with HIV. (UNAIDS)

Immunization rate, measles, child Percentage of children ages 12–23 months who received a vaccination for measles before 12 months of age, or at any time before the survey. A child is considered adequately immunized against measles after receiving one dose of vaccine. (WHO and UNICEF)

Industry Economic activity corresponding to International Standard Industrial Classification (ISIC) divisions 2–5 (ISIC revision 2) or tabulation categories C–F (ISIC revision 3).

Interest payments Payments of interest on government debt—including long-term bonds, long-term loans, and other debt instruments—to both domestic and foreign residents. (World Bank)

International $ An international dollar has the same purchasing power that a U.S. dollar has in the United States.

Internet users Proportion of people with access to the worldwide network. (ITU)

Irrigated land Refers to areas purposely provided with water, including land irrigated by controlled flooding. (FAO)

Labor force participation rate The proportion of the population ages 15 and older that is economically active; all people who supply labor for the production of goods and services during a specified period. (ILO)

Land, arable Land under temporary crops (double-cropped areas are counted once), temporary meadows for mowing or for pasture, land under market or kitchen gardens, and land temporarily fallow. Land abandoned as a result of shifting cultivation is excluded. (FAO)

Land under cereal production Refers to harvested areas, although some countries report only sown or cultivated areas. (FAO)

Life expectancy at birth The number of years a newborn infant would live if prevailing patterns of mortality at the time of its birth were to stay the same throughout its life. (World Bank)

Lifetime risk of maternal death The probability that a 15-year-old female will die eventually from a maternal cause, assuming that current levels of fertility and mortality (including maternal mortality) do not change in the future, taking into account competing causes of death. (WHO, UNICEF, UNFPA, and World Bank)

Low-income economies Those with a gross national income (GNI) per capita of $935 or less in 2007. (World Bank)

Malnutrition, underweight children, prevalence of The percentage of children under-5 whose weight for age is more than two standard deviations below the median for the international reference population ages 0–59 months. The data are based on the new international child growth standards for infants and young children, called the Child Growth Standards, released in 2006 by the World Health Organization. (WHO)

Manufacturing Economic activity corresponding to International Standard Industrial Classification (ISIC) divisions 15–37 or tabulation category D (ISIC Revision 3).

Merchandise trade The sum of merchandise exports and imports measured in current U.S. dollars. Also referred to as trade in goods. (WTO)

Middle-income economies Those with a gross national income (GNI) per capita of more than $935 but less than $11,456 in 2007. (World Bank)

Migration, stock the number of people born in a country other than that in which they live; this includes refugees. (UNSD)

Mobile telephone subscribers Proportion of people who subscribe to a public mobile telephone service using cellular technology. (ITU)

Mortality rate, infant The number of infants dying before reaching one year of age, per 1,000 live births in a given year. (Harmonized estimates of WHO, UNICEF, and World Bank)

Mortality rate, children under-5 The probability that a newborn baby will die before reaching age 5, if subject to current age-specific mortality rates. The probability is expressed as a rate per 1,000. (Harmonized estimates of WHO, UNICEF, UNFPA, UNPD, and World Bank)

Mortality ratio, maternal The number of women who die from pregnancy-related causes during pregnancy and childbirth, per 100,000 live births. The data shown are modeled estimates based on an exercise by the World Health Organization, the United Nations Children's Fund, the United Nations Population Fund, and the World Bank. (WHO, UNICEF, UNFPA, and World Bank)

Multilateral Debt Relief Initiative (MDRI) Further reduces the debt of heavily indebted poor countries and provides resources for meeting the Millennium Development Goals. Under the MDRI the International Development Association, International Monetary Fund, and African Development Fund provide 100 percent debt relief on eligible debts due to them from countries that completed the HIPC Initiative process. (World Bank)

Nationally protected areas Totally or partially protected areas of at least 1,000 hectares that are designated as national parks, natural monuments, nature reserves or wildlife sanctuaries, protected landscapes or seascapes, or scientific reserves with limited public access. The data do not include marine areas, unclassified areas, littoral (intertidal) areas, and sites protected under local or provincial law. Total land area is used to calculate the percentage of total area protected. (WCMC)

Net migration The total number of immigrants minus the total number of emigrants, including both citizens and noncitizens. Data are five-year estimates. (UNPD)

Official development assistance (ODA) Disbursement of loans made on concessional terms (net of repayments) and grants by official agencies of the members of the Development Assistance Committee (DAC), by multilateral institutions, and by non-DAC countries to promote economic development and welfare in countries and territories in the DAC list of ODA recipients. (OECD)

Overqualification rate The proportion of people working in jobs/occupations for which their skills are too high. Education and job qualification levels are grouped into three categories: low, intermediate, and high. An overqualified individual is one who holds a job that requires lesser qualifications than one that would theoretically be available at his or her education level. Overqualification rates are calculated for individuals with an intermediate or higher education. (OECD)

People receiving antiretroviral therapy People living with HIV who are receiving antiretroviral therapy treatment. (UNSD)

Particulate matter concentration Fine suspended particulates less than 10 microns in diameter (PM10) that are capable of penetrating deep into the respiratory tract and causing significant health damage. Data are urban-population-weighted PM10 levels in residential areas of cities with more than 100,000 residents. The estimates represent the average annual exposure level of the average urban resident to outdoor particulate matter. (World Bank)

Permanent cropland Land cultivated with crops that occupy the land for long periods and need not be replanted after each harvest. It includes land under flowering shrubs, fruit trees, nut trees, and vines, but excludes land under trees grown for wood or timber. (FAO)

Population, average annual growth rate The exponential rate of change in population for the period indicated. (World Bank)

Population, total Mid-year population that includes all residents regardless of legal status or citizenship—except for refugees not permanently settled in the country of asylum, who are generally considered part of the population of their country of origin. (World Bank)

Population below $1 a day The proportion of the population living on less than $1.25 a day at 2005 purchasing power parity prices. (World Bank)

Population below $2 a day The proportion of the population living on less than $2 a day at 2005 purchasing power parity prices. (World Bank)

Population density Midyear population divided by land area in square kilometers. (World Bank)

Population, rural Calculated as the difference between the total population and the urban population. (World Bank)

Population, urban The midyear population of areas defined as urban in each country and reported to the United Nations. (UN World Urbanization Prospects, The 2007 Revision, and World Bank staff estimates)

Portfolio equity flow Net inflows from equity securities other than those recorded as direct investment, including shares, stocks, depository receipts, and direct purchases of shares in local stock markets by foreign investors. (World Bank)

Pregnant women receiving prenatal care The proportion of women attended at least once during pregnancy by skilled health personnel for reasons related to pregnancy. (Household Surveys)

Primary completion rate The proportion of students completing the last year of primary school; calculated by taking the total number of students in the last grade of primary school, minus the number of repeaters in that grade, divided by the total number of children of official graduation age. (UNESCO Institute for Statistics)

Private participation in infrastructure Investment commitments in infrastructure projects in telecommunications, energy, transport, and water and sanitation with private participation that have reached financial closure, and directly or indirectly serve the public. All investment (public and private) in projects in which a private company assumes the operating risk is included. (World Bank)

Public sector management and institutions A proxy measure of governance that includes assessments of property rights and rule-based governance; quality of budgetary and financial management; efficiency of revenue mobilization; quality of public administration; and transparency, accountability, and corruption in the public sector. (World Bank)

Purchasing power parity (PPP) conversion factor The number of units of a country's currency required to buy the same amount of goods and services in the domestic market as a U.S. dollar would buy in the United States. (World Bank)

Ratio of female-to-male hourly wage The ratio of the female hourly wage to male hourly wage. (Household Surveys)

Refugees People recognized as refugees under the 1951 Convention Relating to the Status of Refugees or its 1967 Protocol; the 1969 Organization of African Unity Convention Governing the Specific Aspects of Refugee Problems in Africa; people recognized as refugees in accordance with the UNHCR statute; people granted a refugee-like humanitarian status; and people provided with temporary protection. Palestinian refugees (and their descendants) are people whose residence was Palestine between June 1946 and May 1948, and who lost their homes and means of livelihood as a result of the 1948 Arab-Israeli conflict. (UNHCR and UNRWA)

Repeaters, primary The proportion of students enrolled in the same grade as in the previous year as a share of all students enrolled in primary school. (UNESCO Institute for Statistics)

Sanitation, access to an improved facility The share of the urban population with access to at least adequate excreta disposal facilities (private or shared but not public) that can effectively prevent human, animal, and insect contact with excreta. Improved facilities range from simple but protected pit latrines to flush toilets with a sewage connection. (WHO)

Services Economic activity corresponding to International Standard Industrial Classification (ISIC) divisions 6–9 (ISIC revision 2) or tabulation categories G–P (ISIC revision 3). (ILO)

Tariff, simple mean The unweighted average of the effectively applied rates for all products subject to tariffs. (World Bank, UNCTAD, WTO)

Teenage mothers The percentage of women ages 15–19 who already have children or are currently pregnant (Household Surveys)

Trade Refers to the two-way flow of exports and imports of goods (merchandise trade) and services (service trade).

Trade restrictiveness index Measures the impact of each country's trade policies on its aggregate imports, taking into account all types of trade barriers, including tariffs, quotas, non-automatic licensing, antidumping duties, countervailing duties, tariff-quotas, and subsidies. (World Bank)

Treated bednets, use of The proportion of children ages 0–59 months who slept under an insecticide-impregnated bednet the night before the survey. (Household Surveys)

Tuberculosis, incidence of The estimated number of new pulmonary, smear-positive, and extrapulmonary tuberculosis cases. (WHO)

Undernourishment, prevalence of The percentage of the population that is undernourished—whose dietary energy consumption is continuously below a minimum dietary energy requirement for maintaining a healthy life and carrying out light physical activity. (FAO)

Unpaid family worker Unpaid workers who work in a business operated by a relative and live in the same household. (ILO)

Unofficial payments to public officials The percentage of firms expected to make unofficial or informal payments to public officials to "get things done" with regard to customs, taxes, licenses, regulations, and services. (World Bank)

Value added The net output of an industry after adding up all outputs and subtracting intermediate inputs. The industrial origin of value added is determined by the International Standard Industrial Classification (ISIC) revision 3. (World Bank)

Water source, access to an improved The share of the population with reasonable access to an adequate amount of water from an improved source, such as a household connection, public standpipe, borehole, protected well or spring, or rainwater collection. Unimproved sources include vendors, tanker trucks, and unprotected wells and springs. Reasonable access is defined as the availability of at least 20 liters a person per day from a source within one kilometer of the dwelling. (WHO and UNICEF)

Women in parliament The percentage of parliamentary seats in a single or lower chamber occupied by women. (IPU)

Workers' remittances and compensation of employees, received Current transfers by migrant workers, and wages and salaries earned by nonresident workers. (World Bank and IMF)

World Bank Atlas method A conversion factor to convert national currency units to U.S. dollars at prevailing exchange rates, adjusted for inflation and averaged over three years. The purpose is to reduce the effect of exchange rate fluctuations in the cross-country comparison of national incomes. (World Bank)

Data sources

The indicators presented in this *Atlas* are compiled by international agencies and by public and private organizations, usually on the basis of survey data or administrative statistics obtained from national governments. The principal source of each indicator is given in parentheses following the definition.

The World Bank publishes these and many other statistical series in the *World Development Indicators*, available in print, CD-ROM, and online. Excerpts from this *Atlas*, additional information about sources, definitions, and statistical methods, and suggestions for further reading are available at www.worldbank.org/data.

Data notes and symbols

The data in this book are for the most recent year unless otherwise noted.
- Growth rates are proportional changes from the previous year.
- Regional aggregates include data for low and middle-income economies only.
- Figures in italics indicate data for years or periods other than those specified.

Data are shown for economies with populations greater than 30,000, or less if they are members of the World Bank. The term *country* (used interchangeably with *economy*) does not imply political independence or official recognition by the World Bank, but refers to any economy for which the authorities report separate social or economic statistics.

The regional groupings of countries include only low and middle income economies. For the income groups, every economy is classified as low income, middle income, or high income.
- *Low-income economies* are those with a GNI per capita of $935 or less in 2007.
- *Middle-income economies* are those with a GNI per capita of more than $935 but less than $11,456 in 2007.
- *Lower-middle-income economies* and *upper-middle-income economies* are separated at a GNI per capita of $3,705 in 2007.
- *High-income economies* are those with a GNI per capita of $11,456 or more in 2007.

Symbols used in data tables

.. means that data are not available or that aggregates cannot be calculated because of missing data.
o or o.o means zero or less than half the unit shown.
$ means current U.S. dollars.
The methods used to calculate regional and income group aggregates are denoted by:
m (median), s (simple total), t (total including estimates for missing data), u (unweighted average), and w (weighted average).

Abbreviations

AfDF	African Development Fund	ODA	Official Development Assistance
CDIAC	Carbon Dioxide Information Analysis Center	OECD	Organisation for Economic Co-operation and Development
CPIA	Country Policy and Institutional Assessment		
DAC	Development Assistance Committee of the Organisation for Economic Co-operation and Development	PPI	Private Participation in Infrastructure
		PPP	Purchasing Power Parity
DHS	Demographic and Health Surveys	UCW	Understanding Children's Work
FAO	Food and Agriculture Organization of the United Nations	UN	United Nations
		UNAIDS	Joint United Nations Programme on HIV/AIDS
FDI	Foreign Direct Investment	UNDP	United Nations Development Programme
GDP	Gross Domestic Product	UNEP	United Nations Environment Programme
GNI	Gross National Income	UNESCO	United Nations Educational, Scientific and Cultural Organization
HIPC	Heavily Indebted Poor Countries		
ICT	Information and Communications Technology	UNFPA	United Nations Population Fund
IDA	International Development Association	UNICEF	United Nations Children's Fund
IEA	International Energy Agency	UNIFEM	United Nations Development Fund for Women
ILO	International Labour Organization	UNSD	United Nations Statistics Division
IMF	International Monetary Fund	WCMC	World Conservation Monitoring Centre
IPU	Inter-Parliamentary Union	WDI	World Development Indicators
ITU	International Telecommunication Union	WHO	World Health Organization
MDGs	Millennium Development Goals	WRI	World Resources Institute
MDRI	Multilateral Debt Relief Initiative	WTO	World Trade Organization

For more information

- *World Development Indicators* and **WDI Online** are the World Bank's premier compilation of data about development. This *Atlas* complements *World Development Indicators* by providing a geographical view of pertinent data. The *World Development Indicators* is available at: www.worldbank.org/data/wdi
- *Global Development Finance* and **GDF Online** are the World Bank's comprehensive compilation of data on external debt and financial flows. They are available at: www.worldbank.org/data/gdf
- *African Development Indicators*, the World Bank's most detailed collection of data on Africa, available in one volume at: www.worldbank.org/adi
- **The Millennium Development Goals** (MDG) and the data and indicators required to track progress toward them are available at: www.developmentgoals.org
- **The PARIS21 Consortium** and information about how it promotes evidence-based policymaking and monitoring are available at: www.paris21.org
- **The Statistical Capacity Building Program**, which offers tools and advice for statistical capacity building in developing countries, can be accessed at: www.worldbank.org/data/statcap
- **The International Comparison Program** (ICP) and information about the ICP and the final results from the 2005 round can be found at: www.worldbank.org/data/icp

Index

Note: page numbers in **bold** refer to maps, page numbers in *italics* refer to information presented in graphs and tables.